Democratic Moments

TEXTUAL MOMENTS IN THE HISTORY OF POLITICAL THOUGHT

Series Editors:

J. C. Davis, Emeritus Professor of History, University of East Anglia, UK
John Morrow, Professor of Political Studies, University of Auckland, New Zealand

Textual Moments provides accessible, short readings of key texts in selected fields of political thought, encouraging close reading informed by cutting-edge scholarship. The unique short essay format of the series ensures that volumes cover a range of texts in roughly chronological order. The essays in each volume aim to open up a reading of the text and its significance in the political discourse in question and in the history of political thought more widely. Key moments in the textual history of a particular genre of political discourse are made accessible, appealing and instructive to students, scholars and general readers.

Published

Censorship Moments: Reading Texts in the History of Censorship and Freedom of Expression, Geoff Kemp
Feminist Moments: Reading Feminist Texts, Susan Bruce and Katherine Smits
Liberal Moments: Reading Liberal Texts, Ewa Atanassow and Alan S. Kahan
Patriarchal Moments: Reading Patriarchal Texts, Cesare Cuttica and Gaby Mahlberg
Revolutionary Moments: Reading Revolutionary Texts, Rachel Hammersley
Utopian Moments: Reading Utopian Texts, Miguel Avilés and J. C. Davis

Democratic Moments

Reading Democratic Texts

EDITED BY
XAVIER MÁRQUEZ

Bloomsbury Academic
An imprint of Bloomsbury Publishing Plc

BLOOMSBURY ACADEMIC
LONDON • NEW YORK • OXFORD • NEW DELHI • SYDNEY

Bloomsbury Academic
An imprint of Bloomsbury Publishing Plc

50 Bedford Square	1385 Broadway
London	New York
WC1B 3DP	NY 10018
UK	USA

www.bloomsbury.com

BLOOMSBURY and the Diana logo are trademarks of Bloomsbury Publishing Plc

First published 2018

© Xavier Márquez and Contributors, 2018

Xavier Márquez has asserted his right under the Copyright, Designs and Patents Act, 1988, to be identified as Editor of this work.

This work is published subject to a Creative Commons Attribution Non-Commercial Licence. You may share this work for non-commercial purposes only, provided you give attribution to the copyright holder and the publisher. For permission to publish commercial versions please contact Bloomsbury Academic.

No responsibility for loss caused to any individual or organization acting on or refraining from action as a result of the material in this publication can be accepted by Bloomsbury or the Editor.

British Library Cataloguing-in-Publication Data
Names: Márquez, Xavier, editor.
Title: Democratic moments : reading democratic texts / edited by Xavier Márquez.
Description: London UK ; New York, NY : Bloomsbury Academic, 2017. |
Series: Textual moments in the history of political thought |
Includes bibliographical references and index.
Identifiers: LCCN 2017040897 (print) | LCCN 2017052113 (ebook) |
ISBN 9781350006157 (PDF eBook) | ISBN 9781350006188 (EPUB eBook) |
ISBN 9781350006164 (hardback) | ISBN 9781350006171 (paperback)
Subjects: LCSH: Democracy–Philosophy. | BISAC: POLITICAL SCIENCE / Political Ideologies / Democracy. | HISTORY / Social History. | POLITICAL SCIENCE / History & Theory.
Classification: LCC JC423 (ebook) | LCC JC423 .D38135652 2017 (print) | DDC 321.8–dc23
LC record available at https://lccn.loc.gov/2017040897

ISBN:	HB:	978-1-3500-0616-4
	PB:	978-1-3500-0617-1
	ePDF:	978-1-3500-0615-7
	eBook:	978-1-3500-0618-8

Library of Congress Cataloging-in-Publication Data
A catalog record for this book is available from the Library of Congress.

Series: Textual Moments in the History of Political Thought

Cover design: Burge Agency
Cover image © Max Krasnov/Shutterstock

Typeset by Integra Software Services Pvt. Ltd.
Printed and bound in Great Britain

To find out more about our authors and books visit www.bloomsbury.com. Here you will find extracts, author interviews, details of forthcoming events and the option to sign up for our newsletters.

CONTENTS

List of contributors viii
Series editors' foreword xi
Acknowledgements xiii

Introduction 1
Xavier Márquez

1 Herodotus's Political Ecologies 9
  Joel Alden Schlosser

2 Protagoras's Cooperative Know-how 17
  James Kierstead

3 Aristotle on Democracy and Democracies 25
  Kevin M. Cherry

4 Cicero, *On the Republic* 33
  W. Jeffrey Tatum

5 Democracy without Elections: Popular Rule according to Alfarabi 41
  Alexander Orwin

6 Consent and Popular Sovereignty in Medieval Political Thought: Marsilius of Padua's *Defensor pacis* 49
  Takashi Shogimen

7 Machiavelli's Democratic Turn 57
  Catherine H. Zuckert

8   James Harrington and the Rule of King People 65
    J. C. Davis

9   Baruch Spinoza: Radical Republican 73
    Emma Cohen de Lara and Nathan Cooper

10 Thomas Paine and Democratic Contempt 81
    Mario Feit

11 Alexander Radishchev's *Journey from St. Petersburg to Moscow*: The Defence of Natural Rights and the Right to Self-defence 89
    Andrew Kahn

12 Of Postmen and Democracy: Sieyès's Theory of Representation 97
    Lucia Rubinelli

13 'Morals and Enlightenment': Bolívar's Virtuous Democracy in the Angostura Address 105
    Guillermo Aveledo

14 The Puzzle of Political Leadership in Tocqueville's *Democracy in America* 113
    Ryan K. Balot and Zhichao Tong

15 'Family Selfishness' and the Corruption of Public Virtue: Harriet Taylor Mill's *Enfranchisement of Women* 121
    Katherine Smits

16 Lenin: Soviet Democracy in 1917 129
    Paul Blackledge

17 Democracy in the Revolutionary Thought of Rosa Luxemburg 137
    Rosemary H. T. O'Kane

18 Max Weber's Charismatic Democracy 145
    Xavier Márquez

19 An Alternative Democracy: Dissent in Gandhi's Great Trial of 1922 153
Anuradha Veeravalli

20 Sun Yat-sen: People's Democracy and Chinese Democracy 161
Theresa Man Ling Lee

21 Hobson on Democracy and the Humanized Economy 169
Colin Tyler

22 A New Reading on Authority and Guardianship (*wilayah*): Ayatollah Muhammad Mahdi Shamsuddin 177
Hamid Mavani

Conclusion 185

Xavier Márquez

Suggestions for further reading 190
Index 197

LIST OF CONTRIBUTORS

Guillermo Aveledo is Professor of Political Thought at the Universidad Metropolitana, Venezuela. He is the author of the books *Pro Religione et Patria: República y Religión en la Crisis de la Sociedad Colonial Venezolana (1810–1834)* and *La segunda república liberal democrática 1959–1998*.

Ryan K. Balot is Professor of Political Science and Classics at the University of Toronto, Canada. He is the author of several books, most recently *Courage in the Democratic Polis: Ideology and Critique in Classical Athens*.

Paul Blackledge is Professor of Political Theory at London South Bank University, UK. He is the author of *Marxism and Ethics*, *Reflections on the Marxist Theory of History* and *Perry Anderson, Marxism and the New Left*.

Kevin M. Cherry is Associate Professor in the Department of Political Science at the University of Richmond, USA. He is the author of *Plato, Aristotle, and the Purpose of Politics*.

Emma Cohen de Lara is Senior Lecturer in Political Theory at Amsterdam University College, The Netherlands. One of her recent publications is 'Aristotle's *Rhetoric* and the Persistence of the Emotions in the Courtroom', in N. Coelho and L. Huppes-Cluysenaer (eds) *Aristotle on Law and Emotion*.

Nathan Cooper is a graduate from Amsterdam University College and Radboud University, The Netherlands. He has written on the liberal arts and sciences model in the European context. Nathan has a specific research interest in the status of liberal democratic thought in a globalized world, and looks forward to developing this research agenda over the next years in Ghent and Vienna.

J. C. Davis is Emeritus Professor of History at the University of East Anglia, UK. He has published extensively on the political and religious thought of the English Revolution and on the history of utopian thought. A collection of his essays on radicalism and utopianism is in preparation under the title of *Alternative Worlds Imagined 1500–1700*.

LIST OF CONTRIBUTORS

Mario Feit is Associate Professor of Political Theory at Georgia State University, USA. He is the author of the book *Democratic Anxieties: Same-Sex Marriage, Death, and Citizenship*.

Andrew Kahn is Professor of Russian Literature at the University of Oxford, UK. He is the author of the books *Pushkin's Lyric Intelligence* and *Karamzin's Discourses of Enlightenment*.

James Kierstead is Lecturer in Classics at Victoria University of Wellington, New Zealand. He is the author of a number of articles and reviews in the areas of ancient Greek history, the history of democracy, and democratic theory. He is currently working on a book on Athenian democracy and society.

Theresa Man Ling Lee is Associate Professor of Political Science at the University of Guelph, Canada. Lee has published on a wide range of subjects in continental philosophy, modern Chinese political thought and comparative political theory.

Xavier Márquez is Senior Lecturer in Political Science at Victoria University of Wellington, New Zealand. He is the author of *Non-democratic Politics: Authoritarianism, Dictatorship, and Democratization* and *A Stranger's Knowledge: Statesmanship, Philosophy and Law in Plato's* Statesman.

Hamid Mavani is Associate Professor of Islamic Studies at Bayan Claremont Islamic Graduate School/Claremont School of Theology, USA. He is the author of *Religious Authority and Political Thought in Twelver Shi'ism: From Ali to Post-Khomeini*.

Rosemary H. T. O'Kane is Emeritus Professor of Comparative Political Theory at Keele University, UK. She is the author of the books *Rosa Luxemburg in Action: For Revolution and Democracy* and *Paths to Democracy: Revolution and Totalitarianism*.

Alexander Orwin is Assistant Professor at Louisiana State University, USA. He is the author of *Redefining the Muslim Community: Ethnicity, Religion, and Politics in the Thought of Alfarabi*.

Lucia Rubinelli is Fellow in Political Theory, London School of Economics and Political Science, UK.

Joel Alden Schlosser is Assistant Professor of Political Science at Bryn Mawr College and 2016–2017 Fellow at the Harvard Center for Hellenic Studies,

USA. He is the author of *What Would Socrates Do?* as well as numerous articles on ancient political thought.

Takashi Shogimen is Professor of History and Head of the Department of History and Art History at the University of Otago, New Zealand. He is the author of *Ockham and Political Discourse in the Late Middle Ages* and co-editor (with Vicki A. Spencer) of *Visions of Peace: Asia and the West*.

Katherine Smits is Associate Professor of Politics and International Relations at the University of Auckland, New Zealand. She works on political theory, and is the author of *Reconstructing Post-nationalist Liberal Pluralism*, *Applying Political Theory* and the co-editor of *Feminist Moments: Reading Feminist Texts*. She has published in the areas of liberal political theory, multiculturalism, identity politics and nationalism.

W. Jeffrey Tatum is Professor of Classics at Victoria University of Wellington, New Zealand. He is the author of *The Patrician Tribune: Publius Clodius Pulcher*, *Always I Am Caesar*, *A Caesar Reader* and *Plutarch: The Rise of Rome*, with Chris Pelling.

Zhichao Tong is a PhD student in political theory at the University of Toronto, Canada. His essays have appeared in *American Political Thought* and the *Journal of International Political Theory*.

Colin Tyler is Professor of Social and Political Thought and Director of the Centre for Idealism and the New Liberalism at the University of Hull, UK. His most recent books include *Common Good Politics*, *Civil Society, Capitalism and the State* and *The Metaphysics of Self-realisation and Freedom*.

Anuradha Veeravalli is formerly Assistant Professor, Department of Philosophy, University of Delhi, India. She is the author of *Gandhi in Political Theory: Truth, Law and Experiment* and the 'Indian Philosophies' entry in the *Encyclopedia of Religion*, 2nd edition. She is currently working on 'Theories of the Name: Tradition, Modernity and the Vernacular' as guest fellow at the Indian Institute of Advanced Studies, Shimla.

Catherine H. Zuckert is Nancy Reeves Dreux Professor of Political Science, University of Notre Dame, USA. She is the author of *Natural Right and the American Imagination*, *Postmodern Platos*, *Plato's Philosophers* and *Machiavelli's Politics*.

SERIES EDITORS' FOREWORD

At the heart of the serious study of the history of political thought, as expressed through both canonical and non-canonical works of all kinds, has been the question (to which we all too readily assume an answer), 'How shall I read this text?' Answers have varied greatly over time. Once the political works of the past – especially those of Classical Greece and Rome – were read with an eye to their immediate application to the present. And, until comparatively recently, the canonical works of political philosophy were selected and read as expressions of perennial, abiding truths about politics, social morality and justice. The problem was that this approach made little or no concession to historically changing contexts, that the 'truths' we identified were all too often **our** truths. A marxisant sociology of knowledge struggled to break free from the 'eternal verities' of political thought by exploring the ways in which past societies shaped their own forms of political expression in distinctive yet commonly grounded conceptions of their own image. The problem remained that the perception of what shaped past societies was all too often driven by the demands of a current political agenda. In both cases, present concerns shaped the narrative history of political thought off which the reading of texts fed. The last half century has seen another powerful and influential attempt to break free from a present-centred history of political thought by locating texts as speech acts or moves within a contemporary context of linguistic usage. Here the frequently perceived problem has been (a by-no-means inevitable) narrowing of focus to canonical texts, while the study of other forms of political expression in images, speech, performance and gesture – in all forms of political culture – has burgeoned independently.

We have, then, a variety of ways of approaching past texts and the interplay of text and context. The series 'Textual Moments in the History of Political Thought' (in which *Democratic Moments* is the seventh title) is designed to encourage fresh readings of thematically selected texts. Each chapter identifies a key textual moment or passage and exposes it to a reading by an acknowledged expert. The aim is fresh insight, accessibility and the encouragement to read in a more informed way for oneself.

Democracy and democratic institutions – in the prevailing rhetoric if not always in substantive reality – have emerged on such a scale as to encourage us to think of them as natural and readily achievable. As these essays remind us, this has rarely, if ever before in human history, been the case. On the one hand, the links between wisdom, stability, continuity, order and demos, the rule of the multitude, have, in most ages and cultures, appeared far from obvious. At a minimum, the headless multitude have required leadership and hence, so it has frequently appeared, the many have required the collaboration, if not the dominance, of the few. That relationship between the few and the many, has been, and continues to be, central to the possibility and character of democracy; anxiety about the lack of perceived leadership talent is often in tension with the fear of overweening leaders and demagogues. On the other hand, the discussion of democracy has been vexed by the question of who are the 'people'; of how we should define the citizen body? Is it, promiscuously perhaps, the whole population over a certain lower age limit, or, is it more refined and qualified than that? And, if so, how? In other words, how far does the rule of the many incline in the direction of all and how far in the direction of the few? The broader the citizen body the more urgent the issue of representation becomes. Yet representation inevitably involves the mediation of the popular will. Can the authorized actors be trusted to articulate the authentic *vox populi*? As these essays make clear, every expression of 'genuine' democracy involves some engagement with the values and issues of freedom, consent and equality. For much of human history, extending into the present, those values have been regarded as too high a price to pay.

In the present collection of essays, Xavier Márquez has assembled an international team of experts to explore a chronologically, geographically and culturally diverse range of 'democratic moments' in which these questions have been confronted. Both the external threats to and the internal dilemmas facing democratic ideals and institutions in the past and the present are here illuminated. So too are the aspirations to public accountability, liberty of expression, participation in public life and self-rule. Globalization, media manipulation, the sheer complexity of modern commercial life and the ongoing technological revolution, alongside shrinking rates of participation, may make those aspirations appear uncertain if not in jeopardy. Reading, and learning to read, texts like the ones under scrutiny here can bring us both to realize that many of these problems have been seen before and to engage with new ways of thinking about them.

J. C. Davis
John Morrow

ACKNOWLEDGEMENTS

The editor would like to acknowledge the patience and generous assistance of the series editors, J. C. Davis and John Morrow, as well as of the editorial staff at Bloomsbury, especially Beatriz Lopez, who put up with numerous delays and provided helpful feedback at all stages of this project.

Introduction

Xavier Márquez

We live in a democratic age. Constitutional documents throughout the world proclaim their democratic character, and few governments wish to be thought undemocratic. People throughout the world demand democracy, and pro-democracy feeling is high even in the most unlikely places. Indeed, with some very minor exceptions, as the historian John Dunn has noted, the word 'democracy' has come to symbolize the only legitimate political system in most languages.[1] 'Democracy' is today hailed as a 'universal value',[2] and this appears to be the 'democratic moment' *par excellence*.

Yet despite the rhetorical triumph of democracy, its meaning remains disputed, and disappointments with its reality are keenly felt. The standard view of liberal democracy, with its emphasis on electoral institutions, 'checks and balances' and individual rights, has been challenged both by illiberal populists claiming to speak more clearly on behalf of 'the people' and by conceptions of technocratic management reinvigorated by the apparent successes of a Chinese model that still officially wishes to be called 'the people's democratic dictatorship'.[3] The contemporary democratic moment combines high esteem for the vague idea of 'democracy' and surprisingly low esteem for actually existing democracies.

But the idea of democracy has not always been held in high esteem, much less been considered to be a universal principle of political legitimacy and institutional design. On the contrary, up until the nineteenth century, the history of thought about democracy has mostly been the history of arguments against democracy, and the history of democratic practices often a history of fugitive moments, unrecognized as such even by participants. Today's democratic moment masks the fact that democracy has always been a contested concept, controversial from the moment the word was introduced to the Western political tradition in Ancient Greece.

This collection offers new readings of a variety of texts that contributed to the making of our current global democratic moment. Like many such collections, it can hardly aim to be comprehensive. Some classic texts on democracy are omitted, and some less well known and less influential texts included, in an attempt to go beyond the canonical history of democracy, with its beginnings in Ancient Athens and its climax in the French and American revolutions. Along with many classic Western texts, the book thus also includes texts by writers with little experience of institutions of popular participation, from Alfarabi in the Baghdad of the Abbasid Caliphate to Alexander Radishchev in the absolutist monarchy of Catherine II of Russia, as well as from writers not usually considered to be important theorists of democracy, such as Bolívar in nineteenth-century Latin America, Gandhi in pre-independence India, Sun Yat-sen in republican China and Shamsuddin in mid-twentieth-century Lebanon. These essays aim to de-center our understanding of the moments where the idea of democracy was articulated, rejected and appropriated.

The book nevertheless starts, as it must, with Ancient Greece. Though the idea that democracy was invented in a 'small municipality in Southeastern Europe' is exaggerated,[4] almost all systematic written discussion of democracy first emerged from reflection on the Greek, and especially Athenian, experiment. Athens may not have originated the practice of democracy, but it almost certainly inaugurated the practice of written criticism of democracy; textually speaking, this was the first 'democratic moment'. And from the beginning, democracy was faulted for putting power in the hands of the unqualified and destroying natural hierarchies of wealth, prestige or virtue. But these criticisms were tempered by the recognition that some measure of democracy could produce political stability, and that the forms of equality it drew upon could not be simply dismissed. Even Plato, Athens' most famous critic, put in Protagoras' mouth a still striking and powerful defence of democratic equality, in which democracy is made possible by the moral capacities of ordinary people, as James Kierstead's chapter describes.

Athenian democracy was the quintessential 'assembly democracy', where citizens came together to directly decide on most political questions. This was for a long time the only picture of democratic institutions available to later writers, and it remains an inspiration to radical theorists of participatory and direct democracy even today. As Paul Blackledge notes in his chapter on Lenin, Marx and later Marxists took inspiration from the direct democracy of the Greeks even as they sought to transcend its limitations by locating the key locus of democratic power in the economic sphere. Yet even in ancient times democracy was never fully identified with a particular institutional configuration of popular power. As Joel Schlosser's chapter shows, writers from Herodotus onward understood that the forms of equality associated with democracy could be seen in many different regimes, including non-democratic regimes. Democracy as a set of institutions of popular participation was constantly in dialogue with other forms of government, which could and did express, in their own ways, these values, and which were thought to be better adapted to particular cultural and social 'ecologies'.

Nevertheless, already in Herodotus democracy is identified with forms of equality – of power, voice and law – which could not but be in opposition to existing hierarchies of power and status, and which were obviously associated with Athenian institutions. These institutions were in part understood as an outcome of fundamental conflicts between rich and poor, as Aristotle was among the first to emphasize. Disagreements between the rich and the poor about the meaning and appropriateness of political equality were in turn thought to account for the democratic tendency towards disorder and conflict. Yet Aristotle was also aware that democracies were not all identical. As Kevin Cherry describes in his chapter, he carefully considered contemporary forms of democracy to determine their appropriateness to different contexts, noted their differing capacities to preserve the rule of law and justly mediate class conflict, and advised statesmen on how democracy's tendencies to conflict and disorder could be mitigated by mixtures with other forms of government. The eventual result of this line of thought, the theory of the 'mixed constitution', was one way in which democracy was 'tamed' for ancient Republican thought.[5] Even Cicero, that Roman arch-conservative, granted that some degree of democratic participation in rule was necessary to the stability of a constitution, even as he denied that citizens should be considered socially equal, as Jeffrey Tatum discusses in his chapter. On its own, democracy's runaway equality was dangerous; properly tempered by other values and institutions, it was essential for an enduring political regime.

The fall of the Roman Republic led to a decline in writing about democracy in the West except as a historical curiosity. Yet recognizably democratic practices asserting the political equality of the members of a particular community and keeping governors at least morally accountable to a broader public did not disappear completely. They were especially important in the early centuries of Islam, when mosques and other forms of what today we would call 'civil society' helped keep rulers accountable and ensured that the idea of political equality did not die out. Indeed, long after Athens was just a dim memory, preserved only in the writings of Plato and Aristotle, the appeal of democratic equality and its concomitant valuation of a diversity of ways of life could still be understood by thinkers with no experience of institutions of popular participation in rule, as Alexander Orwin's chapter on Alfarabi shows. Alfarabi's discussion of the 'democratic city', drawing both on Plato's *Republic* and on his own experience of tenth-century Baghdad, is perhaps best understood as a description of what Tocqueville would later call the democratic social state, with its levelling of social distinctions and its multiplicity of associations ('cities') and ways of life. And though Alfarabi had no conception of popular consent or sovereignty, he could see how this social state led to the dependence of the ruler on the approval of the ruled, even if for him democracy as a political institution would have been little more than 'monarchy, tempered by riots', to paraphrase Lewis Namier's famous phrase about eighteenth-century England.

The Greek conception of democracy had little to do with the modern idea that legitimate power requires the consent of the citizenry. This latter notion emerges slowly in medieval European political thought, along with the notion of representation. As Takashi Shogimen notes in his discussion of Marsilius of Padua's *Defensor Pacis*, while medieval political thought did not approve of democracy in general, Marsilius' claim that some law is *instituted* rather than divine in origin, and that instituted law requires *consent*, leads to the idea that the community can be *represented* by a part of it. Law is not *discovered* by the citizenry, but it must be *approved* by the 'greater' part of it – the part that can genuinely discern the community's common good – if it is to have authority.

Disapproval of democracy, associated as it was with Athenian tumults and disorder, would nevertheless remain the default position for most writers until the nineteenth century. Indeed, most of the founders of what we now think of as our democratic institutions were no 'democrats' themselves; they were anti-aristocrats and republicans first of all.[6] But the resurgence of republican political thought in Italy in the fourteenth and fifteenth centuries led at least some people to argue for a stronger role for popular participation in politics, even when they still avoided the word 'democracy'. Machiavelli, in this as in many other things an original voice, was among the first to take a decidedly democratic turn, as Catherine Zuckert argues in her essay. 'The people', whose interests primarily lay in not being oppressed, represented a better guarantee of political order than the nobles, who too often wanted to oppress the former. And by competing for the favour of the people, the great would in turn prevent the emergence of tyrants.

Later republicans, including Spinoza and Harrington, further developed the case for granting significant power to the people in a republican context. J. C. Davis notes that Harrington thought democracy was possible in his time because of the spread of land ownership, even as he also worried about how to contain the potential for factionalism that had always been thought to be inherent to the involvement of the people in politics. More importantly, for Harrington, the irrationality of ordinary men was no longer seen as an obviously disqualifying fact about democracy. And as Emma Cohen de Lara and Nathan Cooper argue in their chapter, Spinoza sought to ground political power in the people even while holding a significantly negative view of their individual capacities. Spinoza's radical republicanism is especially notable in this respect; not only does Spinoza argue that democracy is more stable than monarchy, in spite of the ignorance and superstition of most people, he is uncompromising in his defence of the freedom of thought that we now think of as foundational to liberal conceptions of democracy. Monarchy, Spinoza argues, is fundamentally deceptive; the monarch can only keep power by keeping people in a condition of superstition and ignorance, a condition which he thinks democracy mitigates.

A distrust of monarchy and aristocracy soon became a clear theme in the emerging democratic moment of the eighteenth and nineteenth centuries. Paine thought monarchy deserved contempt, and mobilized this feeling rhetorically to support popular participation in government, as Mario Feit shows in his chapter. And Alexander Radishchev, writing in absolutist Russia, mobilized outrage against the depredations of the nobility to argue for the fundamental equality of human beings and an embryonic notion of human rights, as we see in Andrew Kahn's essay. To be sure, unlike radicals like Paine, Radishchev did not think Russia was ready for any kind of representative government, and he did not go so far as to assert that fundamental human equality should translate into political equality or even suffrage. But his vision of how the community retains a fundamental right to hold those who have abused their power to account, and his assertion of a fundamental right to liberty, demonstrates how democratic themes could be appropriated even in the most unfertile soils; it is no wonder that the Bolsheviks would later claim him as a precursor in radical politics.

New democratic ideas at this time were still self-consciously opposed to 'ancient' ideas of democracy (as we see most explicitly in Constant's famous essay contrasting the 'liberty of the ancients' with 'the liberty of the moderns'), but they still offered an initially radical alternative to aristocracy as the rule of inherited privilege. Though most democratic thinkers agreed the people could not rule on their own, given the scale of the political community and the complexity of government, they must at least have an opportunity to consent to the law: no one could have political authority by birth. The alternative to aristocratic monarchy was thus often articulated in the language of representation. And as Lucia Rubinelli shows in her essay on Sieyès, the new notion of representation was part and parcel of an emerging conception of society as a complex division of labour that was self-consciously contrasted to the 'simplicity' of Athens. For Sieyès, society was better off the more individuals were more fully represented by others, not just in politics but in all kinds of activities.

The need for representation by wiser, better others was especially present to the minds of the statesmen who had to deal with the aftermath of the bloody wars of independence in Latin America. These were democratic revolutions in the sense that they were waged for the sake of popular sovereignty and appealed to values of equality and the consent of the governed. But, as Guillermo Aveledo shows in his chapter on Bolívar, while popular sovereignty was widely seen as the only legitimate revolutionary goal, the people themselves seemed unsuited to the responsibilities of government. Factionalism plagued the new republics, and the fault was the people's lack of civic education. The people should be sovereign, not as they were, but as they should be; and education was essential to bring about their enlightenment. But in the meantime, it was still necessary to constitute a people that *could* take on political responsibilities. Bolívar found the right model for the people in his revolutionary army, with its egalitarian mixture of races and its demonstrated virtues; the army could thus represent the people as a whole.

Democracy in any case soon came to mean not just an institutional scheme enabling the representation of the people in government, but an entire culture that levelled social distinctions, and made a democratic people a living reality. The United States was the key exemplar of this new culture; but, as Tocqueville noted, there was a danger that a democratic culture tended to undermine the virtues that preserved democratic government itself. In particular, the democratic citizen, emancipated from hierarchical social ties, had a tendency to narrow the scope of his interests and values, hindering the emergence of the sorts of civic virtues that had made American democracy so lively, and making new forms of despotism possible. As Ryan Balot and Zhichao Tong note in their chapter, Tocqueville thought that in order to preserve democratic government, democratic societies required leaders capable of expanding the horizons of citizens and refining their views. And while his prediction about the kinds of institutions likely to produce such was perhaps misguided, Tocqueville's preoccupation with the privatization of citizenship in the new democratic (and capitalist) age was to remain an enduring concern for democratic theorists.

Excessive concern with narrow private or family interests was a vexing problem for theorists of representative democracies, since their scale, as earlier theorists had usually argued, precluded the kinds of involvement in politics that standard republican thought would have recommended. But the problem could not always be traced to the democratic social state itself. As Katherine Smits shows in her chapter, Harriet Taylor Mill saw the excessive narrowing of citizen interests as one of the evils that flowed from the exclusion of women from the public sphere. Her corrective was to argue for formal inclusion, not only as a matter of basic justice, but precisely as a way to ensure that citizens would care for the common good. Though universal suffrage had to wait until after the end of the First World War in most of Europe, and until the mid-twentieth century in much of the rest of the world, the dynamic of democratic inclusion, with its levelling of arbitrary social distinctions, was already unstoppable.

Formal inclusion, however, was soon believed to be necessary but not sufficient to realize democratic self-rule. For Marx and later Marxist thinkers, including Lenin, capitalism seemed to make a mockery of representation. In particular, if economic power was also political power, it followed that it was necessary to democratize economic power, starting at the locus of production. Marxists did not necessarily dismiss the emancipatory power of representative democracy, but they did seek to supplement it by democratizing other spaces. The 'soviet' vision of democracy, though grotesquely distorted in the Soviet Union, did have its origins in a genuine account of democracy and the state, as Paul Blackledge argues in his chapter.

And Rosa Luxemburg's concern with the democratizing power of the people in the street bears more than a family resemblance with earlier views of the power of civic engagement, if in a stronger fashion more appropriate to the revolutionary period she lived through, as we see in Rosemary H. T. O'Kane's chapter.

Marxists were not the only people concerned with the corrosive power of capitalism, and more broadly modernity, on democracy. J. A. Hobson, writing in the 1930s, did not think democracy could survive unless it could address the broader problems of global capitalism and imperialism, as Colin Tyler notes in his chapter. The complexity of the economy and the international system meant that all visions of direct democracy were doomed; but the scope of the regulatory state and international institutions could only be safely enlarged if it was subject to democratic control by a properly educated electorate. The same complexity of modern government had led Max Weber to argue that democracy required charismatic leadership. Like other modern social orders, democracy was subject to pressures towards bureaucratization that made genuine popular control impossible. Democracy, on this view, is a matter for elites, a view that would be further articulated by Schumpeter and the proponents of the 'minimalist' conception of democracy. But Weber also stressed that properly structured democracies were also better able than the alternatives to produce responsible leaders and keep them accountable.

In the twentieth century democratic ideas came to resonate far beyond the European core, the Anglosphere, and Latin America. Even before the end of the Cold War, elections with universal suffrage, the primary mark of modern representative democracy, had become ubiquitous, even if they were not always meaningful or fair. But they were also reinterpreted in new ways. Today's democratic moment is resolutely post-Western. Gandhi's struggle against the British empire, for example, led him to put 'dissent', rather than collective control, front and centre in his conception of democracy, as we see in Anuradha Veeravalli's chapter. The individual conscience, speaking truth to power, was also to be a part of the democratic resistance to totalitarian states. Sun Yat-sen saw democracy as the best way to build a strong national state, capable of resisting the depredations of imperial powers while ensuring welfare for the people, but self-consciously drew on Chinese ideas of meritocratic selection to argue for a balance between competence and popular control in democratic states, as Theresa Man Ling Lee shows in her chapter. And many Muslim thinkers came to see democracy, understood as popular sovereignty, as fundamentally compatible with Islam, given the fallibility of human rulers, as we see in Hamid Mavani's chapter on Muhammad Mahdi Shamsuddin.

A collection like this necessarily has some important limits. Democracy, as an idea and as a practice, developed not just through the ideas of elite writers but also through the actions of many ordinary people who did not care to theorize their activity. Democratic moments are not all textual. Yet this work focuses mostly on theoretical elaborations (and critical discussions) of the idea of democracy: its meaning, its reach, the principles and institutions that express it. Despite their limits, we think these texts are illuminating about the history of democracy and its power.

Notes

1 John Dunn, *Democracy: A History* (New York: Atlantic Monthly Press, 2005).
2 Amartya Sen, 'Democracy as a Universal Value', *Journal of Democracy* 10, no. 3 (1999): 3–17.
3 See, for example, Daniel Bell, *The China Model: Political Meritocracy and the Limits of Democracy* (Princeton: Princeton University Press, 2015).
4 Adam Przeworski, *Democracy and the Limits of Self-Government* (New York: Cambridge University Press, 2010), 4. Assembly forms of government are attested in the Syria-Mesopotamia region and the broader Mediterranean before the classical age of Athens. See John Keane, *The Life and Death of Democracy* (New York: W.W. Norton & Co., 2009), chapter 2. There is also evidence that such forms of government have been independently re-invented multiple times in world history.
5 See Xavier Márquez, 'Cicero and the Stability of States', *History of Political Thought* 32, no. 3 (2011): 397–423.
6 Przeworski, *Democracy and the Limits of Self-Government*, 5–8.

CHAPTER ONE

Herodotus's Political Ecologies

Joel Alden Schlosser

Rule by the majority on the other hand, bears that fairest of all titles: 'Equality before the law'. Not only that, but it has this second quality: it gives rise to none of the actions which a monarch characteristically takes. Those in office have their authority courtesy of a lottery, and wield it in a way that is strictly accountable. Every policy decision must be referred to the commonality of the people. That is why I give it as my opinion that we should abolish monarchy and foster the rule of the masses. Everything, after all, is contained within the multitude.[1]

Democracy began in ancient Greece and Herodotus's *Histories* offer the first description of democracy in Greek literature. The *Histories* chronicle the interactions between the Greek city-states and their powerful neighbours in the Near East, interactions that culminated in the Persian invasions of Greece in 490 and 480 BCE. Herodotus delves far into the past to explain this conflict, following the Persians' rise to mastery over a multi-ethnic and multi-continental empire. Herodotus himself was born on the edge of this empire, along the eastern coast of the Mediterranean in what is now Turkey. While we have few details of his life, the *Histories* testify to his travels: visits to the Black Sea region and Scythia, perhaps Babylon, Phoenicia, Palestine and especially Egypt where he sailed up the Nile to Elephantine. He also shows great familiarity with the Greek world, and became a citizen of Thurii, a pan-Hellenic colony in southern Italy, later in his life.

While tracing the long development of conflict between the Greeks and the Persians, Herodotus develops a distinctive approach to understanding a wide variety of human and non-human phenomena, including political phenomena. In what commentators have called the 'Constitutional Debate', Herodotus transcribes a discussion he purports took place among a group of seven Persian elites after they had taken power from a usurping group, the Magi. In this episode, three Persians – Otanes, Megabyzos and Darius – argue for a democracy, oligarchy and monarchy, respectively, as the new regime they should adopt. These arguments offer the first comparative approach to political regimes in ancient Greek political thought. They also anticipate many of the key concepts and arguments that would develop and flower in the centuries to follow.[2]

At the present moment, democracy is often considered the only legitimate political regime. Encouraging democracy abroad is regarded as a worthwhile endeavour; no one would wish to be known as opposing democracy. Herodotus's treatment of democracy merits our attention because it stands against these conventional opinions. In the Constitutional Debate, democracy does not emerge as the most choiceworthy regime, both in the particular moment of the narrative and across the whole of Herodotus's *Histories*. Herodotus instead illuminates the specific ecologies, that is, the interdependent physical, intellectual and cultural factors that make different political regimes possible and desirable for a given situation. And he introduces principles of balance and equality – *isonomia*, *isēgoria* and *isokratia* – that can orient successful political life within a given political ecology. Herodotus thus develops a view of democracy as situated in a particular ecology and not always the best or only way of achieving a sustainable and fair regime.

In the first of the speeches, the Persian noble Otanes introduces democracy with a flourish: the rule of the many, he says, has the fairest of names – *isonomia*. *Isonomia* might best be translated 'equality of law'.[3] Everyone makes the law and everyone is subject to it. As we see in the passage at the beginning of this chapter, Otanes elaborates the meaning of *isonomia* through its three constituent parts: rule by lot, accountability procedures and making all resolutions refer to the public.

While Otanes speaks as a Persian, these three components of a regime took fullest form in the Athens of Herodotus's day.[4] 'Rule by lot' meant that nearly all political offices were filled by lotteries. The agenda-setting Council of 500 was filled by lot, the administration of law was in the hands of the People's Courts (also chosen by lot) and juries had extensive discretionary scope. Accountability procedures meant that all government officials were subject to giving an account of their tenure both before and after their terms of office. They were also liable to recall and punishment. Orators could be held to account for advice through other laws. All resolutions were referred to the public. Each of these measures lay within the power of the people as embodied in the Assembly and the law courts.

Otanes's allusions to Athens also bespeak the contingency of the Athenian democracy – and of successful democracies more generally. At this point in the narrative, Herodotus's account has already given us many stories about how Athens became Athens. Athens' distinct topography, including coast, plains and hills, created the possibility for three different factions (1.59). When these came into conflict, Peisistratos, the famous Athenian tyrant, took power in large part because of his ability to trick the Athenians using their own customs. In one of these instances, Peisistratos returned from having been driven out of power by dressing a tall and strikingly beautiful women in a full suit of armour, placing her in a chariot and declaring that Athena herself was bringing Peisistratos home to her acropolis (1.60). The Athenian democracy, however, only came about when the Peisistratids were overthrown, a defeat instigated by the chance event of the capture of their children, which threw them into such confusion that they were forced to accept terms (5.65). Cleisthenes, who emerged as the leader after the Peisistratids were deposed, enlisted the common people and created the organizational structure that became emblematic of democracy.

The example of Athens suggests the accidents and contingencies that inform any particular democracy. Indeed, *isonomia*, the word Otanes uses to describe democracy, does not necessarily equate to the democratic institutions he lists.[5] Equality under law could well exist within an oligarchical regime: power is distributed in the state on the basis of equality yet the authority to issue law and be bound to it could well exist in representative systems with strong executives, as we see today.

When Otanes concludes that 'the many is the whole', it points to the indeterminate nature of democracy. Majority rule, *isonomia*, rule by lot, accountability procedures and popular sovereignty name components that may or may not be sufficient for democracy. Herodotus makes his readers extraordinarily aware of the particular conditions that create a democracy as well as the paradoxes involved. Athenian democracy arose in a dynamic ecology of geography, history, personality and contingency.

The subsequent speech by Megabyzos responds directly to Otanes's claims. This speech ostensibly advocates an oligarchy, yet much of it focuses on the negative aspects of empowering the people (*dēmos*). The people cannot be easily subdued, let alone directed or governed. They are like 'a stream swollen in the winter'.[6] They lack education and have never seen anything good or decent. Let the enemies of Persia be ruled by democracies, Megabyzos declares. The Persians themselves should choose the best men to rule.

This speech is full of critiques of democracy common during the fifth century BCE, and many commentators pass over it to focus on Darius's. Yet the choice of language here is important: the image of a stream swollen in winter is Homeric. Homer uses it to describe the irresistible vehemence of heroes, while Theognis employs it to indicate the overflowing, impulsive mass of people.[7] With this metaphor, Megabyzos invokes a broader sociological phenomenon. Megabyzos describes the *nature* of crowds.

Megabyzos's claim about crowds has support elsewhere in the *Histories*. One of Athens' first acts as a democracy is to punish and enslave the neighbouring Boeotians and Chalcidians for aiding Kleomenes in his attack (5.77); their freedom seems to include the freedom to dominate others, flooding over them like a swollen river. Nor is the Athenian *dēmos* predictable: We already encountered the story of the Athenians' being tricked by Peisistratus; Herodotus offers a corresponding story later when he describes the Athenians falling for the claims of Aristagoras of Miletus when he inveigles the Athenians to join the Ionian revolt against the Persians. Herodotus comments: 'This seems to suggest . . . that a crowd is more easily fooled than a single man' (5.97). Even the Persians, who with Cyrus can collectively preserve their status as rulers (9.122) also hold that rule by one man is necessary to drive people past their natural inclinations (7.103). Herodotus raises the question of the nature of crowds but doesn't answer how they can be directed or predicted.

The metaphor of the swollen stream suggests a *natural* tendency, one that can perhaps be diked or dammed but only so far. At the foundation of Megabyzos's argument for an oligarchy, then, is the idea that this structure would provide the most effective crowd control. The Constitutional Debate is an oligarchy already in action. The best men deliberate and vote on the proper course of action. There's no consideration of what the Persians in general think or of rivalries within the group. And the assembled seven arrive at an acceptable answer that allows the Persian empire to survive.

Darius's speech builds on the political ecologies of Otanes and Megabyzos by adding another dimension: history. 'Where does freedom come from?' asks Darius after he has argued for the inevitability of monarchy. Answering his own question, Darius points to the founder of the Persian empire, Cyrus, who freed the Persians from the Medes. The custom, or *nomos*, of the Persians is monarchy. Ignoring the criticisms of Otanes and Megabyzos, Darius points to the particular appropriateness of this regime for the Persians. It is the ancestral tradition and the source of their freedom.

Alongside his praise of monarchy for Persia, Darius introduces a new and important form of argumentation: a *historical* argument, one that takes into account contingency – namely, that regimes change with time, despite commitments otherwise. The Constitutional Debate as a whole reminds us of the importance of contingency: Otanes's speech alludes to the Athenians, who had only recently freed themselves from a tyrant; Megabyzos notes the inherently discontinuous nature of the people, which we can observe throughout the *Histories*; Darius warns against introducing more contingency. The Constitutional Debate as a whole creates a moment of potential discontinuity when the assembled consider a radical change to their customs of governance. While Darius's argument succeeds, Herodotus's attention to contingency reminds us that it could have been otherwise.

The Constitutional Debate itself puts the contingencies that shape political reflection on display. In the mouths of Otanes, Megabyzos and

Darius, the regime categories appear much less separable in practice than in theory. Otanes appears as much less of a committed democrat than he makes himself sound: When his proposal is not selected by the seven, he withdraws from participation, in effect refusing to 'rule and be ruled in turn'; later, Darius calls on Otanes to command the invasion of Samos where he orders the massacre of the Samians, violating Darius's instructions to the contrary (3.141, 3.147). Darius's trickery wins him the kingship and seems to suggest that the deliberations were for naught.

Here *isonomia* returns. Remember that Otanes used this term rather than *dēmokratia* to describe the regime to which he ascribed democratic institutions. *Isonomia* characterizes first of all an opposition to tyranny; we see this in Maiandros's attempt to reestablish freedom in Samos (3.142) and Aristagoras's abdication of his tyranny in Miletus (5.37). Yet as Vlastos and other commentators have pointed out, opposition to tyranny only captures one half of *isonomia*.[8] It also involves a principle of balance: *isonomia* emerged from Presocratic reflections on justice and equality in the cosmos; in the first use of the term, medical writer Alcmaeon defines health as 'equality [*isonomia*] of the powers'.[9] *Isonomia* thus points to the possibility of equilibrium. The health of the polity depends on a multitude of factors, not all of which lie within the domain of political control or power. Thinkers such as Empedocles, Parmenides and Anaximander saw natural events united in a common law of *isonomia*: Equality can prevent injustice; the earth owes its stability to this equality. *Isonomia* does not prescribe specific actions yet it provides a rule of thumb for maintaining balance and harmony, a rule of equality that can achieve justice.

Athens would seem to offer the best example of a sustainable *isonomia*, yet the *Histories* do not use this word to describe her. That is, *isonomia* is only used in Otanes's speech and the efforts of Miltiades and Aristagoras to establish *isonomia* in Ionia. Instead, the Athenian democracy following Cleisthenes's reforms has its own corresponding language of equality: equal voice (*isēgoria*) and equal power (*isokratia*). The differences among these *iso-* compounds suggests important distinctions among Herodotus's political ecologies determining where and how democracy might arise.[10]

After the Athenians are freed from their tyrants, the narrator explains its strength in terms of *isēgoria*:

> So Athens came to flourish – and to make manifest how important it is for everyone in a city to have an equal voice [*isēgoriē*], not just on one level but on all. For although the Athenians, while subjects of a tyrant, had been no more proficient in battle than any of their neighbours, they emerged as supreme by far once liberated from tyranny. This is proof enough that the downtrodden will never willingly pull their weight, since their labours are all in the service of a master – whereas free men, because they have a stake in their own exertions, will set to them with enthusiasm. (5.78)

The logic of *isēgoria* appears different in important respects from that of *isonomia*. The emphasis is not on something institutionalized but rather a broader political culture: *isēgoria* creates the conditions where everyone strives for what is best, with the assumed reward being theirs; yet while each pursues his own cause, this leads to the strength of the whole. *Isēgoria* makes possible collective self-actualization.

Athens also earns another distinctive name for its equality: *isokratia*. Freed from the tyrants, Athens demonstrates its strength with immediate conquests of the Boeotians and the Chalcidians. The Spartans wish to restore the Athenian tyranny lest the Athenians begin to match their own strength and influence. The Spartans summon their allies and Sokleas, a Corinthian, speaks against the restoration:

> 'So the sky is to be placed below the earth, is it, and the earth to hover above the sky?' he demanded. 'Humans are to gain their livelihood in the sea, are they, and fish in the former haunts of mankind? I only ask because it is you, the Lacedaemonians, who are planning to deny people an equal share of power [*isokratias*], and to foist tyrannical regimes upon them, when there is nothing more offensive to justice than a tyrant, not in all the affairs of man, nor anyone more steeped in blood!' (5.92)

Sokleas proceeds to describe the horrors of the tyranny in Corinth, illustrating his claim against it. Much like *isonomia* and *isēgoria*, *isokratia* is set off in contrast to tyranny. Yet these are not identical terms. The narrative context suggests a distinction: *isokratia* involves not the individual's pursuit of his own cause that redounds to the good of the whole but instead the equal power of each individual that leads to collective strength. The Spartans' abolition of *isokratia* would turn the world upside-down because this would involve destroying their own principle of political organization and success.

The likening of Athens to Sparta by Sokleas suggests a broader point applicable to *isonomia, isēgoria* and *isokratia*. These are general terms and not particular to Athens's style of democracy. Persians, Ionians, Athenians and Spartans can all have some variety of one of the three, although each has its specific emphasis. *Isonomia* names a principle of political equality; *isēgoria* invokes the need for deliberation and the effectiveness of equal voice in promoting individual efforts for the common weal; the equal power involved in *isokratia* prevents the rise of tyrants while promoting the strength of collective action.

Extrapolating from Herodotus's references, we might consider the politics of these principles of equality – *isonomia, isēgoria* and *isokratia* – in terms of the yielding and adjustment necessary for maintaining balance in the face of disrupting and discontinuous contingency. As the preceding discussion shows, associating any of these principles of equality with a specific regime misses their broader applicability and relevance for considering different political ecologies: each names not a set of practices or institutions but a 'political principle', as Ostwald puts it.[11] Herodotus puts democracy in a broader context of political ecology; with *isonomia*, *isēgoria* and *isokratia* he offers principles and practices for sustaining political life without necessarily becoming democratic.

This language of yielding and adjustment appears in another context roughly contemporary to the *Histories*: Sophocles's *Antigone*. There Haemon implores his father to reconsider the decision to execute Antigone:

> It is not shameful for a man, even if he is wise, often to learn things and not to resist too much. You see how when rivers are swollen in winter those trees that yield to the flood retain their branches, but those that offer resistance perish, trunk and all.[12]

The 'swollen river' echoes Megabyzos's criticism of the *dēmos* while Haemon's broader plea resonates with Otanes's concern for the potential hubris of the tyrant. Haemon advocates yielding, bending as the tree in a river's flood. Of course, Creon did not bend; we know the ultimate result. So too the *Histories* end with Xerxes' tyrannical madness and an allusion to how much Persia has transformed since the days of Cyrus. *Isonomia*, *isēgoria* and *isokratia* offer repertoires of response to these tendencies toward destruction; Otanes's praise of equality sounds a democratic note that persists throughout the *Histories*. Yet Herodotus does not seem to view democratic government as a solution. This Sophoclean insight casts a shadow on the hopes of staying ahead of the nature of things – be it the rising waters of the unwieldy rabble or the unruly desire of the tyrannical soul.

Notes

1 Herodotus, *The Histories: A New Translation*, trans. T. Holland (New York: Penguin, 2014), 3.80. Translations of the *Histories* will come from this text unless otherwise noted. Greek references are to *Herodoti Historiae*, 2 vols, ed. C. Hude (Oxford: Oxford University Press, 1990 [1908]).

2 It is important to note in advance that this comparative political assessment takes place through particular characters depicted with their own desires, orientations and relative power. In other words, the comparative politics is not disinterested.

3 M. Ostwald, *Nomos and the Beginnings of Athenian Democracy*. See further discussion and citations in J. Lombardini, 'Isonomia and the Public Sphere in Democratic Athens', *History of Political Thought* XXXIV, no. 3 (Autumn 2013): 393–420.

4 S. Forsdyke, 'Athenian Democratic Ideology and Herodotus' *Histories*', *The American Journal of Philology* 122, no. 3 (Autumn 2001): 329–58.

5   J. Schlosser, 'Herodotean Democracies', *The Bulletin of the Center for Hellenic Studies* 5, no. 1 (2017). http://www.chs-fellows.org/2017/04/17/herodotean-democracies/ [accessed 14/7/2017].

6   Herodotus, *The Histories*, trans. G. Rawlinson (New York: Knopf, 1997).

7   D. Asheri, *A Commentary on Herodotus Books I–IV* (Oxford: Oxford University Press, 2007), 475.

8   G. Vlastos: 'Isonomia', *The American Journal of Philology* 74, no. 4 (1953): 337–66; 'Isonomia Politike'. *Isonomia: Studien zur Gleichheitsvorstellung im Griechischen Denken*, ed. J. Mau (Berlin, 1964): 1–36.

9   G. Vlastos, 'Equality and Justice in Early Greek Cosmologies', *Classical Philology* 42, no. 3 (July 1947): 156–78, 156. See also L. MacKinney, 'The Concept of Isonomia in Greek Medicine', in *Isonomia: Studien zur Gleichheitsvorstellung im Griechischen Denken*, ed. J. Mau (Berlin, 1964): 79–88.

10 The next five paragraphs draw on Schlosser, 'Herodotean Democracies'.

11 Ostwald, *Nomos and the Beginnings of Athenian Democracy*, 97.

12 Sophocles, *Antigone*, trans. H. Lloyd-Jones (Cambridge: Harvard University Press, 1994), lines 710–14.

CHAPTER TWO

Protagoras's Cooperative Know-how

James Kierstead

So Zeus, afraid that our species might go extinct, sends Hermes to bring a sense of conscience and justice to humans, so that political communities could be organized and people could be brought together in joint activity. And Hermes asks Zeus how he should give out the sense of conscience and justice to humans. 'Should I hand them out like the other types of know-how? They get handed out like this: one person knowing medicine is enough for lots of people who don't, and it's the same for the other types of practical know-how. Is that how I should put a sense of justice and conscience into humans, or should I deal those out to everyone?' 'To everyone', says Zeus, 'and let everyone have a share of them; for political communities could not come into being, if only a few had a share of them like with the other types of know-how. And make a law for me that anyone who doesn't have a share of conscience and justice should be killed as a cancer on the body politic'. That's why, Socrates, when there's a question about how to do carpentry or any other sort of practical know-how, the Athenians and everyone else think that only a few people should have a part in the discussion, and if anyone else from outside those few

> *people offers advice, they don't put up with it, like you say – rightly, too, I'd say – but when it comes to a discussion about what's best for the political community, which has to go through a sense of what's right and people's common sense, then they're right to accept advice from everyone, since everyone has to have a part in this sort of thing; otherwise there'd be no political communities at all.*[1]

At the beginning of Plato's *Protagoras*, Socrates asks the celebrated sophist what it is he claims to teach. After some discussion, Protagoras agrees with Socrates that what he teaches is a kind of cooperative know-how (*politikē technē*), later also referred to as cooperative ability (*politikē aretē*) (314c–319a).

Socrates then asks Protagoras to explain something he has noticed about the Athenians. In the Assembly, Socrates observes, 'when the political community has to do something that has to do with construction, they send for construction engineers to give their advice about the construction, and when it has to do with building ships they send for the shipwrights', and so on; and 'if anyone else tries to give them advice who they don't think has that practical know-how, even if he's really hot or rich or from a great family, they'll have none of him, and they'll mock him and shout him down' (319b). In contrast to that, 'when they have to discuss something to do with the direction that the political community is going in, anyone can get up and give their advice, the carpenter just as much as the metal-worker or shoemaker, the merchant just as much as the ship-owner, the poor just as much as the rich, the common man as much as the aristocratic type, and nobody complains' (319d).

Protagoras's lengthy response to this has come to be known as the 'Great Speech' (320c8–328d2), and it contains one of the earliest defences of popular rule that we have from ancient Greece. For Cynthia Farrar, the speech shows that Protagoras was 'the first democratic political theorist in the history of the world' – at least 'as far as we know'.[2] Even this speech, of course, is really a product of Plato's mind rather than Protagoras's, but most scholars now seem happy to take it on trust that the speech reflects the thought of the historical Protagoras, or at least captures the gist of some of his main arguments.[3] Even if it does not, it would still represent a rare example of an ancient *apologia* for democracy.[4] On top of this, Protagoras's approach to democracy is an unfamiliar and insightful one. His key argument is that in order for the essential good of political community to be secured, it must be both possible and obligatory for all of us to practice political virtue. So let us now look at the Great Speech in more detail.

The speech begins with two titans, Prometheus and Epimetheus (Forethought and Afterthought), handing out capacities to the various species of mortal beings. Epimetheus distributed strength, speed, 'flying with wings, or the ability to live underground', as well as other attributes and abilities, to the various newly-created species (320d–321a), but he forgot to give any of these capacities to man, so that Prometheus was forced to steal 'technical smarts' (*entechnon sophian*) along with fire from Hephaestus and Athena, to ensure that humans survived (321c–d). And humans did survive, mainly because their 'practical know-how' (*dēmiourgikē technē*) enabled them to develop language and to figure out how to make clothing and homes for themselves, as well as to produce their own food through farming (322a).

The only problem was that humans lived 'scattered about the place, and there were no political communities; so they started to be killed by wild animals' (322b). As Protagoras explains, 'their practical know-how was enough to get them food, but not enough for fighting against the wild animals – they didn't have cooperative know-how yet, and knowing how to fight together (*polemikē technē*) is part of that' (322b). In reaction to this, 'they tried to get together and be safe by starting up political communities' but 'they did unjust things to each other because they didn't have cooperative know-how; so they scattered about the place and started to be killed again' (322b). At which point our passage begins.

Protagoras himself almost certainly did not believe that the events described in his story actually happened, but we can understand the story as a way of talking about certain natural characteristics of human beings. We can also see the stages of human development as a series of counterfactuals, designed to explore what life would have been like if we had not been endowed with certain characteristics.

So, for example, since we lack great size or claws or the ability to fly, we probably would have perished without a) fire and b) the practical know-how to learn how to use words and to produce clothing, shelter and food for ourselves. And we would not have been able to get political communities going without cooperative know-how. Cooperative know-how is one part *aidōs* (a sense of conscience) and one part *dikē* (a sense of justice). These enable us to live together because they force us to moderate our actions in response to the reactions of others.

A crucial part of Protagoras's argument is that we *all* have to have cooperative ability if our political community is going to survive (and here we might add 'and to flourish'). Why do we *all* have to exercise our cooperative know-how? Because cooperative know-how is the kind of know-how that, unless it is practiced by everybody, will not do the community any good. This is why Zeus tells Hermes to share out conscience and justice to everyone 'since everyone has to have a part in this sort of thing; otherwise there'd be no political communities at all' (322d). That makes them different to other types of know-how, like medicine; as Hermes says, 'one person knowing medicine is enough for lots of people who don't' (322c).

We do not all need to be doctors to have the benefits of medicine; indeed, although it is usually considered a good thing for a country to have more doctors rather than fewer, a society that consisted entirely of doctors would not be a flourishing one. But a society in which everybody had a sense of justice and conscience *would* be a flourishing one; in fact, if we believe Protagoras, *everybody* having some sense of justice is a necessary condition for the existence of political community in the first place. Here we might well wonder whether Protagoras has been over-ambitious. Surely all that he needs is the proposition that lots of people, or most people, have to have a conscience and a sense of justice if political community is to be possible. And that condition might seem more easily attainable.

This would be to misunderstand what Protagoras means by 'cooperative ability'. Everyone does not have to act perfectly the whole time for political community to function. They just all have to have a conscience and a sense of justice, and they need to be surrounded by people who also have those qualities. A person who commits a crime is not necessarily lacking in cooperative ability. They are lacking in cooperative ability only if they feel no remorse for the act and if they fail to react to the kind of rehabilitative punishment advocated by Protagoras (323d–324d).

On the other hand, if they do feel no remorse and have no ability to learn from their punishment, then they might well be lacking in cooperative ability. In this case, the punishment is death. Zeus himself, after all, lays down the law that 'anyone who doesn't have a share of conscience and justice should be killed as a cancer on the body politic' (322d). This might seem a bit harsh, and to be out of kilter with Protagoras's otherwise enlightened views on punishment. In fact, it is perfectly in accordance with them. It is precisely because Protagoras views punishment as moral teaching that there is no point in punishing someone who has no capacity for moral learning. (It might help to say that in modern terms, Protagoras is talking not about criminals, even hardened criminals, but psychopaths and sociopaths, that is, individuals who appear to have been born without the capacity to feel guilt.) This is why nobody admits that they have no cooperative ability, in the way that you can admit to not being able to play the flute; because 'everyone has to have some kind of cooperative ability, or they're not part of the human race' (323b).

The fact that we *all* need to have cooperative ability if the political community is to survive and flourish explains why we all need to monitor one another (at least, that is what Protagoras thinks; we will discuss more hierarchical ways of monitoring citizens in a minute). It is in every person's interest to make sure that everybody else is employing their cooperative ability, since if only a few people do not do so, our ability to operate as a complex whole is compromised. Moreover, monitoring the cooperative know-how of others is a way of employing our own; and at the same time as we are giving feedback to others about their cooperative know-how, we will inevitably be receiving feedback about our own. We are all constantly both teaching and learning the skill of doing things with others.

At this point, we may detect a similarity with Aristotle's account of man as a *zōon politikon*, that is, a political animal, or (less succinctly) an animal whose nature is to live in a political community (*Pol.* 1253a). Protagoras's emphasis on cooperative know-how or ability may also remind us of Aristotle's statement that political knowledge (*politikē epistēmē*) is the 'most authoritative and architectonic' (*Nic. Eth.* 1094a) sort. Ober has even developed an Aristotelian defence of democracy in which engaging in political activity is a way of exercising one of our essential capacities as political beings, and is thus a kind of good in itself.[5] Protagoras instead values political skill or virtue as a necessary condition for the creation of states, which are in turn necessary for our survival, rather than as a good in itself.

Protagoras's theory thus has a pragmatic and even consequentialist cast to it: the point of exercising our cooperative faculties is because if we fail to do so we will perish. In this his account of the creation of states is reminiscent of Thomas Hobbes, who postulated a stateless 'State of Nature' in which a continual 'war of every man against every man' rendered human life 'solitary, poor, nasty, brutish, and short' (*Lev.* 13). At the same time, in his concept of a universal moral/political capacity, Protagoras's account differs from that of Hobbes. For Hobbes, the only escape from the State of Nature is for individuals to give up their freedom to a sovereign capable of imposing order and security (*Lev.* 14). Once the Leviathan we have pledged our obedience to has started to make laws, we can begin to speak of justice; for Hobbes, 'no law can be unjust' because justice is whatever the Leviathan does (*Lev.* 30). For Protagoras, by contrast, the sense of justice inherent in each of us in what enables us to construct states. And because justice is inherent in each of us, the states that we can construct are cooperative endeavours, not hegemons to which we have ceded power.

Protagoras thus conceives of the state, not as a separate coercive apparatus imposing order on a subject population, but as a continual form of collective action carried out by the citizens themselves. In other words, Protagoras lacks the modern conception of the state as it is found, for example, in the work of Max Weber. For Fred Rosen, this is a limitation of his theory; but we may prefer to consider the possibilities that it opens up. As Cynthia Farrar suggests, for Protagoras, 'Society is social interaction [and] social harmony is the result of internal (not institutional) constraints. . . . Political interaction . . . is self-sustaining, for it fosters the very qualities and attitudes on which free social order depends.'[6]

In other words, social interaction is the state and the state consists of social interaction. Once we accept this as a feature of Protagoras's way of seeing things, it becomes easier to understand his concept of *politikē technē* or *aretē*, which runs over the division we might like to make between 'moral sense' and 'political expertise' (hence my translation, 'cooperative know-how' or 'ability'). Arthur Adkins's main complaint about Protagoras's speech was precisely that it conflates 'an assemblage of moral excellences' with what is required to give 'skilful advice', and 'co-operative excellences with administrative and political skills'.[7] But the point of the conflation was not, as Adkins suggests, to enable the sophist to offer something both to administrative elites and to the ordinary citizen. Morality and politics are brought together by Protagoras because there is, in his view, no firm boundary between them.

As citizens of a modern, representative democracy, this last point may seem hard to swallow. Surely, it might be said, we cede power to various representatives and civil servants precisely because voters are too ignorant, irrational and indifferent to make decisions on complex issues for themselves.[8] But we should consider the particular kinds of decisions Protagoras is evoking when he talks about the *politikē technē* or *aretē*. These are political and/or moral questions, and should be contrasted with merely technical matters, the province of practical know-how. If we consider that in modern democracies there is (at least in theory) a distinction between policy-*making*, which is the province of the people's representatives, and the *implementation* of policy, which is the province of civil servants, Protagoras's views may not seem so alien after all. And this is because genuinely political questions are not merely technical or factual in nature, but are rather ethical or normative: they are not questions about how the world is, but about what we ought to do.

And deciding what to do as a community will call on the same inborn qualities of conscience and justice that govern our relationships with our fellows in our day-to-day lives. Rather than seeing democratic practices as a means of attaining an ideal form of reasonable discussion (as theorists of deliberative democracy do), Protagoras sees democracy as a consequence of the kinds of moral communication we engage in every day. We do so naturally, because we are all endowed with a moral sense (psychopaths excepted); but also because *politikē aretē* is the sort of virtue that everybody must practice if any of us are to enjoy its benefits. In this respect, Protagoras joins forces with the political scientists who argue that democracy is superior in securing various sorts of goods (security, prosperity and so on).[9] Protagoras's *apologia* thus has a double aspect, combining as it does a naturalistic claim about equal political capacities with a consequentialist claim about the benefits of political virtue.

For one of our earliest known democratic theorists, then, democracy is a consequence of the nature of human beings and of the cooperative ability with which we are all endowed. We need political community for our survival and flourishing; in turn, if the political community is to survive and flourish, we need to exercise our cooperative ability. We can do this in a number of different ways, from engaging in moral communication with our fellows in social settings, to participating in the formal institutions of the state. But we *all* need to take part, and we need to encourage and enable *all* of our fellow citizens to take part too. This is the final message of Protagoras's theory of democracy for us today – and its real challenge.

Notes

1. Plato, *Protagoras*, 322c–323a. All translations are my own. I thank the editors of this volume, especially Xavier Márquez, for asking me to write this essay and for their feedback on it. I also thank Stephen Lambert for his comments and encouragement.
2. For this proclamation (and others along similar lines), see Fred Rosen, 'Did Protagoras Justify Democracy?', *Polis* 13, no. 1–2 (1994): 12–30.
3. See e.g. Rosen, 'Did Protagoras Justify Democracy?', 16.
4. Peter Nicholson, 'Protagoras and the Justification of Athenian Democracy', *Polis* 3, no. 2 (1981): 14–24, is among a dwindling minority of scholars who have denied that the Great Speech is about democracy at all.
5. Josiah Ober, 'Natural Capacities and Democracy as a Good-in-itself', *Philosophical Studies* 132, no. 1 (2007): 59–73.
6. Rosen, 'Did Protagoras Justify Democracy?', 19.
7. Arthur Adkins, 'ἀρετή, τέχνη, Democracy and Sophists: Protagoras 316b–328d', *Journal of Hellenic Studies* 93 (1973): 3–12.
8. See e.g. Bryan Caplan, *The Myth of the Rational Voter* (Princeton: Princeton University Press, 2007).
9. See e.g. Morton Halperin, Joe Siegle, and Michael Weinstein, *The Democracy Advantage: How Democracies Promote Prosperity and Peace* (New York: Routledge, 2004).

CHAPTER THREE

Aristotle on Democracy and Democracies

Kevin M. Cherry

The first sort of democracy, then, is that which is particularly said to be based on equality. The law in this sort of democracy asserts that there is equality when the poor are no more preeminent than the well-off, and neither have authority but both are similar. For if freedom indeed exists particularly in a democracy, as some conceive to be the case, as well as equality, this would particularly happen where all share in the regime as far as possible in similar fashion. But since the people are a majority, and what is resolved by the majority is authoritative, this will necessarily be a democracy. This is one kind of democracy; another is the kind where offices are filled on the basis of assessments, but these are low, and it is open to anyone possessing the amount to take part, while anyone losing it does not take part. Another kind of democracy is where all citizens of unquestioned descent take part, but law rules. Another kind of democracy is where all have a part in the offices provided only they are citizens, but law rules. Another kind of democracy is the same in other respects, but the multitude has authority and not the law. This comes about when decrees rather than law are authoritative, and this happens on account of the popular leaders. For in cities under a democracy that is based on law a popular leader does not arise, but the best of the citizens preside; but where the laws are without authority, there popular leaders arise. For the people become a monarch, from many combining into one – for the many have authority not as individuals but all together. . . . At any rate, such a people, being a sort of monarch, seek to rule monarchically on account of their not being ruled by law, and become like a master: flatterers are held in honor, and this sort of rule of the people bears comparison with tyranny among the forms of monarchy.[1]

It is a commonplace that Aristotle, like his teacher Plato, was a critic of democracy. This is, to a certain extent, true: Plato and Aristotle both saw democracy, at least as practiced in Athens, as prone to tumultuousness and imprudence. The failed Sicilian expedition, the execution of Socrates, the failure to heed Demosthenes's warnings about Philip of Macedon and Aristotle's own reported flight from Athens all highlighted the weaknesses of Athenian democratic institutions. Yet Aristotle's understanding of political science requires him to consider not only what the simply best regime might be, as Socrates purports to do in the *Republic*, but also the characteristic advantages and disadvantages of all kinds of regimes, including democracy. This is, in fact, particularly true with regard to democracy: Aristotle suggests that it is unlikely that any regime other than democracy will come into being (*Pol.* 1286b20–22) and, insofar as his political science is intended to be practical, understanding its strengths and limitations is of great importance.

Yet any account of Aristotle's views about democracy is complicated by the fact that there are different kinds of democracy. In Books IV, V and VI of the *Politics*, he explains why these different kinds arise and evaluates them, with a view toward helping statesmen improve the cities in which they live. Aristotle explicitly notes that many others have failed to recognize the varieties of democracy and oligarchy (1289a8–10). He makes similar claims about the importance of properly understanding the difference between oligarchy and democracy (1279b11–15), about the constituent features of political inquiry (1288b35–39), and about the importance of the regime generally referred to as polity, too often overlooked by those who look at regimes (1293a39–b1). Placing these hints of originality together reveals the core contribution of Aristotle's practical political science: an improved understanding of oligarchy and democracy as they exist in various cities in order to bring about better forms of those regimes (1289a1–4, 1289a20–22). From there, a prudent statesman may even be able to move the regime toward a polity, which is a combination of oligarchy and democracy (1293b33–36).

The textual source for Aristotle's criticism of democracy is found in Book III of his *Politics*. Aristotle there outlines a sixfold typology of regimes, dividing them first according to whether they rule for the common advantage or that of the rulers and then according to the number of rulers: one, few or many. A democratic regime is thus one in which 'the free and poor, being a majority, have authority to rule' for their own advantage (1290b17–19). It is a perversion of the 'regime called regime', often translated as 'polity', in which a multitude possessing 'military virtue' rules for the common advantage (1279a37–79b4).

The concept of regime is central to Aristotle's political science. By regime, Aristotle means the arrangement of the most authoritative offices in the city (1278b8–10) but also the way of life characteristic of the city, what the end of the city is (1289a15–18). Aristotle argues that the particular arrangement of offices in a city reflects a presumption about the best way of life. In an oligarchy, for instance, the purpose of life, and so of the city, is to make money, and therefore those who excel at making money hold political power. In a democracy, the assumption is that those who are equally free-born citizens ought to be equal in everything and so should share in the city's offices.

Aristotle thus quickly refines the initial division of regimes based on number of rulers, observing that what really distinguishes democracy from oligarchy is not whether the rule is by many or few but whether the poor or rich have authority. Because of the way politics is constituted by claims about justice, both rich and poor seek to justify their authority. Although the rich claim authority on the basis of their wealth, the poor do not justify their claim on what they lack but rather on what they share: the freeborn status of citizens (1279b34–80a6, 1301a28–35).

Aristotle emphasizes that these differences are not based simply on economic position but rather beliefs about justice. Oligarchs believe that, being superior in wealth, they ought to be superior in everything; democrats believe that, being equal in free birth, they ought to be equal in everything. The problem is that both oligarchs and democrats articulate a partial view of justice that they mistake for the whole, largely because they tend to judge in their own interest (1280a7–25). More important, both oligarchs and democrats overlook the true purpose of politics: living well. The political community is not primarily about avoiding injustice or acquiring wealth but about 'living happily and finely'. It is those who contribute most to this higher purpose who ought to have a greater, though not exclusive, share of power in the city (1280a25–40, 1280b40–81a8). Resolving these competing claims about justice and equality is no simple matter; it is, indeed, the chief task of 'political philosophy', a phrase Aristotle uses but once in the works we possess (1282b16–23).

Until Books VII and VIII, however, much of the *Politics* develops the contrast between oligarchy and democracy. Although presented as deviations, they were the more realistic alternatives for Greek statesmen insofar as they represented two enduring and competing claims to rule found in every city (1290a13–29, 1291b7–13, 1296a22–36, 1301b39–02a4).[2]

Although democracy as such is a deviant regime, that its view of justice is partially correct means that not every regime with democratic elements will be similarly deviant.[3] Much, therefore, depends on the evaluation of particular democracies and oligarchies in Aristotle's thought. We cannot adequately evaluate democracy and oligarchy in the abstract, insofar as they take different forms depending on the particular circumstances of given cities. In the passage above, Aristotle identifies five kinds of democracies that range from a regime that treats rich and poor equally under the law to a demagogic mob. These various democracies reflect to a certain extent the prudence of the statesman who gave the city its laws, but they also reflect the existence and prominence of various 'parts' of the city.

Aristotle identifies a variety of parts that exist in every city, ranging from the farmers, artisans, labourers and traders to soldiers, deliberators and judges. Many of these parts can overlap; farmers, for instance, can also be soldiers and judges. However, Aristotle observes, because the rich and the poor cannot be the same and, moreover, because the rich tend to be few and the poor many, most people mistakenly reduce the parts of the city to these two (1291b2–13). Recognizing the wider variety of the parts found in every city allows the prudent political scientist to understand the varieties of oligarchy and democracy that can arise, as these regimes will reflect the social and economic forces at work in the city.[4]

Aristotle offers two different enumerations of the varieties of democracy; in the passage at the beginning of this essay, he focused on the political institutions but in a later enumeration he focuses instead on the parts of the city and the way they affect those institutions through their sharing, or not sharing, in the regime (1292b22–25).[5] A democracy with a preponderance of farmers generally leads to the rule of law, insofar as farmers have enough property to provide for sustenance but lack leisure to assemble frequently. Other democracies allow citizens to participate even without sufficient property but if they are not paid to assemble, the regime will still be governed by law. Once a city becomes large and wealthy enough to pay the poor for attending the assembly, they have the leisure necessary to do so. The regime is thus increasingly in the hands of the lower classes, as they begin to outnumber the wealthy in the assembly. Holding more frequent assemblies leads to less reliance on the rule of law and, ultimately, the transformation of democracy into something else, the lawless – tyrannical – power of the assembly (often influenced by a demagogue). Such a city may not have a regime at all, for without law there is no regime (1292a30–32), and it is closer to a 'dynastic oligarchy and a tyrannical majority' (1298a32–33).[6]

Despite its deviant character, Aristotle holds that it is natural for a democracy to exist in those cities where the poor multitude exceeds in influence those of wealth or good birth (1296b24–26). Indeed, the various kinds of democracy reflect the relative influence of the various parts of the city. The best form of democracy involves a large middle class, composed primarily of farmers (1295b3ff., 1296b28–29, 1318b9–17). In this democracy, the farmers will generally select the wealthy to hold office, auditing them after their terms end (1318b27–19a4).[7] Ironically, this best form of democracy departs significantly from the best regime more broadly: farmers are good citizens because their lack of leisure prevents them from engaging actively in political life, yet such leisure is not only necessary for the cultivation of complete virtue but also for the activity one would think necessary for the fulfillment of our nature as political animals. In what appears to be a sketch for a simply best regime in Books VII and VIII, Aristotle explicitly states that farmers – along with merchants and labourers – will be refused citizenship (1328b41–29a2).

Although they fall short of the best regime, Aristotle offers two additional arguments in favour of moderate democratic regimes. The first of these occurs in a dialectical investigation of whether the best man or the many ought to be authoritative. Though Aristotle does not deny that some are more prudent than others or that such persons ought to rule, he does contend that the people – provided they are of a certain character – are capable of, and so ought to share in, selecting those who will occupy the highest offices of the city. This is no small matter but rather a 'very great thing' (1282a27). Although the political art is not one each citizen possesses individually, Aristotle suggests that citizens, when taken together, are capable of judging well the results of this art.[8] There is nothing that prevents the multitude, taken collectively, from exceeding the few in wealth, virtue or wisdom (1283b30–35, 1286a26–b7). Sharing in deliberative assemblies and juries is something the multitude can do without harm to the city.

It is important to note that the justifiable claim of some multitudes is not made on the basis they themselves advance, i.e. their equality as freeborn citizens. It is, rather, made in terms that are potentially acceptable to the wealthy, the virtuous and the wise. It is, moreover, immediately tempered by Aristotle's observation that it would be dangerous to exclude the multitude from some share of authority (1281b25–30). The argument based on the collective excellence of certain multitudes is not a straightforward argument for democracy.

Although not all multitudes will merit sharing in ruling, Aristotle acknowledges that democracy has another advantage in that it is generally more stable than oligarchy, at least in its moderate forms (1302a8–15). This is partially because of the obvious strength of numbers: insofar as most people tend to be poor rather than rich, more people are likely to be democratic than oligarchic. Precisely because democracy includes more citizens, in pursuing the good of the poor majority, it may more closely approximate the common advantage than oligarchy, especially if the middle class is included alongside the poor. Aristotle holds that successful regimes require a kind of friendship and regimes characterized by equality better promote friendship (1295b23–27). Moreover, oligarchs not only are opposed by partisans of democracy but also tend to fight among themselves for pre-eminence. Democracy is thus generally the 'most moderate' of all deviant regimes, although Aristotle pointedly refuses to call it 'the best' of these, perhaps because of its potential to become tyrannical (1289b4–11).

This sympathetic understanding of democracy also harkens back to the beginning of the *Politics*, in which Aristotle emphasizes the communal character of politics: a political community is one that looks to the benefit of all of its members. This purpose is more easily achieved when rule is shared among the broader populace rather than restricted to a particular class. Hence a political community is distinguished from a kingly community in that it is composed of citizens who are 'free and equal' (1255b20).[9] The people's conviction that they ought to share in ruling is, Aristotle suggests, why it is difficult for any regime other than democracy to arise in the future. At its core, Aristotle says, the city 'is a community of free persons' (1279a21).

Yet precisely because of its emphasis on freedom and equality, democracy does not promote among its citizens the virtues necessary for living well. Rather, many democrats understand freedom as the ability to live as one wants; to be free is not to be a slave, ruled by another (1310a26–36, 1317a40–17b17). Because no political community can exist without rule, and because it would be all but impossible for everyone to rule at once, the institutional expression of not being ruled is to share in ruling in such a way that 'what is resolved by the majority must be final and must be justice'. Yet insofar as they allow citizens to live as they wish, democracies will be characterized by immoderation, which is more pleasant to most people than moderation (1319b30–32). The great danger of democracy is therefore the use of the majority's power to do whatever it wishes, a power Aristotle explicitly compares to tyranny (1281a15–24).[10] Precisely because of the way in which democracy tends to foster class division, there is a constant danger of the majority using its power to confiscate the wealth of the few. This is not only unjust, Aristotle notes, but tends to destroy democracy by prompting the wealthy to unite against the poor. Nothing is more destructive of democracy than its tendency to engage in class warfare with the rich, and the same is true of oligarchy with respect to the poor. The institutions too often taken as characteristic of democracy do not conduce to good government or stability. Indeed, democrats, seeing themselves as opposed to oligarchy, tend to value those traits that are antithetical to oligarchy and thus elevate those who are of low birth, poor and vulgar (1317b40–41).

To avoid this, it is necessary for democratic citizens to receive a democratic education, an education relative to the regime.[11] Aristotle suggests, however, that most cities fail to do this, instead encouraging citizens to pursue the principle of the regime to its fullest. What they ought to do, according to Aristotle, is not to teach citizens to be as much of a democracy as possible – for to do this would result in the elevation of the assembly over law, ultimately ceasing to be a regime at all – but rather to teach them to do what is necessary to enable a democracy to endure (1320a2–4). In this way, Aristotle counsels democracies, much as he counsels tyrannies and oligarchies, how to be more stable, but to be more stable requires of them to be more moderate and more just. They do this, at least originally, not out of a sense of moderation and justice but rather out of self-interest. Aristotle explicitly promises that a tyrant who moderates his rule for the sake of remaining in power will cease to be entirely vicious and will become, if not virtuous, at least merely half-vicious (1315b4–10). There is no reason democracy could not progress in the same way, moving closer toward a polity. In its extreme form, democracy is highly unstable – ripe for revolution, whether from excluded oligarchs or its descent into what would later famously be called a tyranny of the majority. The more moderate form of democracy, however, preserves democracy by making it more like the blend of oligarchy and democracy that is a polity.

Aristotle's frequent enumeration of the varieties of democracy indicates the importance of such knowledge for political science as well as political practice. A democratic statesman who understands the various kinds of democracy that arise, and why they do so, would know 'which of the characteristically popular things preserve democracy and which destroy it' (1309b35–37). He would be able to perceive which regime would be best for a particular city and the parts and institutions necessary for it. Such a statesman would gradually improve the democracy, moving it from one kind to another and, as far as possible, toward polity.

Notes

1 Aristotle, *Politics* IV.4, 1291b30–92a18. Translations are taken from *Aristotle's Politics*, edn trans. Carnes Lord, 2nd edition (Chicago: University of Chicago Press, 2013). References to the Greek lines are from Aristotelis, *Politica*, ed. W. D. Ross (Oxford: Oxford University Press, 1957). I would like to thank Joanne Ciulla and the members of the Political Philosophy Learning Community at the University of Richmond for helpful comments on an earlier draft of this chapter.

2 Indeed, Aristotle describes polity – often taken to be the best regime generally possible for most cities – as a mixture of oligarchy and democracy, if tilting more toward the latter (1293b31–38, 1294b13–18).

3 See Mary P. Nichols, *Citizens and Statesmen* (Lanham: Rowman and Littlefield, 1992), especially Chapter 3.

4 Awareness of the parts of the city is also necessary to preserve existing regimes, as unnoticed and disproportionate growth of certain parts can lead to revolution (1302b33–3a13).

5 This second enumeration (see also 1298a9–34, where Aristotle discusses the extent to which the assembly or magistrates decide matters) presents four types rather than five, and Aristotle later states explicitly that there are but four sorts of democracy (1318b6). Most (e.g. Lord, in his translation [175 n. 12]) take the first variety to represent a mixture that somehow transcends democracy as such (perhaps through the combination of rich and poor outlined in VI.3).

6 Although Aristotle's account of the kinds of democracy focuses on the extent to which law rules, one must remember that the rule of law, though valuable, is insufficient, for much depends upon the kind of laws that rule (1294a4–9).

7 Aristotle's definition of citizenship at the beginning of Book III is importantly democratic in this way: it defines a citizen as one who is *eligible* to share in ruling and being ruled in turn (1275b17–21); it does not require one to hold office to be a citizen. Thus a democracy that tends to elect magistrates from the wealthy remains a regime in which the poor are truly citizens.

8 This argument has been the subject of much scholarly debate. See, most recently, Melissa Schwartzberg, 'Aristotle and the Judgment of the Many: Equality, not Collective Quality', *Journal of Politics* 78 (2016): 733–45 and the earlier literature she helpfully surveys.

9 Indeed, one of the merits of polity as a regime is that it allows more citizens to share in ruling and thus to fulfill their nature as political animals. See Kevin M. Cherry, 'The Problem of Polity: Political Participation and Aristotle's Best Regime', *Journal of Politics* 71 (2009): 1406–21.

10 As Thomas Pangle notes, Aristotle 'speaks at greater length and more emphatically of the tyrannical proclivity of democratic law' than oligarchic law in raising questions about the claim of any regime to rule (*Aristotle's Teaching in the* Politics [Chicago: University of Chicago Press, 2013], 139).

11 This is not something taught exclusively in a formal educational setting but rather the creation of a certain cultural understanding along the lines, perhaps, of Walter Lippman's 'public philosophy' (*The Public Philosophy* [New Brunswick: Transaction, 2009]).

CHAPTER FOUR

Cicero, *On the Republic*

W. Jeffrey Tatum

In no other state than that in which supreme power belongs to the people can liberty find any place to dwell – and surely nothing can ever be sweeter than liberty. But liberty, if it is not equal, is not actually liberty. But how can it be said to be equal in states in which men are only nominally free? I am not talking about autocracy, in which servitude is neither disguised nor even ambiguous. I mean states in which men vote, invest leaders with military commands and magistracies, are canvassed by office seekers, and have bills submitted to them for legislative approval – but under circumstances in which they must grant what is sought, whether they want to or not, and in which they are asked to give to others what they do not possess themselves. Such men have no share in magisterial power, in public deliberations, in the panels of men who are chosen to be jurors in court, for all these privileges are granted on the basis of birth or wealth.[1]

Cicero, usually a rapid writer, took three years (54 BC–51 BC) in completing the six books of the *Republic*, which now survives only in extended fragments. Plato is the work's obvious model, though by no means its only influence. The *Republic* represents a fictitious conversation among several distinguished senators that took place in 129 BC, at the estate of Scipio Africanus Aemilianus, twice consul and the conqueror of Carthage and Numidia – and the principal interlocutor of the dialogue.

This setting is by no means merely decorative. Instead, it orients the reader's interpretation of the work as a whole. Four years before the conversation depicted in the *Republic* takes place, Scipio's cousin, Tiberius Gracchus, enacted legislation that redistributed state-owned land to poor citizens. He was soon accused by his enemies of demagogy and of aiming at autocracy. In the end, he was lynched by a gang of senators who claimed to be champions of a free state. Nevertheless, Tiberius's law subsisted and a commission, endowed with extensive judicial powers, was established to oversee Tiberius's redistribution. But its operations aroused profound discontents, and in 129 BC Scipio took up the cause of rolling back its authority. When Scipio perished in the night, not long after the dramatic date of the *Republic*, it was widely believed that he had been murdered by demagogic forces.[2] By way of its literary setting, then, the demands of social harmony and the dangers of demagogy are each of them underscored for the reader from the very start: these issues animate Cicero's idea of what is good – and what is bad – about democracy.

Although Rome never embraced the idea of radical democracy, Romans nonetheless appreciated how important it was for any state's success that it enjoy the robust participation of a free citizenry, an observation that had not eluded Greek political scientists. There existed three kinds of constitution according to the theoretical analysis that was standard in ancient political thought: government by the one, the few or the many, and each kind existed in two species. Monarchy, aristocracy and democracy were viewed as positive forms of government, each of which was liable to degenerate into tyranny, oligarchy or ochlocracy. The ideal constitution, by general consent, combined the best features of the positive forms of government. This so-called mixed constitution was supple enough to avoid the pitfalls of mob rule, oligarchy or tyranny, and it supplied stability and justice because it was predicated, if not on social cooperation, then at least on a balance of powers.[3]

When the Greek historian Polybius, a personal friend of the Scipio who leads the dialogue in the *Republic*, sought an explanation for the Romans' spectacular success as an international power, he found his answer in their constitution, which he described as a consummate specimen of a mixed constitution. In Rome, he argued, the monarchical powers of the consuls rendered them effective executives whose brief tenure in office prevented their seizing permanent dominion. In the senate Polybius found the aristocratic element in the Roman state; composed of men of superior merit, this body dispensed wise counsel to magistrates and public alike. As for the people, owing to its participation in Rome's assemblies, the only bodies in Rome which could make laws or elect magistrates, they were furnished with an essential agency in the fundamental operations of the republic. Competition between the three elements of Rome's constitution, in Polybius's view, was tempered by necessity: each required the cooperation of the other and consequently Rome's constitution was not monarchic, aristocratic or democratic: it was a mixed constitution.

In the first two books of the *Republic*, which recount the first day's conversation at Scipio's estate, the speakers rehearse various constitutional theories, ultimately and unsurprisingly agreeing on the superiority of the mixed constitution. In making their way to this conclusion, they examine the merits and the failings of democracy, first by way of praise for its merits, then of blame for its defects. Scipio expands himself on the virtues of democracy (*Rep.* 1.47–50), and our passage is excerpted from what remains of his speech. Here emphasis is placed on equality, inclusion and independence in every aspect of civic life, and Scipio's view reflects a tradition of democratic justification that reaches back to fifth century Greece. Democracy, in Scipio's account, requires a form of *libertas* (liberty) that is *aequa* (equal), a reprise of the Greek democratic formula *eleutheria kai isonomia*, freedom and equality under the law. And this form of government, Scipio goes on to maintain, is rightly deemed a commonwealth (*res publica*) because under a democracy the commonwealth is truly 'the property of the people' (*res populi*) (*Rep.* 1.48). Indeed, when later in the work Scipio compares democracy with monarchy and aristocracy, he concedes that its singular attraction lies in its undiminished *libertas* (*Rep.* 1.55). But Scipio's commentary is made complicated for any reader by his later criticisms of democracy and his confession that, of the three positive forms of government, he regards monarchy as the best – and democracy as the worst (*Rep.* 1.54; 3.46–7). In the *Republic*, it is Cicero's view that 'the common good' cannot be preserved by deferring to the wishes of a simple majority of the people's membership: for good government, Cicero insists, it is vital that 'the greatest number not have the greatest power' (*Rep.* 2.39). Hence the attraction of a mixed constitution, which, for Scipio, is better even than monarchy (*Rep.* 1.54).

Greek criticisms of democracy tended to concentrate on the perils of entrusting civic affairs to a public who were ignorant and capricious.[4] Lacking wisdom and freed from any real responsibility for its decisions, the people, it was claimed, too often proved unreliable in practice, and democracy was always liable to descend into mob rule. Plato, in his *Republic*, was troubled by the excesses of freedom in a democracy, whereas Aristotle, in the *Politics*, objected to the democratic notion that equality obliged a state to follow the decisions of the majority simply because they were the majority and not because they were in any degree prudent or sound. Another danger of democracy, and one following from the rashness attributed to the masses, lay in its potential for giving rise to demagogues, who might subsequently become tyrants.

Cicero takes up Plato's depiction of democracy's collapse into tyranny owing to the baleful influence of demagogues (Plato, *Republic* 562c–566e). He puts Plato's account, however, to a significantly different purpose. Scipio is discussing the transformation of one constitution into another: kings become tyrants, he observes, and tyrants are expelled. But, he points out, the moral calculus of constitutional change is not a simple one. Righteous kings and sound aristocracies are also overthrown by the people when, its passion for liberty excited by demagogy, it erupts into an arrogant mob (*Rep.* 1.65). In order to lend vividness to such a catastrophe, Scipio offers his companions his own extended translation of Plato's depiction of the freedom-loving masses when they throw off any restraint. In Plato's *Republic*, however, it is not a monarchy or aristocracy which falls. Instead, it is a democracy which is corrupted by demagogues, whom Plato describes as 'wicked wine stewards' intoxicating the people with heavy draughts of liberty (*Republic* 562c). Soon the people recklessly regards any leaders who refuse to truckle as traitors and oligarchs, and public perturbation leads to the installation of tyranny. Although he alters the context, Scipio preserves many colourful instantiations of the outrages associated by Plato with unbridled democracy, including the breakdown of any traditional social order: 'slaves conduct themselves with undue liberty, wives possess the same rights as their husbands, and owing to these enormities of liberty, dogs, horses and asses race here and there – free! – and men are obliged to get out of their way'. In the end, government and law are dissolved into anarchy (*Rep.* 1.66–67). A close comparison of Scipio's translation with its original reveals how much more strongly than Plato Cicero emphasizes the unacceptability of the democratic ideal of equality.[5] In a democracy, Scipio concludes, *libertas* (liberty) too easily becomes *licentia* (licence). In his *Republic*, then, Cicero renders democracy not merely a danger to itself but also a levelling impulse which remains vulnerable to the manipulations of demagogy and therefore a potential threat to any constitutional form.

This was a sentiment that reflected Roman sensibilities, and not only at elite levels of society, because all Romans, so far as we can tell, accepted the necessity of social distinctions. Indeed, hierarchy is inherent even in the very word *libertas*, which fundamentally indicates the status of a person who is free over against one who is a slave. This is made clear, for instance, by the pervasive employment in Rome of the *pilleus* as a symbol of freedom: a *pilleus* was a cap awarded to a slave on the occasion of his manumission, when he was translated from the condition of property into a freedman (*libertus*) – and a Roman citizen. Liberty, for the Romans, then, did not intrinsically entrain absolute equality, which is why Scipio, in another passage of the *Republic*, elects to criticize democracy by asserting that 'whenever all public affairs are conducted by the people, however just and moderate its administration, such equality is none the less inequitable because it does not recognize distinctions in social standing' (*Rep.* 1.43). *Aequa libertas*, equal liberty, was, for the Romans, not equality in every sense of the word but rather equality before the law. The equality that is praised by Scipio in our passage, however, is a comprehensive equality. This all-encompassing notion of equality was regarded by Cicero and his Roman audience as a distinctive feature of democracy. It was also regarded, in important respects, as profoundly unfair, since not all men were equal in their contribution to the commonwealth (*Rep.* 1.43; 1.51–53).[6] Indeed, Scipio's formulation of democratic liberty in our passage could only have been provocative.[7]

Still, as Scipio suggests, there is something unjust in an aristocratic or oligarchic government that, although it allows the people to participate in the pageantry of government, affords it no real power. Such a government, in Scipio's exposition, is not merely as undemocratic as an autocracy that reduces its subjects to the condition of slavery, it is insidious in its disguise – and the reader cannot help but find the two constitutions equally distasteful. This was certainly Cicero's expectation. Even those Romans whose temperament was most fiercely aristocratic were obliged to concede the majesty of the Roman people and recognize its legitimate right to select magistrates and to carry or reject laws. As Cicero puts it elsewhere, in a public oration addressed to a noble who failed to win election to office, 'the people judged poorly you say? Nevertheless, the people passed its judgement. It ought not to have judged as it did? Nevertheless, it had the power to judge as it did' (*In Defence of Gnaeus Plancus* 7).

This state of affairs was not, as Ronald Syme has described it, 'a screen and a sham'.[8] Although most Roman citizens could not in practice stand for office or serve in a jury, or even address the Roman people during debates over legislation, it was nevertheless the case that the citizenry played a vital and independent part in Roman government. Scipio asserts that a democratic constitution is rightly denominated *res populi* in no small part because in its operations the public are masters (*domini*) of the law and the courts, decide matters of peace and war, and hold the ultimate authority in capital cases (*Rep.* 1.48): so, too, did the Roman people, if not in the unrestricted style of a radical democracy. Cicero expected his Roman readers to appreciate how their constitution, their mixed constitution in the world of the *Republic*, was something very different from the shell-game state Scipio describes in our passage. In a mixed constitution, Scipio observes, true equity (*aequibalitas*) requires that the masses (*multitudo*) play a very real role in the exercise of government (*Rep.* 1.69).

Although the *Republic* views the commonwealth as *res populi*, the Roman people, in matters of government, was not identical with the citizenry as a whole. The people operated in defined assemblies, which were further articulated by way of civic units like tribes and centuries. It was only when configured as assemblies that the Roman people could execute its vast power – and assemblies could only be called into existence by magistrates, a dynamic that invested the individual aristocrats who held office with significant authority over the public and its actions. For this reason, even in a mixed constitution like Rome's, because the power of the people was very real, and because the Roman public were by definition every bit as rash as the peoples populating the democracies criticized by Cicero, demagogy remained a constant anxiety throughout the republic. In Rome's mixed constitution, however, unlike a democracy, the responsibility for sound government resided not with the people but with their leadership: a stable order demanded good magistrates and a wise senate.

Here Cicero's Scipio diverges from Polybius. For Polybius, the genesis, development and decline of constitutions were inevitable, unrelenting and determined by the essential structure of each constitution. Notwithstanding differences in particulars, the pattern remained the same: monarchy declines into tyranny, which is subsequently overthrown by aristocracy; aristocracy descends into oligarchy, doomed to be swept aside by a democracy; democracy collapses into mob rule, a catastrophe the only cure for which is monarchy. This cycle could not be broken. It could, however, be retarded in the case of a mixed constitution, which, in Polybius's view, was held together more strongly than other constitutions because the self-interest of its elements in combination with the limitations constitutionally imposed on each compelled their cooperation. Cicero rejects this mechanical view of government.

For Cicero, it is the civic morality of the actors that matters most to the success of any constitution (e.g. *Rep.* 2.30; 2.45; 2.57). The *Republic* opens with a preface in which Cicero, addressing his brother Quintus, emphasizes the importance of personal civic responsibility and stresses the role of individual virtue in public life (*Rep.* 1.1). In the closing sections of Book Two, which draws to a close the *Republic*'s first day of conversation, Scipio underscores the primacy of personal moral values in the operation of any constitution (*Rep.* 2.69–70). This assertion prepares the reader for Books Three and Four, a central point of which is the moral superiority of the ideologies and practices that constitute the Roman constitution. But even the Romans' constitution demanded responsible citizens. This point is emphasized in the preface to Book Five, where Cicero quotes with approval a famous line from Ennius's *Annals*:

moribus antiquis res stat Romana virisque
(the Roman commonwealth rests on its traditions and its men)

The ideal but necessary figure is described by Cicero as a man who is morally good, intelligent and experienced in the operations of dignified statecraft: he is, for Cicero, the guide and helmsman of the state (*Rep.* 2.51). This is an attainment beyond the reach of the many, but remains an aspiration that must influence the governing class who supply the senate and magistrates in Rome's mixed constitution. The true statesman achieves a kind of divinity, a version of which is observed in the final book of the *Republic*, the so-called Dream of Scipio, Cicero's reworking of Plato's Myth of Er (*Republic* 10.614–21), in which it is revealed that the reward for the virtuous statesman is immortality. From beginning to end, then, the

Republic, notwithstanding its extensive constitutional analyses, insists that, in the matter of a successful state, individuals matter more than systems. Hence Cicero's description of his *Republic*, in a letter to Quintus, as a work concerned 'with the best constitution and the best citizen' (*Letters to His Brother Quintus* 3.5.1).

Still, in the *Republic*, even a virtuous citizenry cannot redeem democracy. True, in Book Three Scipio adduces Rhodes as a tolerable specimen of radical democracy (*Rep.* 3.47–48). And in his account of democracy in Book One, Scipio points out how its proponents insist that one should not reject democracy on account of the evils associated with mob rule: discord occurs only when there are conflicts of interest, but, in an ideal democracy, there can be none, owing to the equality that defines it (*Rep.* 1.49). But such equality cannot, in Cicero's view, be sustained in the real world: in a democracy, the people honour some of its citizens over others and therefore introduce significant discrepancies in terms of social standing and prestige (*Rep.* 1.53). Even if this were not the case, the equality that marks Scipio's ideal democracy remains contrary to Roman sensibilities, a measure that matters in the *Republic*. Near the end of Book Two, Quintus Aelius Tubero, the most philosophical of the dialogue's interlocutors, draws the reader's attention to this: it is not commonwealths abstractly that constitute the real subject of *Republic*, he observes, but the *Roman* commonwealth (*Rep.* 2.64). And it is by way of this distinctly Roman perspective that Cicero's view of democracy, the most extended Roman discussion of democracy that survives from antiquity, was self-consciously refracted.

Notes

1 Cicero, *On the Republic* 1.47. A standard English edition of Cicero's *Republic* (also cited in English as *On the Commonwealth*) is J. E. G. Zetzel, *Cicero: On the Commonwealth and On the Laws* (Cambridge: Cambridge University Press, 1999). In this chapter, all translations are my own.

2 On these matters, see C. Steel, *The End of the Roman Republic, 146 to 44 BC: Conquest and Crisis* (Edinburgh: Edinburgh University Press, 2013), 15–20.

3 K. von Fritz, *The Theory of the Mixed Constitution in Antiquity* (New York: Columbia University Press, 1954); A. Lintott, *The Constitution of the Roman Republic* (Oxford: Oxford University Press, 1999), 214–32.

4 See the evidence assembled by J. Ober, *Political Dissent in Democratic Athens: Intellectual Critics of Popular Rule* (Princeton: Princeton University Press, 1998); E. Harris, 'Was All Criticism of Athenian Democracy Anti-democratic', in *Democrazia e antidemocrazia nel mondo Greco*, ed. U. Bultrighini (Alessandria: Edizioni dell'Orso, 2005), 11–24.

5 J. Gregory, 'Cicero and Plato on Democracy: A Translation and its Source', *Latomus* 50 (1991): 639–44.

6 E. Fantham, '*Aequabilitas* in Cicero's Political Theory, and the Greek Tradition of Proportional Justice', *Classical Quarterly* 23 (1973): 285–90; cf. Zetzel, *Cicero: On the Commonwealth and On the Laws*, 140–3.
7 For a very different view of Roman concepts of equality, see T. P. Wiseman, *Remembering the Roman People: Essays on Late-Republican Politics and Literature* (Oxford: Oxford University Press, 2009), 81–98, with my review in *Hermathena* 186 (2009): 101–6.
8 R. Syme, *The Roman Revolution* (Oxford: Oxford University Press, 1939), 15.

CHAPTER FIVE

Democracy without Elections: Popular Rule according to Alfarabi

Alexander Orwin

As for the democratic city, it is a city every one of whose inhabitants is unrestrained, left to himself to do whatever he wants. Its inhabitants are equal, and their custom is that nobody is superior to anyone else with respect to anything at all. Its inhabitants will be free men doing whatever they want, but nobody from among themselves or others has authority over anyone of them except insofar as he does what removes their freedom. Many moral habits arise amongst them, along with many concerns, many desires, and delight in many things too numerous to count. Its inhabitants consist of many groups, similar and dissimilar, also too numerous to count. Whatever was separate in all of the other cities, be it high or low, will come together in this city, and rulership will come about through whichever of the rest of the things that we have mentioned happens to figure in it.[1] Its multitude does not have what the rulers have, but enjoys authority over those who are said to be their rulers, since whoever rules them does so only in compliance with the wishes of the ruled, and the rulers are subject to the inclinations of the ruled. If their situation is examined closely, neither ruler nor ruled will truly be found among them. . . . Among the cities, this city is the wonderful and happy city: on the surface, it is like an embroidered dress with colorful figures and dyes. It is beloved, and beloved to every one of its residents, since everybody who has an inclination or desire for something is able to attain it in this city. The nations flock to live in it, and its size grows beyond all bounds. People of all dispositions are born in it, by every sort of coupling and marriage. Children of very disparate nature, education, and upbringing arise in it. This city becomes many cities, not distinguished from one another but intermingled, the parts of one dispersed among the parts of another, and the foreigner is not distinguished from the native. All the inclinations and ways of life come together in it, so that it is not impossible for the virtuous to grow up in it with the passage of time. There may even chance to exist in it wise men, rhetoricians, and poets of every kind of subject. It is possible to gather from it the parts of the virtuous city, and this is the good that grows up in this city. So of the ignorant cities, this one has both the most good and the most evil, and as it becomes greater, more prosperous, more populous, more fertile, and more perfect for people, these two [good and evil] become greater and more numerous as well. . . . The leader whom they consider virtuous is capable of excellent deliberation and cunning in attaining for them [the objects] of their desires and inclinations in all of their difference and variety, and preserving these things from their enemies, while not depriving them of any of their money, but restricting himself only to what is necessary for his power. But the virtuous man who is truly virtuous, who, if he ruled them, would determine their actions and direct them toward happiness, would never be made a ruler by them. And if he chanced to rule them, he will soon be deposed, killed, or have his rulership disturbed and challenged. . . . So they refuse the rule of the virtuous and denounce it. However, the establishment of the virtuous city and rulership of the virtuous comes most plausibly and easily from the necessary and democratic cities.[2]

Alfarabi (870–950) is a formative figure in the development of philosophy in Islam. He successfully adapted the thought of Plato and Aristotle for a Muslim readership and was revered by his successors, including Avicenna, Averroes and Maimonides, as a great philosopher in his own right. His account of democracy in a treatise titled '*The Political Regime*' has two principal sources: Greek philosophy on the one hand and Islamic thought and practice on the other. The debt that Alfarabi's description of democracy's licentious diversity owes to Plato is evident,[3] while his emphasis on its vast size and cosmopolitan character alludes to contemporary Baghdad, in which Alfarabi spent most of his productive career.

Alfarabi's account nevertheless goes far beyond merely summarizing Plato or describing Baghdad. Its peculiarity is indicated partly by what Alfarabi does not include. Direct popular control of the governmental offices characterizes democracy in Plato,[4] but not in Alfarabi, who never speaks of elections of any sort. Neither political representation nor the rule of law, key features of modern democracy, play any role in Alfarabi's account. Indeed, even Islamic deliberative concepts such as *shūra* (council) and *ijmāʿ* (consensus), which occur frequently in discussions of democracy by modern Muslim authors such as Fazlur Rahman and Muhammad Iqbal,[5] are absent from it. Unlike these authors or Muhammad Mahdi Shamsuddin, who appears later in this volume, Alfarabi makes no explicit attempt to discuss Islam or its compatibility with democracy, an issue that would not have resonated with his contemporaries, who knew and accepted only the absolute rule of sultans and caliphs.

The term translated into English as 'democratic', *jimāʿiyya*, is the classical Arabic equivalent of the Greek *demokratia*; however, in modern Arabic political discourse it has given way to another term, *dīmuqrāṭiyya*, imported directly from modern Europe rather than ancient Greece. Unlike the Greek original, the etymology of *jimāʿiyya* has nothing to do with popular rule: it could be literally translated as 'associational', as Butterworth proposes in a footnote,[6] and signifies a vast number of people living and mixing together without any defined political structure. In contemporary Arabic, *jimāʿiyya* has come to mean 'collective' and appears mainly in expressions that pertain more to economics than politics, such as 'collective farm' and 'collective agreement'.

The modern Arabic term for 'republic' is *jumhūriyya*, signifying the new regimes that followed the overthrow of monarchies in places like Egypt and Iraq, in which 'the people' allegedly ruled. It is derived from the older word *jumhūr*, which occurs frequently in Alfarabi and is usually translated as 'multitude'.[7] Alfarabi does indeed associate democracy with the rule of the *jumhūr*, but argues that the *jumhūr* in itself fails to generate any principle of rule, since its unpredictable passions do not suffer any kind of consistent governmental authority. At the end of the first paragraph, Alfarabi claims that in a society dominated by the *jumhūr*, 'neither ruler nor ruled will truly be found', leaving the impression that the vast, teeming city defined by the adjective *jimāʿiyya* subsists and even flourishes in a state of near anarchy.

Alfarabi partially corrects this impression in the following paragraph by introducing rulers.[8] The necessity of maintaining some kind of government requires a modification of the democratic principles of complete freedom and equality, as laid out in the first paragraph. Yet these rulers are single and hereditary, and their subjects are relatively free only because they themselves are relatively weak. The so-called democracy therefore turns out to be a monarchy, in which the ruler has lost his ability to vigorously exercise his power. The status of democracy as a weak version of monarchy is confirmed by Averroes (1126–1198), author of the second substantial treatment of democracy in medieval Islamic thought, in which he invokes as examples of democracy 'the entirely domestic . . . associations of many of the Muslim *kings* today' and emphasizes that most democratic governments 'perish rapidly'.[9]

The claim that democracy is in fact a form of monarchy may at first appear strange. However, we recall that the Arabic *jimā'iyya* does not really signify any direct popular participation in government. Alfarabi lived in a time and place that knew of no such participation, so he conceived of popular power in the only way that would have been familiar to himself and his contemporaries. His notion of such power is indirect but brutal: a ruler who runs afoul of the passions of the people risks being 'deposed, killed, or have his rulership disturbed and challenged'. The ruler is kept in check not by elections but by the ever-present threat of riots. To demonstrate the plausibility of Alfarabi's view, we need to look no further than the Arab Spring, in which the latest crop of Middle Eastern autocrats has been either deposed or weakened by massive popular demonstrations. Western democrats, of course, continue to hope that regular elections along with freedom of speech will render more disruptive manifestations of popular power superfluous.

Alfarabi's account of democratic rulership may seem somewhat anachronistic from a modern Western standpoint, but his account of democratic society does not. Alfarabi's starting point, to be sure, remains the societies that he observed with his own eyes. His memorable depiction of a vast, diverse, colourful city clearly resembles the Baghdad in which he lived: by some estimates, it had over a million inhabitants, hailing from all regions of the Abbasid empire.[10] Alfarabi himself, who may have been born in what is now Kazakhstan, must have ranked among the more exotic arrivals.[11] We shouldn't conclude, however, that Alfarabi constrains himself to a merely historical description of Baghdad. He permits his imagination to unfold the consequences of democracy's principle of freedom. Most notably, he includes among the characteristics of the democratic city 'people of all dispositions' and 'every sort of coupling and marriage', from whom 'children of very disparate nature, education, and upbringing arise'. The reader is led to imagine non-conventional families, brothels and every sort of religious heterodoxy. The historical Baghdad was not quite that libertine: morals were regulated by a *muḥtasib*, a public official whose job was not only to prevent cheating in markets but also to watch over mosques and baths, as well as strict, sectarian Islamic groups who sometimes sought to impose their will by force.[12]

Although some readers may be ashamed to admit it, Alfarabi's focus on the moral licentiousness of democracy is part of what makes his description so enticing. Who wouldn't dream of living in a society that permits such religious, intellectual and erotic fulfilment? Alfarabi's democracy is so charming precisely because it promises more freedom than any government of his time could ever hope to deliver. Yet Alfarabi's account seems altogether less hyperbolic in our own time, which has witnessed both a dramatic expansion of the metropolis and a considerable increase in moral and sexual freedom, well beyond the limits accepted by our grandparents. Alfarabi's exaggerated depiction of Baghdad may turn out to be a more accurate portrayal of contemporary New York or London. Whatever the exact municipal ordinances may be, the basic phenomena described by Alfarabi are indeed present in those cities: gigantic size, immigrants from all the nations, enormous diversity of sexual practice, every imaginable cultural group or sub-group, a flourishing art scene and varied intellectual life. Contemporary readers may discover in Alfarabi's portrayal of democratic society alluring images of the excitement that radiates from the modern metropolis. The questions Alfarabi asks about the health and happiness of such a city therefore concern us as well.

Alfarabi introduces his ode to the city's diversity by calling the city 'wonderful and happy', but proceeds to cast some doubt on this description. He immediately adds the expression 'on the surface', as if this may be a matter of appearance rather than truth. The city is 'beloved, and beloved to every one of its residents', but is their love justified? Although Alfarabi does not quite follow Plato in attributing the attraction of the multi-coloured garment of democracy to the whims of 'children and women',[13] he raises similar concerns. The love felt by such a diverse and capricious populace, consisting of all manner of characters and dispositions, is an ambivalent phenomenon. They adore this permissive, free-wheeling city for allowing them to pursue their own interests, passions and activities, but there is no guarantee that these pursuits will actually bring them happiness. Alfarabi makes it quite clear that the aims pursued in the democratic city are bound to be both noble and base: it 'has both the most good and the most evil' of all the ignorant cities, and the larger and richer it grows, the greater its quantity of both opposites. Besides, the frenetic pursuit of ever-changing desires may lead not to happiness, but something closer to a nervous breakdown. New Yorkers may delight in the liveliness and sophistication of their city and refuse to pass more than a few days anywhere else, but in some cases a quiet, meditative stay in Vermont might be the best way to restore their spirits.

In the concluding paragraph, Alfarabi distinguishes clearly between democracy and the kind of governance most likely to make its subjects happy. The 'truly virtuous' ruler directs citizens toward happiness instead of permitting them to pursue their own whims. In democracy, however, a ruler who makes such an effort is likely to be deposed for his pains. The weak monarchs who manage to retain power in such a society will have little capacity to rein in the diverse passions of the people. The same difficulty weighs on elected representatives today: at party conventions and campaigns, any criticism of the voters themselves is usually taboo. Whatever the political arrangement, leaders who depend primarily on the people for support are understandably reluctant to challenge or improve them.

Alfarabi nonetheless concludes that the virtuous city is more likely to emerge from a democratic city than from the other kinds of ignorant city. Such optimism seems quite peculiar, coming as it does immediately after Alfarabi's admission that a truly virtuous ruler is bound to be deposed by the unruly democratic populace. It makes sense only if 'city' is an equivocal term, referring both to a geographically contiguous settlement encompassing many neighbourhoods and quarters, as it does earlier in the *Political Regime*,[14] and a group of people who share a common way of life. The latter definition is reflected in Alfarabi's claim that 'This city becomes many cities, not distinguished from one another but intermingled, the parts of one dispersed among the parts of another.' It is according to this statement that the notion of a virtuous city emerging from the democratic city is most plausibly understood. The virtuous city that emerges from within the democracy is the city of Alfarabi and his associates, who have succeeded in establishing a virtuous city within a city 'with the passage of time'. If Alfarabi himself perfected the development of philosophy in Baghdad in the tenth century, he did so almost 200 years after the founding of the city in 756. Such an interpretation is corroborated by what little we know of Alfarabi's life: by devoting himself to quiet pedagogy rather than politics, he gradually became one of Baghdad's most influential inhabitants, whose name would be remembered long after the oblivion of its lackluster tenth-century rulers.

If this interpretation is correct, then Alfarabi's account of the emergence of the virtuous city within democracy is indeed inspired by Plato: 'The man who wishes to organize a city [should] go to a city under a democracy. He would choose the sort that pleases him . . . and thus establish the regime.'[15] Just as the conversation about the various kinds of cities in the *Republic* could only take place in Athens, where these cities could be viewed and examined in all their diversity, so the *Political Regime* could have been written only in a city such as Baghdad. In that cosmopolitan capital, Alfarabi could observe the inhabitants of each and every city intertwined, thus permitting him to compose a description of every kind of government, virtuous and ignorant. Whatever the political deficiencies of democracy, its intellectual advantages are very real.

Alfarabi's treatment of democracy was taken up directly by Averroes, who begins his own discussion of democracy with an obvious paraphrase from Alfarabi.[16] Like Alfarabi, Averroes emphasizes the freedom, equality and diversity that pervade democratic society. However, the Andalusian soon veers off in his own direction, by introducing the notion of primary laws, whose main purpose is to protect household property, as well as secondary laws regulating commerce and tertiary laws regulating moral dispositions. With these crucial additions to Plato and Alfarabi, Averroes declares that evils such as robbery and murder should be strictly forbidden in democracy, and strongly implies that marriage, sex and education should be regulated.[17] He thereby tempers democracy's freedom and diversity, conferring upon it an orderly, even bourgeois feel that is entirely absent from Plato and Alfarabi's free-wheeling democratic societies. It could be said that Averroes takes a step, somewhat unwittingly of course, toward more modern theories of democracy, which emphasize public order as well as individual freedom. Perhaps it is the concern with order so pervasive in modern democracy that makes Alfarabi's account appear entertaining but quaint. Alfarabi's lively description of democracy may make fascinating reading, but it certainly does not provide any blueprint for setting up the strong, stable society that modern democracy aspires to be. As far as I know, modern authors, be they Muslim or Western, have not drawn much inspiration from it.

The lack of influence exercised by Alfarabi's account of democracy in modern times should not detract from its inherent value. Alfarabi provides a compelling example of how a classical Greek concept may be reinterpreted in order to fit an alien civilization. In doing so, he shows how popular power inevitably affects political life even in the absence of institutions that channel it. He also offers an enduring description of how our longing for freedom and diversity would manifest itself if unregulated by society. Insofar as these aspirations for an infinite variety of people, ideas and intercourse are nurtured most fully by the modern metropolis, Alfarabi not only portrays the society of his time, but also offers a window into our own.

Notes

1. Presumably necessary goods, money, pleasure, honour or tyranny, discussions of which precede the discussion of democracy and form the basis of governance in the other ignorant cities.
2. Alfarabi, *Political Regime*. My translation. For Arabic, see *Kitāb al-Siyāsa al-Madaniyya*, ed. Fauzi M. Najjar (Beirut: Dār al-Mashriq, 1993), 99–102. Butterworth provides an excellent English translation of the entire passage, from which my own has greatly benefitted. See Alfarabi, *The Political Writings*, vol. 2, trans. Charles Butterworth (Ithaca: Cornell University Press, 2015), 86–8.
3. As for Aristotle's *Politics*, discussed earlier in the volume, it is by no means clear that Alfarabi had access to it. See Shlomo Pines, 'Aristotle's *Politics* in Arabic Philosophy', *Israel Oriental Studies* 5 (1975): 150–60.
4. Plato, *Republic*, 557a.

5　Fazlur Rahman, *Major Themes in the Qur'ān* (Chicago: University of Chicago Press, 1980), 43; Muhammad Iqbal, *The Reconstruction of Religious Thought in Islam* (Stanford: Stanford University Press, 2012), 137–40.
6　Alfarabi, *The Political Writings*, 86, n. 46.
7　Butterworth prefers 'Public': see Alfarabi, *The Political Writings*, 86.
8　For reasons of space I omitted this passage from my translation. It is ably translated by Butterworth in Alfarabi, *The Political Writings*, 86–7.
9　Averroes, *On Plato's Republic*, trans. Ralph Lerner (Ithaca: Cornell University Press, 1974), 112, 127.
10　A. A. Duri, 'Baghdad', in *Encyclopaedia of Islam*, vol. 1, ed. B. Lewis, Ch. Pellat and J. Schacht (Leiden: E.J. Brill, 1960), 898–9.
11　See Muḥsin Mahdi, 'Al-Fārābî', in *Dictionary of Scientific Biography*, vol. IV, ed. Charles Coulston Gillispie (New York: Charles Scribner's Sons, 1971), 523–6.
12　Duri, 'Baghdad', 898, 900.
13　Plato, *Republic*, 557c.
14　Alfarabi, *Political Writings*, 60–1.
15　Plato, *Republic*, 557d.
16　Averroes, *On Plato's Republic*, 110.
17　Ibid., 110–11.

CHAPTER SIX

Consent and Popular Sovereignty in Medieval Political Thought: Marsilius of Padua's *Defensor pacis*

Takashi Shogimen

The primary human authority, simply speaking, to pass or institute human laws belongs to that from which alone the best laws can result. But this is the universal body of the citizens or its prevailing part, which represents the whole of that body: since it is not always easy or even possible for all persons to agree upon one opinion because some individuals have a stunted nature, which through singular malice or ignorance is out of harmony with the common view. But things that are to the common advantage should not be impeded or neglected because of the irrational objection or opposition of these people. The authority to pass or to institute laws belongs, therefore, solely to the universal body of the citizens or its prevailing part.[1]

Marsilius of Padua (*c*.1275–*c*.1342) is undoubtedly one of the best known political thinkers in medieval Europe, along with Thomas Aquinas in the previous century and William of Ockham in his own time. In his academic career Marsilius was trained as a physician before serving as rector of the University of Paris. His major political treatise, *The Defender of the Peace* (*Defensor pacis*), which was completed in 1324, drove him into a life of exile as the papacy regarded it as heretical. The work consisted of three parts or 'discourses': Discourse 1 presented his 'generic' theory of the political community, which relied on rational arguments derived from Aristotle and Cicero; Discourse 2 turned to a critique of the contemporary papacy's interventions in secular affairs with a recourse to biblical and patristic authorities; and Discourse 3 summarizes the preceding arguments, serving as a manifesto or a call for action. Discourse 2 was clearly problematic, to say the least, from the viewpoint of the papacy.

But one might wonder why a chapter on medieval European political thought is included in this volume on 'democratic moments' in the history of political thought. Historians of political thought are often skeptical about the existence of political thought in the European Middle Ages because political thought is typically a theory about the state that did not exist in the Middle Ages. Even those who are not so skeptical would associate medieval political thinking with hierarchical authoritarianism and theocracy rather than with democracy. Indeed, democracy was not an idea that medieval political thinkers endorsed. To be sure, medieval intellectuals were aware of the concept of democracy through Aristotelian categories of political constitutions. In the Book 5 of his *Politics*, Aristotle posited that there are three legitimate constitutions that serve the common good, monarchy, aristocracy and polity, while there are, correspondingly, three illegitimate constitutions that do not serve the common good: tyrannical monarchy, oligarchy and democracy. Democracy was not counted among the legitimate political constitutions.

So where can we find any 'democratic moments' in medieval political thought? Walter Ullmann once argued that the rediscovery of Aristotelian political science in the middle of the thirteenth century secularized and democratized European political thinking: from Aristotle came the new idea of the citizen as an active participant in politics. The entry of this concept onto the stage of thirteenth-century political thought undermined the Christian hierarchical model of government.[2] This thesis, widely known as Ullmann's 'Aristotelian revolution' thesis, has since been subjected to criticisms and is now largely discredited.[3] Perhaps we find a better guide for medieval 'democratic moments' in Alexander Passerin d'Entrèves. He wrote: 'it was only when the idea of consent finally came to be associated with that of an equal right in each individual to share in the establishment and exercise of power, that the distinctive features of modern democratic theory began to emerge into full daylight'.[4]

Again, it was not in the Middle Ages that the association between the idea of consent and that of human equality first occurred in the European political tradition. However, both ideas were definitely present in medieval political conceptions. The notion of human equality, which was foreign to the rediscovered political philosophy of Aristotle, belonged to the Stoic and patristic traditions. The doctrine of the natural equality of human beings was expounded by Cicero and Seneca and was later inherited by the early Christian Fathers, thus constituting an essential part of the natural law tradition, which was not at all new to medieval intellectuals. What was more original to medieval European political thought was the other central idea: consent. Marsilius was a key thinker who viewed consent as the cornerstone of his political theory. The purpose of the present chapter is to show how Marsilius's discussions of consent constituted a democratic moment in the history of medieval political thought.

As I wrote earlier, his *Defender of the Peace* consisted of three 'discourses'; many of the ideas that are relevant to what we today call political theory are found in Discourse 1, which opens with a discussion of the origin and the development of the political community. Marsilius considered that the end of the political community is peace and order because in the orderly society the citizens can 'live well (*bene vivere*)' – and a 'sufficient life', Marsilius argued, is achievable through the satisfaction of a wide range of human desires by the concerted activities of diverse functional groups in the community (I, iv, 5). The role of the government is, according to Marsilius, to envisage and enable the diverse functions of the political community through legislation in order to ensure the materialization of a sufficient life (I, iv, 4). To achieve this, the government regulates the 'human civil acts' of individuals based on private interests according to a 'standard of justice' (I, x, 1) – that is, law – thereby ensuring the maintenance of 'civil justice and the common advantage' (I, xi, 1). Indeed, the government – the 'judicial or princely' part – of the political community is the first to emerge in the making of the community (I, v, 7).

Marsilius maintained that those who create the diverse functional parts of the community are 'the legislator', which he equated with 'the people or the universal body of the citizens or else its prevailing part' (I, xii, 3). The opacity of Marsilius's notion of 'legislator' has long invited debate, but recent scholarship suggests that the 'legislator' is not coextensive with the whole community of citizens; rather, 'the community of citizens is the *legislator humanus* only when its members congregate for the express purpose of debate and decision about the common benefit'.[5] And the key business of the 'legislator' is to institute laws to design how the community should be diversified and how the various functional parts should operate and cooperate with each other. Marsilius also viewed the function of law as regulatory and coercive. An important implication of this is that, for Marsilius, the type of law that occupies the most exalted status in this-worldly life is human law. Divine law only regulates spiritual matters that belong to the other world and Marsilius hardly discussed natural law. Human law is the unrivalled standard of justice in the civil community.[6]

So how is (human) law instituted? The quotation in the opening of this chapter epitomizes Marsilius's vision of the legislative mechanism. First, he acknowledges the difficulty in reaching a unanimous decision in collective deliberation. Such an acknowledgement is predicated on the assumption that an essential requirement for collective decision-making about law is consent: the agreement of those who are concerned. Second, such decision-makers are 'the universal body of the citizens or its prevailing part, which *represents* the whole of that body' (emphasis mine): they may not be the entire body of citizens but their representatives. Third, Marsilius's vision is guarded against the intrusion of irrationality into collective decision-making about law through the 'malice or ignorance' of some individuals. The key issue here is how to ensure the rationality of the content of legislation. What follows will discuss these points in turn.

As I discussed earlier, human law is the only 'standard' that regulates human actions in this world. So what is the source of such an unrivalled status for human law? Marsilius's answer is unequivocal: the supreme authority of human law derives from the will of the people – the universal body of the citizens or its prevailing part. In referring to the will of the people, Marsilius did not have in mind the establishment and exercise of power in terms of the contractual association of equal individuals; rather, he was thinking of the whole people as a corporation (*populus*). The idea that the people as a whole is the source of legitimate power, according to Brian Tierney, derived from the twelfth-century Roman lawyer Azo. Azo argued that the people as a whole instituted imperial power by ceding, not transferring, power. Hence the people retain the power to legislate and abrogate laws. From this, Azo inferred that individual members of the people are less than the emperor but the emperor is less than the people as a whole.[7]

This idea of the corporate body of the people as the source of legitimate power has often been described as 'popular sovereignty' (or 'populism').[8] However, this appellation may be misleading because the above notion of the popular corporate authority does not presume any involvement of the people in the public decision-making process. The term 'popular sovereignty' obviously entails modern connotations but the active participation of individuals in the public decision-making was typically not a part of medieval political thinking.[9] So what did Marsilius mean when he attributed the source of legislative authority to the will of the people? The key to answer this question lies in Marsilius's idea of consent.

It is widely known that consent was integral to medieval political practice. Feudal vassalage is based on mutual consent between lord and vassal. Parliaments were summoned by the king to obtain consent for taxation. In the European tradition of political theory, Cicero envisioned that a political community was a multitude associated by consent.[10] The Ciceronian notion that through linguistic communication individuals consented to enter collective life forms a sharp contrast to the Aristotelian model that humans entered a collective life by nature. Medieval political thinkers were often aware of both Ciceronian and Aristotelian arguments, and Marsilius was no exception.

Marsilius considered consent to be the cornerstone of the legislative procedure. He argued that the universal body of the citizens has the final say about legislation as the expression of their 'common advantage', and what gives legitimacy to legislation procedurally is the consent of the citizens.[11] What underpins Marsilius's emphasis on consent is his division of legislative process into two stages: the first stage is the *discovery* of law and the second is the *authorization* of law. He attributed the discovery of law only to those who have legal expertise and prudence, while he insisted that the law discovered by the experts must be authorized by the consent of the entire body of the citizens. Marsilius held that citizens, who are not equipped with legal expertise, were generally rational and sufficiently capable of judging whether or not the law in question would serve their common advantage.

But how does the universal body of citizens make a collective decision? This leads to two further questions: first, did Marsilius think that each and every citizen must participate in the authorization of legislation? Second, if each and every citizen is expected to give consent unanimously, what if a collective decision-making process fails to reach a unanimous decision? Both questions allude to the possibility of representation.

Representation may be viewed as a second salient feature of the Marsilian 'democratic moment'. As is already noted, Marsilius maintained that in the political community legislation derives from the consent of the whole community or its 'prevailing part (*valentior pars*)'. He wrote that the prevailing part 'represents the whole of the community (*totam universitatem repraesentat*)' (I, xii, 5). As he conceptualized the political community in generic terms, he did not only discuss representation within the civil community but also with reference to the Church. The general council consisted of priests and experts in divine law who are elected by all the communities in the Church, thus 'representing the universal body of the faithful through the . . . authority granted them by those other universal bodies' (II, xx, 2). His argument for conciliar supremacy in Discourse 2 of the *Defender of the Peace* was anchored in his generic theory of the political community in Discourse 1. But before we investigate what Marsilius meant by 'representation', we need to clarify his notion of the 'prevailing part'.

Marsilius did not define the 'prevailing part' explicitly. In order to highlight key issues, we might first examine another similar concept that is widely used in the context of collective decision-making in medieval texts: *maior et sanior pars*, which may be translated as 'a greater and wiser part'.[12] Historians have explored this concept, along with the Marsilian 'prevailing part', in relation to the historical origins of the majoritarian principle.[13] The 'greater' could of course have either a quantitative or a qualitative meaning: one could interpret the 'greater' part as a numerical majority whose decision is presumed to carry weight. This understanding can be warranted by the fact that the electoral process within the medieval Church often adopted the principle that two-thirds of the entire number of votes determined the outcome of ecclesiastical elections. However, one could also interpret 'greater (*maior*)' in a qualitative sense because the medieval concept of *maioritas* could mean not only majority but also authority. The qualitative interpretation of 'greater' would be reinforced by the subsequent phrase 'and wiser (*et sanior*)'. In this case, the 'greater and wiser' part would underscore the authoritative and prudent, not the numerically 'greater', nature of the decision-makers. The ambivalence of the idea of the 'greater and wiser part' can be witnessed in medieval canonist scholarship on ecclesiastical elections. The early-thirteenth-century canon lawyer Johannes Teutonicus advocated a clear numerical majority, while the contemporary canon lawyer Bernardus Parmensis and Pope Gregory IX rejected the majoritarian interpretation.[14] A survey of the history of the concept of the 'greater and wiser part' does not suggest that majoritarianism had gained wide support in the Middle Ages.[15]

Viewed in this light, it would be rather imprudent to surmise that the Marsilian idea of the prevailing part is a manifestation of majoritarian rule. Indeed Marsilius noted: 'I say "prevailing part" taking into consideration both the quantity and quality of persons in the community upon which the law is passed' (I, xii, 3). Clearly *both* the number of votes *and* prudence and expert knowledge carry weight in his conception of the 'prevailing part'. This seems to imply that for Marsilius a majority is collectively a rational decision-maker. The rationale for singling out the 'prevailing part' as representatives of the universal body of the citizens is that they should collectively reach a common decision on 'common advantage'; the reverse side of this is that it is necessary to exclude some individuals of 'a stunted nature' from the public decision-making process because they, due to their malice or ignorance, might obstruct decision-making for the 'common advantage' (I, xii, 5). The prevailing part represents the voice of rational individuals, which can prevail if the noise of irrational voices is eliminated.

Thus, it becomes clear that the 'representative' nature of the 'prevailing part' is different from the modern democratic conception. What the political philosopher Hannah Pitkin calls 'political' representation is predicated on the idea that representatives need to act at the behest of the body they are representing in the context of negotiating the conflicting interests and desires of various groups that constitute the entire community.[16] Cary J. Nederman relies on Pitkin to argue that the concept of 'political' representation is absent from medieval political thought. At the heart of the 'political' idea of representation is that representatives must concern themselves simultaneously 'with the interests of constituents (regardless of their wishes) and the wishes of constituents (regardless of their interests)'.[17] 'Political' representatives, therefore, who act at the behest of the constituents, have discretionary power in order to act for the interest of the constituents, which may be against their wishes. The Marsilian notion of representation, by contrast, envisages that laws, which embody the common advantage, emerge not from negotiations between representatives who represent diverse interests and desires but largely by excluding individuals of 'a stunted nature'. The Marsilian 'representatives' are rational enough to discover laws that serve the common good of the community; human interests and desires are rather the objects of legal control, and legislation is not viewed as a process where diverse and often mutually conflicting interests and desires are negotiated.

It is clear by now that identifying a 'democratic moment' even in a radical medieval thinker such as Marsilius requires caution. The passage cited at the opening of this chapter has prompted intellectual historians to suggest a similarity to the modern language of democracy. However, what Marsilius meant by 'the representation of the entire body of citizens by the prevailing part' still remained within the orbit of medieval political culture that did not view democracy in a favourable light. Yet Marsilius's recognition of the intellectual capabilities of a multitude, perhaps even a majority, for judging the suitability of proposed legislation for the common advantage certainly points to a democratic future. In this, the Marsilian emphasis on human consent – a significant departure from the traditional reliance on divine authorization[18] – constituted an important 'democratic moment'.[19]

Notes

1 Marsilius of Padua, *The Defender of the Peace*, ed. and trans. Annabel Brett (Cambridge: Cambridge University Press, 2005), I, xii, 5 (which refers to Discourse 1, chapter 12, section 5), 68. The original Latin text of this English translation is: *Defensor pacis*, ed. C. W. Previté-Orton (Cambridge: Cambridge University Press, 1928).

2 Walter Ullmann, *Principles of Government and Politics in the Middle Ages* (London: Methuen, 1961), 232 and Ullmann, *A History of Political Thought: The Middle Ages* (Harmondsworth: Penguin, 1965), chapter 2.

3 An up-to-date reappraisal of Ullmann's scholarship is found in Cary J. Nederman, *Lineages of European Political Thought: Explorations along the Medieval/Modern Divide from John of Salisbury to Hegel* (Washington, DC: Catholic University of America Press, 2009), chapter 1.

4 Alexander Passerin D'Entrèves, *The Notion of the State: An Introduction to Political Theory* (Oxford: Clarendon Press, 1967), 197.

5 Cary J. Nederman, *Community and Consent: The Secular Political Theory of Marsiglio of Padua's* Defensor Pacis (Lanham: Rowman & Littlefield, 1995), 69–70.

6 Francis Oakley, *The Watershed of Modern Politics: Law, Virtue, Kingship, and Consent (1300–1650)* (New Haven: Yale University Press, 2015), 189–90.

7 For example, see Brian Tierney, *Religion, Law, and the Growth of Constitutional Thought, 1150–1650* (Cambridge: Cambridge University Press, 1982), 56–60.

8 Tierney, *Religion, Law, and the Growth of Constitutional Thought*, 56–60.

9 Nederman, *Community and Consent*, 74–5.

10 Tierney, *Religion, Law, and the Growth of Constitutional Thought*, 40.

11 Nederman, *Community and Consent*, 77.

12 See L. Moulin, '*Senior et Maior Pars*: Note sur l'évolution des techniques électorales dans les Ordres religieuses du VIe au XIIIe siècle', *Revue historique de droit français et étranger*, 4th ser., 36 (1953): 368–98, 491–530.
13 J. H. Burns, 'Majorities: An Exploration', *History of Political Thought* 24 (2003): 66–85.
14 K. Pennington, 'Representation in medieval canon law', in *Repraesentatio: Mapping a Keyword for Churches and Governance*, eds Massimo Faggioli and Alberto Melloni (Münster: LIT, 2006), 21–40 at 26.
15 See Burns, 'Majorities: An Exploration'.
16 See H. F. Pitkin, *The Concept of Representation* (Berkeley: University of California Press, 1967).
17 Nederman, *Lineages of European Political Thought*, 102.
18 Francis Oakley, *The Mortgage of the Past: Reshaping the Ancient Political Inheritance (1050–1300)* (New Haven: Yale University Press, 2012), 222.
19 I am grateful to Stephen Conway for his help during the preparation for this chapter.

CHAPTER SEVEN

Machiavelli's Democratic Turn

Catherine H. Zuckert

Against the common opinion that says that peoples, when they are princes, are varying, mutable, and ungrateful, I affirm that . . . a prince unshackled from the laws will be more ungrateful, varying, and imprudent than a people. The variation in their proceeding arises not from a diverse nature – because it is in one mode in all – but from having more or less respect for the laws. . . . A people is more prudent, more stable, and of better judgment than a prince. . . . If a people hears two orators who incline to different sides, when they are of equal virtue, very few times does one see it not take up the better opinion. . . . If it errs in mighty things or those that appear useful, . . . often a prince errs too in his own passions, which are many more than those of peoples. It is also seen in its choices of magistrates to make a better choice by far than a prince; a people will never be persuaded that it is good to put up for dignities an infamous man of corrupt customs – of which a prince is persuaded easily. . . . Beyond this, one sees that cities in which peoples are princes make exceeding increases in a very brief time, and much greater than those that have always been made under a prince. . . . This cannot arise from anything other than that governments of peoples are better than those of princes. . . . If princes are superior to peoples in ordering laws, forming civil lives, and ordering new statues and orders, peoples are so much superior in maintain things ordered that without doubt they attain the glory of those who order them.[1]

In this statement drawn from Book 1, Chapter 58 of his *Discourses on Livy* Machiavelli makes what I have called his 'democratic turn'. He declares that popular or democratic governments are better than princely or aristocratic ones. He recognizes that he is making a revolutionary statement in maintaining that 'the multitude is wiser and more constant than a prince', because he is defending 'a thing that . . . has been accused by all the writers'.[2] Writers such as Plato, Aristotle, and Aquinas had argued that the only means of securing good government was to educate a few virtuous men to control the unruly, tumultuous many. Machiavelli contends not merely that political leaders who always attempt to do what is right and good will necessarily fail, but also that popular governments last longer and are more glorious.[3]

Like his better known and shorter treatise entitled *The Prince* (composed between 1513 and 1516), Machiavelli's *Discourses on Livy* (composed between 1515 and 1519) were published posthumously in 1532 with papal permission, but were placed twenty-five years later on the Index, that is, the list of readings prohibited by the Roman Catholic Church. On the basis of the more widely read *Prince*, Machiavelli has often been castigated as a teacher of tyrants, if not of evil simply. In fact, however, in both his *Prince* and *Discourses* Machiavelli tries to convince those who have or aspire to possess political power that they will attain it best by trying to satisfy their people's desires for the preservation of their lives, families and properties. Popular governments are better than princely governments because they preserve the liberties of the people as well.

The common view of Machiavelli as a proponent of 'Machiavellian politics' is based to a large extent on another even more famous statement of the way in which he understood himself to be differing from all previous writers. In Chapter 15 of *The Prince* he declares:

> I fear that . . . I may be held presumptuous. . . . But since my intent is to write something useful to whoever understands it, it has appeared to me more fitting to go directly to the effectual truth of the thing than to the imagination of it. Many have imagined republics and principalities that have never been seen or known to exist in truth; for it is so far from how one lives to how one should live that he who lets go of what is done for what should be done learns his ruin rather than his preservation.

To show a prince how he can maintain his state, Machiavelli thus proposes to teach him how 'to be able not to be good, and to use this and not use it according to necessity'.[4]

To teach a political leader 'to be able not to be good' and to use that ability 'according to necessity' is not, however, simply to teach him to be bad. Who would need to learn 'to be able not to be good'? Not those who are already bad, but those who would like to do good. Machiavelli has thus often been cast as a 'realist' thinker who recognizes the weaknesses of human nature and advocates the necessity of using harsh measures, upon occasion, especially in foreign policy. But this 'realist' understanding can also be shown to be partial and thus flawed by the fact that Machiavelli's two major works, *The Prince* and *Discourses on Livy*, are as much about domestic policies and institutions as they are about the use of arms.

Machiavelli announces his great moral (or perhaps we should say immoral) revolution in politics in *The Prince* in order to make governments serve the interests of most ordinary people and not the aristocratic – or rich – few. The core of his teaching princes 'to be able not to be good' and to use that knowledge 'according to necessity' is to be found in his re-definition of the traditional virtues of liberality, mercy and faith in Chapters 15–19. Re-defining these traditional virtues in instrumental terms, Machiavelli advises a political leader that if he wants to preserve himself, he should do what is necessary to secure the lives, families and property of his many subjects or fellow citizens, not seek to reward or otherwise favour his relatively few aristocratic supporters or partisan cronies. Machiavelli is not simply a populist or democratic political thinker, however. In his *Discourses* he shows that this 'popular prince' poses the greatest threat to the preservation of republican or free government. In his *Discourses* Machiavelli thus tries to persuade other politically ambitious young men to compete with the 'prince' for popular favour and so prevent any one individual from gaining unchecked power.

The basis of Machiavelli's re-definition of the traditional virtues in *The Prince* and his advocacy of republican institutions in the *Discourses* is to be found in a general observation he makes – both in his discussion of 'civil principalities' in *The Prince* (Ch. 9) and in his praise of the Roman republic in his *Discourses* (1.4–5) – about the existence of two 'humours' in every city. There are 'the people [who] desire neither to be commanded nor oppressed by the great, and the great [who] desire to command and oppress the people' (39). These two 'humours' are obviously opposed, so that neither can be satisfied except at the expense of the other. Because they are divided into these two 'humours', all political associations are characterized by a fundamental conflict between those who want to rule and those who do not want to be ruled.

Depending on the relative strength of these two 'appetites', as Machiavelli also calls the 'humours', there are three possible results: principality, liberty or license. In a book purportedly devoted to the education of a prince, Machiavelli does not explain how 'liberty' can be achieved through a balancing of the two humours; that is the subject of Book 1 of his *Discourses on Livy*. In *The Prince* Machiavelli confines himself to urging the prince, whether he comes to power with the aid of the great or of the people, once in power to seek the support of the people. The reasons he gives are telling.

First, Machiavelli points out, the great will always see themselves as the prince's equals and demand ever more offices and goods as the price of their support. Attempts to satisfy them will necessarily fail and, in failing, add to the prince's enemies. It is possible, however, for a prince to satisfy the people, because 'the end of the people is more decent (*onesto*) than that of the great, since the great want to oppress and the people want not to be oppressed' (P 9, 39).[5]

The second reason Machiavelli gives as to why it is better to seek the support of the people than of the great is even more fundamental. There is strength in numbers and the people are many whereas the great are few. As Machiavelli reminds his readers with the examples of 'lovely' fellows like Cesare Borgia, Agathocles and Oliverotto, the great in any particular city can be brought together under false pretences and slaughtered; but a prince will have no one to rule if he murders all or most of his people. To be sure, Machiavelli acknowledges, a prince needs subordinates to help him rule, but he observes that a prince can do perfectly well without any given set of 'great' persons, since the prince 'can make and unmake them every day' (P 9, 40). He makes some 'great' by giving them lands and offices or, conversely, 'unmakes' them by taking away their lands and offices along with their lives. Machiavelli thus shows his reader that the 'great' are not different from the many by nature. 'Greatness' is a product of a person's position. As he states in the *Discourses* (1.58), human nature is the same in all. Because those granted high offices have more power and goods, however, they no longer feel as liable to oppression as those subject to the government. Rather than desiring merely not to be oppressed, they come as a result of their 'great' positions to wish to acquire more by oppressing others.

In redefining traditional virtues such as liberality, mercy and faith in calculating, instrumental terms, Machiavelli shows that the best way for a political leader to satisfy his own desire to maintain his own dominion is to satisfy his people's desire to have their lives, families and properties protected. A political leader who depletes his own resources by generously granting offices, lands and titles to his aristocratic friends or partisans will lose their support and acquire their contempt, he observes, unless that leader acquires new funds by taxing his people and so arouses their hatred. Rather than squander his capital by rewarding an ungrateful few, a leader will prove himself truly liberal to the many he does not have to tax by conserving his own resources so that he will be able to defend them when needed. Likewise, Machiavelli argues, a political leader who pardons criminals may appear to be merciful to a few, but he is cruel to his many subjects or fellow citizens who fear for their lives and property when the law is not vigorously enforced. Leaders have to use both force and fraud in order to acquire and maintain power; but they must always strive to appear to be full of mercy, faith, honesty, humility and religion. If a prince does what is necessary to 'win and maintain his state', Machiavelli assures his readers, 'the means will always be judged honourable, and will be praised by everyone' (*P* 18, 71). Why will everyone not merely believe, but praise a head of state when he claims to be waging war, rigorously enforcing the law or raising taxes for the sake of the true faith or humanity? It is difficult, if not impossible for observers to discover what a person's true motives are. In fact, political leaders act in order to acquire and maintain power for themselves. But if they act to maintain a state that protects the lives and property of their subjects or fellow citizens from external aggression and domestic crime, people will believe them when they declare that they are acting for the common good. In other words, people judge a leader's character and words by the effects of his deeds.

People gather together and form political communities to protect themselves from the aggression of others, Machiavelli points out in his *Discourses* (1.1). In order to do so effectively, however, they need a leader to organize or 'order' them. Unfortunately, having seized the opportunity to free his people from the oppression of others, that leader often uses the opportunity to command and oppress them himself. In order to preserve the liberty of all, it thus becomes necessary to devise 'modes and orders', i.e. laws and institutions, that enable the two 'humours' that grow up in all cities to check the excesses of the other. In urging his readers to imitate the Roman republic, but to avoid the excesses that led to its demise, Machiavelli argues that the best way to prevent the emergence of a new tyrant is to make the ambitious *grandi* compete with each other for popular favour in elections. Public offices should have specified powers and individuals elected to them for short terms. All citizens should be eligible to be elected to the highest public offices, and there should be what we call 'rotation in office', so that older and more experienced leaders will be able to counsel and restrain more impetuous and ambitious youths. Rather than castigating the ingratitude, if not the vanity and inconstancy of the multitude for their willingness to condemn individuals to death whom they previously glorified for deeds of extraordinary public service, Machiavelli suggests that people ought to be made more suspicious of 'merciful works of citizens' which conceal the beginning of tyranny. To deter and punish such tyrannical ambitions, public trials ought to be held in which individuals would be formally accused and able to defend themselves in front of large popular juries.

To justify granting such fundamental decisions with regard to who should rule and what constitutes treasonous activity to the multitude Machiavelli explicitly disagrees with all previous writers by maintaining that 'the multitude is wiser and more constant than a prince' (*D* 1.58, 11). Recognizing that all human beings are misled by their passions, Machiavelli qualifies that judgment by explaining that he is speaking about a people restrained by law. In other words, the characteristic excesses or weaknesses of the popular humour also need to be checked. 'A multitude without a head is useless', he bluntly declares (*D* 1.44, 92). 'There is nothing more formidable than an unshackled multitude', but there is also 'nothing weaker. . . . For when the spirits of men are cooled a little and each sees he has to return to his home, they begin to doubt themselves and to think of their safety, either by taking flight or by coming to accord. Therefore a multitude so excited . . . has at once to make from among itself a head to correct it, to hold it united, and to think about its defence' (*D* 1.57, 115).⁶ In sum, peoples need leaders (princes). Nevertheless, Machiavelli concludes that 'if princes are superior to peoples in ordering laws, forming civil lives, and ordering new statues and orders, peoples are so much superior in maintaining things ordered that without doubt they attain the glory of those who order them' (*D* 1.58, 118).

In a properly structured republic where the people feel secure in their lives, families and property, individuals and the community as a whole both grow and prosper:

> Larger peoples are seen there, because marriages are freer and more desirable to men since each willingly procreates those children he believes he can nourish. He does not fear that his patrimony will be taken away, and he knows not only that they are born free and not slaves, but that they can, through their own virtue, become princes. Riches are seen to multiply there in larger number, both those that come from agriculture and those that come from the arts. For each willingly . . . seeks to acquire those goods he believes he can enjoy once acquired. From which it arises that men in rivalry think of private and public advantages, and both . . . grow marvelously. (*D* 2.2, 132)

The criterion by which governments should be judged to be good or bad, Machiavelli contends, is not the moral character or intelligence of the person or persons who rule. It is the common good that results from a government that secures the lives, families, liberty and property of its citizens. Machiavelli thus advocates a thoroughly democratic end or purpose for government. But he does not think that purely democratic processes or means are always the best or even adequate ways of achieving that end. Leaders who understand that the best way to fulfil their own desire to rule is to satisfy the desires of their people for security, prosperity and advancement are also needed.

Notes

1 Niccolò Machiavelli, *Discourses on Livy*, trans. Harvey C. Mansfield and Nathan Tarcov (Chicago: University of Chicago Press, 1996), 117–18, slightly modified on the basis of the Italian text.
2 Machiavelli, *Discourses on Livy*, 116.

3 Leo Strauss, *Thoughts on Machiavelli* (Chicago: University of Chicago Press, 1958) has been widely criticized for his expressed sympathy for the simple and old-fashioned view of Machiavelli as a 'teacher of evil' (e.g. by Quentin Skinner, *Machiavelli: A Short Introduction* [Oxford: Oxford University Press, 1981], 99; Barbara Spackman, 'Machiavelli and Maxims', *Yale French Studies* no. 77, *Reading the Archive: Old Texts and Institutions* [New Haven: Yale University Press, 1990], 137.) However, Strauss explicitly finds that simple view inadequate and declares, 'Machiavelli was the first philosopher who questioned in the name of the multitude or of democracy the aristocratic prejudice or the aristocratic premise which informed classical philosophy' (127).

4 Niccolò Machiavelli, *The Prince*, 2nd edn, trans. Harvey C. Mansfield (Chicago: University of Chicago Press, 1998), 61.

5 Pierre Manent, *An Intellectual History of Liberalism*, trans. Rebecca Balinski (Princeton: Princeton University Press, 1995), observes that 'by radically depreciating the pretensions to "virtue" of the nobility, and simultaneously making the people "honest", Machiavelli becomes the first *democratic* thinker' (16).

6 In emphasizing the democratic character of Machiavelli's politics, Miguel Vatter, *Between Form and Event: Machiavelli's Theory of Political Freedom* (Dordrecht: Kluwer, 2000) overstates the importance of popular uprisings in destroying old orders and creating openings for the construction of new ones. Likewise, John McCormick, *Machiavellian Democracy* (Cambridge: Cambridge University Press, 2011) overstates Machiavelli's advocacy of 'ferocious populism' in countering the oppression of the 'great'. The conflict between the two humours that arise in every city threatens to become a civil war, which will in turn give rise to a tyrant, Machiavelli argues, unless the two humours are channelled by laws and institutions that enable them to check one another. As he shows repeatedly in his *Florentine Histories*, periodic rioting results in the destruction of property and deaths of citizens, but it does not produce beneficent institutional changes.

CHAPTER EIGHT

James Harrington and the Rule of King People

J. C. Davis

This free born nation liveth not upon the dole or bounty of one man but, distributing her annual magistracies and honours with her own hand, is herself King People. [. . .]
The people for the rest shall elect their own magistrates, and be governed by their own laws having power also to appeal from their native or provincial magistrates, if they please, unto the people of Oceana.[1]

However sympathetic James Harrington might have been to the royal predicament in the run up to the regicide, in defiantly democratic statements like these he applauded the vesting of those early modern marks of sovereignty, official appointments and the distribution of honours, as well as final judicial appeals, in the people rather than a single person ruling over them. Then, in 1648–9, he may have been attendant on the doomed King, now, in 1656, he was writing in the face of the Protectorate's moves back towards the rule of a single person with a council and parliament. England, in 1656, continued to wrestle with the instabilities consequent upon a series of viciously divisive and partisan civil wars and revolution. No one questions Harrington's preoccupation with that instability and its causes, nor his determination to provide structural and procedural solutions. Debate has swirled around the material basis of his analysis of England's troubles and prescribed remedies, whether his thought is republican or utopian, his debt to Machiavelli and whether the primary influences upon him were Greek, Roman or Hebrew. Less attention has been given to his extolling the virtues of popular authority, to Harrington as a theorist of democracy. Confronted by England's chronic instability and in an age deeply suspicious of the many and profoundly hierarchical in its social attitudes and practices, how much of a democrat was Harrington?

There are a number of ways in which the Oceanic constitution he was proposing in 1656 appears quintessentially democratic. For instance, civil society was constructed and annually renewed by the full participation of all citizens in a sequence of ritualized decision-making processes rising from the parish to the national level. Annual musters of citizens or their representatives, at the parish, hundred (groups of ten parishes), county or national levels, elected civil office holders and representatives, as well as a militia, out of which was generated a sizeable standing army, with their officers (I–XII). Decision was invariably in the hands of popular assemblies at the national, county, hundred or parish levels. Such authority as was invested upwards was always at the will of the generality of the citizens, was revocable by them and was accountable to them. All officeholders (from parish constables and church wardens to judges, ambassadors and members of the Council of State) were elected for limited terms and obliged to vacate office for a period at the end of those terms. Rotation of office holders and representatives was for Harrington a key device to ensure the widest participation and to prevent the formation of cliques or parties amongst officeholders or even the development of an officeholder interest against the public interest. It guaranteed a perpetual or spherical motion, the circulation of the commonwealth's political lifeblood.

Military provision was by way of a democratic militia accountable to the people and in marked contrast with the armies which had emerged out of the recent civil wars (and indeed most armies since).[2] Parishioners voted to confirm the appointment of parochial clergy after one year's probationary service and the gathered congregations, to which liberty of conscience was extended, were also expected to elect their pastors (VI). A similar democratization of the judicial system was anticipated with juries as well as the judiciary elected and with the ultimate determination of judicial appeals by the popular assembly (169, 171: *A System of Politics*, 279–80, 289–90). The democratically elected administration of the county would, in the first instance, try all 'Crimes against the Majesty of the People', in particular high treason and the theft or misuse of public funds.[3] All conciliar decrees were subject to confirmation by the popular assembly and, even *in extremis* the Dictator, charged with dealing with emergencies, was subject to the approval and review by that body (XIX).

Not only was citizen control maximized but the qualification for citizenship, although, as we shall see, limited, was politically, religiously and – to a degree – economically inclusive. Indeed Harrington was very sensitive to the potential of deference in seventeenth century society (149–50) and took steps to mitigate it. The majority of seats in the popular assembly were reserved for representatives of the less affluent, and the secret ballot (XIV) and salaries for official duties were designed to prevent undue influence by the rich. Yet the leisure for study and travel (and thence the acquisition of political wisdom) which wealth could confer also had a political importance for him. The purpose of his Agrarian Law (XIII) was to maintain the balance of land ownership on a popular basis while preserving an aristocracy, incapable of overbalancing the many but equipped to provide wisdom and direction in formulating the public interest (23, 141, 280). Above all, Harrington was antipathetic to party (which reduced the public interest to partisan interest) and to demagoguery (which could divert the popular will from its instinct for the public interest). Frequent elections, rotation and vacation of office were designed to eliminate party while the restriction of debate to the senate and decision to the popular assembly in a bicameral division of function were arranged to limit the scope for rhetoricians to influence, and possibly distort, the popular will. Over a triennial cycle, half of all adult citizens would be required to discharge some office in an administration run completely by the citizens and with some considerable local discretion.[4] Such levels of participation in themselves embodied the will of the people in the operation of government and were intended to ensure a democratic ethos and ownership of the state.

Harrington was explicit about the theoretical underpinning of such a state. He drew the distinction between empire, or power, and authority. Empire was, he believed, in a reflection of the landed society he inhabited, a function of the ownership of land, which commanded obedience because of its potentially inexhaustible capacity to feed. If one person owned the balance of land, absolute monarchy was possible. If the few owned such a balance, oligarchy or, more likely, regulated monarchy should follow. Both those systems were unstable. Since the dissolution of the monasteries and the secularization of church property in the sixteenth century, the balance of land in England had swung on to a popular basis and therefore a commonwealth or rule of the many was possible.

But the stability of such a commonwealth (and commonwealths had failed throughout history) was dependent on skill in political architecture or constitutional design. Such design had to stabilize the balance of property and ensure the decisiveness of a popular will guided by, but not dominated by, the political wisdom of an elite whose fortunes would be protected while being prevented from subverting the popular balance of land ownership (11–18). His proposed republic was unique because it was an 'Equal Commonwealth' combining bicameral division of function, rotation, the secret ballot and an agrarian law constraining the transmission and acquisition of landed property so as to preserve the balance of land ownership in the many while sustaining a non-dominant landed elite. It was the historical good fortune of England in the 1650s that such a popular distribution of property also provided a basis in empire underwriting the superior legitimacy or authority of a popular commonwealth. Harrington argued that all law arose from will and that formative will was the more legitimate if it were the will of the whole rather than of the part, just as the interest (which drove the will) of the whole was more legitimate than the interest of the one or the few.[5] Like an interest theorist *avant la lettre*, he answered the question as to how irrational men could make a commonwealth of rational laws by pleading for a constitutional arrangement which would always give the upper hand to the common interest (19–23).

On the other hand, Harrington did set limits, or apparent limits, to what might today be regarded as democratic rights. The underlying criterion for citizenship was a good degree of self-rule or independence. Accordingly, not only children but women, servants (I), wastrels (III), bachelors (XII) and those who refused public or military service were excluded from citizenship as were those who were assumed to be *parti pris* (in the sense of already having a committed position which might blind them to the public interest). Amongst the latter, priests, physicians and lawyers were also deprived of citizenship (203–4). Those who remained as citizens were divided into the youth (aged 18 to 30) and the elders (those over 30). The militia was organized by and around the youth, while responsibility for civil office holding and representation were confined to the elders. What is extraordinary, and almost unique to Harrington (and we shall return to this later), is that he did not exclude former royalists or neutrals, who might have been expected to be hostile to a republican constitution, from citizenship.

In what might be seen as a further restriction on democratic freedoms, Harrington also limited political discussion. In the formal sense it was restricted to the Senate, whose members were elected from the wealthier equestrian class. They were to debate and propose. The more popularly based assembly was to decide ('yes', 'no' or 'not persuaded') on the Senate's proposals without further discussion. Canvassing and caballing were forbidden (XXIII, 167). The atmosphere of this republic was to be much more constrained and formal than that of most modern democracies but of course Harrington was seeking to avoid demagoguery, as well as partisan and confusing politics. There was some mitigation of the political silence outside of the Senate, some provision for a limited public sphere. The Academy of Provosts was to provide an open salon every evening for the informal but orderly exchange of political news and discussion by all comers (XIX) and every Tuesday the popular assembly attended a lecture on the constitution and its workings (XXIII). Moreover, the state made provision for two national theatres, four poets and a poet laureate (260–1). While protecting and funding a national religion, *Oceana* made widespread provision for the liberty of protestant consciences – Roman Catholics, Jews and the more extreme protestant sects being excluded. Finally, while a democratic and very intensive citizen engagement with office holding was a core operating principle, rotation and vacation of office, which were intended to prevent the development of parties, excluded some citizens, at least temporarily, from office.

It can be argued then that there was a balance, or tension, in Harrington's thought between democratic empowerment and limitations on political conduct in the name of political stability and the public interest. In part this might be explained by acknowledging that he was attempting to create a new second nature for man as a political animal (or an alternative political culture). The difficulty he saw was that

> be the interest of popular government right reason, a man does not look upon reason as it is right or wrong in itself, but as it makes for or against him, wherefore unless you can show such orders of government as, like those of God in nature, shall be able to constrain this or that creature to shake off that inclination which is more peculiar unto it and take up that which regards the common good or interest, all this is to no more end than to persuade every man in a popular government not to carve himself of that which he desires most, but to be mannerly at the public table, and give the best from himself unto decency and the common interest. (22)

In any case, there was, as he put it in *The Art of Lawgiving*, no such thing as 'pure' democracy; the rule of the many would always require the input of the few.[6] In the end it was the institutional and procedural structures of a well-designed or equal commonwealth (32–4) which would prevent anyone having either the power or the interest to disturb the government and go against the common interest.[7]

To fully appreciate Harrington's balancing of democratic freedom and its limitation, to grasp his thinking's singularity and what it shared with his contemporaries, we should locate it in its historical context. In the early 1640s the government of the Stuart monarchs dissolved into competing factions and civil war ensued. As well as wreaking havoc, that prolonged war embraced all four of their kingdoms in a massively punishing, internecine struggle which transformed many of the processes and institutions of government – eventually abolishing the Church of England, the monarchy and the House of Lords. But stability did not follow from the victory of parliament's armies in the civil war. Resistance continued and the victors fell out amongst themselves. In the seven years after 1649, the regicide and the declaration that England was a 'Free State' there had been five 'parliaments' under five different parliamentary systems, and in the autumn of 1656 yet another new constitution was under consideration. Loyalty to what existed was hard to come by and one response was to exclude those – and there were obviously many – who were of doubtful loyalty from citizenship. This might be done by direct exclusion or by the use of oaths or avowals to create a subscriptional civil community. So the Levellers – once much vaunted as advocates of democracy – in their final Agreement of the People excluded not only children, women, servants and alms takers, from citizenship, but also those unwilling to endorse the Agreement, thus creating something equivalent to a one party state. Harrington criticized this kind of exclusion as divisive and creative of parties; the included and the excluded. In turn, his critics almost universally saw him as dangerously inclusive. The more famous republicans, like Milton and Sir Henry Vane, believed that stability, and probably virtue, required the exclusion of the majority from citizenship. Marchamont Nedham was deliberately blunt in pointing to his differences with Harrington:

> To take off all misunderstandings; when we mention *the People*, observe all along, that we do not mean the confused promiscuous Body of the People, not any part of the people who have forfeited their Rights by Delinquency, Neutrality, of Apostasy, &c. in relation to the divided state of any Nation; for they are not to be reckon'd within the Lists of the People.[8]

Others like Henry Stubbe and Richard Baxter deplored the inclusiveness of *Oceana*'s provision for citizenship, either because the time was not ripe for such generosity or because the ungodly would never be fit for civic responsibility.[9]

Harrington was equally concerned to offer guarantees of stability but he offered them in forms other than citizen exclusivity. His principal means were institutional structures and the processes, operating around and through them, which were designed to generate a convergence of practice, scripted, enacted and re-enacted in grand, almost-theatrical, annual, quasi-ritualistic cycles. It was 'not the people that are trusted, but the orders of the commonwealth'[10] and, accordingly, an inclusive approach could be adopted in classifying people as citizens. The function of his political architecture was, in this respect, threefold. It guaranteed stability by ensuring that all citizens had some share in the exercise of power, some prospect of riches and some considerable freedom, the deprivation of any of which could lead to instability. Secondly, all citizens were engaged in functionally differentiated cycles of deliberation, decision or administration. The design was to 'take in the whole body by parts' (33), creating such a level of participation amongst citizens as to create a sense that the people were in possession of their own government, making all those qualified complicit in the operation of Oceana's political system. Finally, the system with its bicameral separation of debate from decision and its measures against party formation and a culture of partisanship was designed to ensure that the public interest would always prevail over private interests.[11]

In classical political literature the rule of the many had frequently been associated with the threat of instability if not anarchy. For Machiavelli, Harrington's teacher, republican self-rule was inevitably associated with popular tumults. Harrington's approach to this perceived problem of democracy was to devise means to limit and control the people while giving expression and force to their collective will, to the rule of King People.

But, in doing this, he also protected them against deference, demagoguery, parties and their own ignorance, as well as against real power moving away from them in movements in the ownership of landed property. It was necessary to divide the people geographically and socially but by the standards of his time they were generous divisions and, by the same standards, his was an extraordinarily inclusive democracy. But, if it was to operate effectively, democracy could not be simply reducible to an inclusive franchise. Believing that it was the legislator's duty to presume all men wicked, he had a democratic faith that the people would choose the public interest, once it was identified and articulated for them and provided that they were protected from demagoguery and their manipulation by partisan interests. Most impressively, he attempted to design the constitutional machinery which would guarantee those protections. In an age of all-pervasive media manipulation and democratic deficit, this should be worth reflecting on.

Notes

1. References to *Oceana* and *A System of Politics* will be to J. G. A. Pocock, ed., *James Harrington: The Commonwealth of Oceana and A System of Politics* (Cambridge: Cambridge University Press, 1992). The two extracts heading this chapter will be found at pages 98 and 215 respectively. Page references to this edition will be given in parentheses throughout the text of this essay. The orders or constitutional rules of Oceana are similarly referred to in roman numerals.
2. For the context here see T. R. W. Kubik, 'How Far the Sword? Militia Tactics and Politics in the *Commonwealth of Oceana*', *History of Political Thought* 19, no. 2 (1998): 186–212.
3. See Charles Blitzer, *An Immortal Commonwealth: The Political Thought of James Harrington* (New Haven: Yale University Press, 1960), 245.
4. See J. C. Davis, 'Narrative Constitutionalism and the Kinetics of James Harrington's *Oceana*', in *Constitutions and the Classics: Patterns of Constitutional Thought from Fortescue to Bentham*, ed. D. J. Galligan (Oxford: Oxford University Press, 2014), 178–9; J. C. Davis, 'Reassessing Radicalism in a Traditional Society: Two Questions', in *English Radicalism 1550–1850*, ed. Glenn Burgess and Matthew Festenstein (Cambridge: Cambridge University Press, 2007), 360–2.
5. For a succinct statement of this position see James Harrington, *The Prerogative of Popular Government* (1658), in *The Political Works of James Harrington*, ed. J. G. A. Pocock (Cambridge: Cambridge University Press, 1977), 401.
6. Pocock, *Works*, 611.
7. Ibid., 658.

8   [Marchamont Nedham], *The Excellencie of a Free-State* (London, 1656), 71.
9   Henry Stubbe, *An Essay in Defence of the GOOD OLD CAUSE* (London, 1659), Preface; William Lamont, ed., *Richard Baxter: A Holy Commonwealth* (Cambridge: Cambridge University Press, 1994), 12, 40, 80–1, 102-8, 128.
10 Harrington, *Valerius and Publicola* (1659), in Pocock, *Works*, 795.
11 J. C. Davis, 'Equality in an Unequal Commonwealth: James Harrington's Republicanism and the Meaning of Equality', in *Soldiers, Writers and Statesmen of the English Revolution*, ed. Ian Gentles, John Morrill, and Blair Wooden (Cambridge: Cambridge University Press, 1998), 138–40.

CHAPTER NINE

Baruch Spinoza: Radical Republican

Emma Cohen de Lara and Nathan Cooper

> *Human society can thus be formed without any alienation of natural right, and the contract can be preserved in its entirety with complete fidelity, only if every person transfers all the power they possess to society, and society alone retains the supreme natural right over all things, i.e., supreme power, which all must obey, either of their own free will or through fear of the ultimate punishment. The right of such a society is called democracy. Democracy therefore is properly defined as a united gathering of people which collectively has the sovereign right to do all that it has the power to do.*[1]

In this chapter, we seek to explain how Spinoza's low opinion of the masses can be reconciled with his affirmation of democratic self-rule as the best form of government. We also seek to show that Spinoza was, in fact, a radical republican.[2] He is a republican in virtue of his opposition to monarchical government. He is a *radical* republican because, unlike ancient republicans like Aristotle, Polybius and Cicero, Spinoza does not advocate a mixed regime composed of democratic, aristocratic and monarchical elements. Rather, Spinoza is committed to a strictly egalitarian foundation for society and government. This distinguishes Spinoza from contemporary British republicans such as James Harrington who favoured a mixed regime with a monarch deprived of absolute power. Harrington is still closer to the ancient understanding of government, whereas Spinoza is one of the first moderns on account of his unyielding emphasis on egalitarianism. Spinoza's political and philosophical corpus remains radical even today, although it also contains elements that resonate with modern democracies.

The masses constitute the main political challenge according to Spinoza. He considers the masses to be superstitious, capricious, fickle, motivated by passion rather than reason, easily corrupted and angered because of their poverty, and generally predisposed to wish ill towards others. In particular, the masses' susceptibility to superstition poses a problem. Political instability, conflict, scarcity and the uncertainty of human knowledge cause most people to live in a state of doubt and, in this condition, '[n]o suggestion they hear is too unwise, ridiculous or absurd to follow' (preface, 2). In his *Ethics*, Spinoza explains how human beings have developed the imagination in order to provide a response to potential threats to one's self-preservation with fear and superstition. It is under the physical contingency of war, scarcity or petulance, that human beings easily accept superstition or religious dogmatism to offer an explanation of these conditions.

In the *Theological-Political Treatise*, Spinoza blames religious agitators for manipulating the masses. By religious agitators, he denotes the contemporary Calvinist clergy as well as the rabbinical authority of his time and the Catholic ecclesiastical authorities who 'fill the minds of every individual with so many prejudices that they leave no room for sound reason' (preface, 6). Instead of teaching Christianity's universal values of neighbourly love and natural justice, they generate conflict, rivalry and resentment by articulating new and controversial interpretations of the Bible. In this way, the religious agitators take advantage of the fears and weaknesses of the masses while undermining state authority and profiting from lucrative positions they obtain in the church.

There are two ways in which Spinoza aims to free the masses from the subversive influences of the religious agitators. First of all, he argues that the social relevance of the Bible should be understood purely in terms of the moral message of Christ, whose core message was one of charity and justice. The Bible conveys these universal principles through parables and narratives, which make them accessible to the common people who are not competent to perceive things clearly and distinctly by the use of reason. The clergy should restrict themselves to this core message and not engage in religious disputes. The social relevance of the Bible as a document that cultivates obedience to the universal moral law of charity and justice is enormous. Spinoza's interpretation of the Bible contributes to making the masses 'safe' for democracy.

The second way in which Spinoza seeks to free the masses from the subversive influences of the religious agitators is by subjecting religion to state authority. In order to secure the laws of the civil state, by means of which stability and safety is obtained, 'the supreme right of deciding about religion, belongs to the sovereign power' (16:21). Those who hold sovereign power must be both the interpreters and guardians of things sacred. They must offer this religious interpretation in light of the peace and security of the state. Those who advocate a separation of civil and divine authority simply seek to devise a path of worldly power for themselves (19:1; 19:16).

Spinoza's argument in favour of providing the state with authority over religious matters may seem inconsistent with his commitment to religious tolerance and freedom of thought. For Spinoza, however, there is no contradiction. The state has authority to judge over the actions of people, including religious actions such as external religious worship and every expression of piety (cf. 19:9). People's *thoughts* remain free. It may be naïve to think that people's thoughts can be divorced from people's actions. But Spinoza shows himself to be part of a liberal tradition that separates the private – an individual's thoughts and judgments – from the public – the individual's actions insofar as they have a public impact.

Spinoza's account of the social relevance of the Bible and his argument for subjecting religious authority to the state are not the only ways in which he is paving the way for democratic rule. It is also the other way around: Spinoza favours a democratic government by virtue of the very fact that the masses are susceptible to being deceived and are prone to be fickle and egocentric. Democratic government actually responds best to the incapacity of the masses for sound reasoning; it provides the most stability given the tendency of the masses to follow passion instead of reason and, on top of that, it provides the most freedom of thought, which in turn supports good governance because it generates knowledge. In order to see how this argument works, we will first look at why Spinoza rejects an alternative form of government, namely, monarchy.[3]

According to Spinoza, a monarchy is a regime defined by a lack of freedom. Monarchs are predisposed to seek too much power because the security of their government depends on the one ruler. This makes monarchies unnatural, or at least less natural than republics. Nature dictates that absolute power is an unattainable goal; the natural freedom of people will always resist such concentration of power. Monarchs, however, will strive endlessly for the accumulation of power in order to secure their regime.

For people to sacrifice their natural freedom, a monarchical government needs to keep the subjects in a permanent state of deception (preface, 7). Monarchies thus manipulate the people into loyalty to the regime, and this loyalty extends as far as believing that one should fight for the glorification of a single man at the risk of losing one's life. This is an irrational proposition as far as Spinoza is concerned, especially because monarchs are likely to start and continue wars for irrational reasons such as pride and glory instead of peace and liberty (18:5). Out of the constant and essential need for deceiving the people, kings use religion to channel the fear that the subjects experience. Spinoza points out that false prophets eagerly feed into this strategy and flatter kings and promise them to subdue the people

(18:5). In short, monarchies by definition promote people's susceptibility for superstition and religious falsehoods. These regimes maintain the people in a less rational state than they could be.

In a democratic republic, deception is no longer essential to exact the obedience of the people and to ensure stability. Instead, obedience and stability is much more easily maintained in a democratic republic because the people are the authors of their own laws. Spinoza develops this argument by means of a social contract theory. This theory warrants more attention than we can provide here, but a few key aspects should be highlighted.

The first is that Spinoza starts from the premise of the natural equality between people. In the natural condition, by which Spinoza indicates a hypothetical, pre-societal and pre-political condition, all human beings are equally free to ensure their individual self-preservation. Some people may be stronger, more rational or cleverer than others, but this makes no difference for the normative premise that *everyone* has the natural right to do what it takes to survive.

People come together and 'contract' with one another in order to guarantee their own survival more effectively. Without political organization, people 'lead wretched and brutish lives' (5:7). Contracting with one another is the best way to ensure security and prosperity. The contract establishes a political society where the people agree to live according to laws and certain dictates of reason, by which Spinoza means general principles such as not harming others, not treating others like one would not want to be treated oneself, and defending other people's rights as their own (16:5). Importantly, with the social contract, sovereign right – that is, the right that trumps any other right – is now held collectively. This right, the right to all things that each individual had from nature, is now no longer determined by the force and appetite of each individual but 'by the power and will of all of them together' (16:5). In other words, human society is formed not by alienation of each individual's natural right, but by exercising natural right collectively. This, Spinoza writes, is properly called a democracy: 'Democracy therefore is properly defined as a united gathering of people which collectively has the sovereign right to do all that it has the power to do' (16:8).

Spinoza argues that the people have an interest in obeying the collective, sovereign right. We should note that people's psychology does not change; everyone, in particular the masses, remain guided by self-interest, pleasure, greed, glory and so forth. However, laws that provide security and prosperity *are* in each individual's interest. A properly functioning democratic citizen obeys the command of the sovereign and, by doing so, does what is useful for the community and consequently also for himself (16:10). In principle, this means that the democratic citizen should carry out 'absolutely all the commands of the sovereign power however absurd they may be' (16:8). However, Spinoza is keen to point out that democratic governments never issue absurd or irrational commands for a sustained period of time. Democratic governments govern by majority rule and although Spinoza does not use the word 'elections' it is clear that everyone who has submitted to the democratic government is periodically consulted: 'In a democracy no one transfers their natural right to another in such a way that they are not thereafter consulted' (16:11). Furthermore, one person or a few may be caught by the whim of the moment, but deliberations by a large group of people are likely to be more rational and conducive to wise decision-making.[4]

The key insight guiding Spinoza's social contract theory is that democratic republics are more stable than other forms of governments. In a way, the problem of the masses remains; they are still predisposed to act irrationally and in their self-interest. However, by submitting oneself to the rule of the majority in a democratic regime, 'all remain equal as they had been previously, in the state of nature' (16:11). In other words, a democratic republic is most natural, requiring the least amount of coercion and deception to maintain its condition. People in general are unlikely to be obedient to rules or to others but in the state of political equality that a democratic republic most closely approximates, the people are *most* likely to obey the laws and rules. In a society where the laws are made by common consent, 'the people remain just as free [as in the natural state], since they are not acting under the authority of another but by their own proper consent' (5:9). It would indeed be reprehensibly irrational to act 'contrary to the decree and dictate of one's own reason' (20:8). People contracting into a democratic society actively consent to being governed by their own reason, which is now exercised collectively. People may not be inclined towards the common good, but it *is* more rational to obey a law if one is its own author even though one may still be inclined to do the opposite. Furthermore, manipulation of the masses is less necessary because they will obey the laws (more often) out of their own free will.

In short, compared to monarchies, democratic republics are less violent, more rational and more free. The masses, no longer manipulated by religious agitators, receiving an uncorrupted Christian message from the clergy, and with a stake in governmental decision-making, have become capable of political agency. Still, this is not Spinoza's final argument as to why democracy is a better and more natural form of government than other kinds. Democracy is most natural not only because it most closely approximates man's natural state of equality, but also because it approaches most closely the state of freedom that nature bestows on every person (16:11). By freedom, Spinoza means the freedom to govern oneself and, importantly, the freedom to think and judge for oneself. Unlike Hobbes, who proposes an absolute government in order to guarantee peace and stability, Spinoza understands freedom of thought as the main purpose of political association, second only to stability.

The value of freedom of thought and toleration is arguably the closest to Spinoza's heart. As a philosopher with radical ideas, he must have longed to live in a freer society. He calls the city of Amsterdam 'a fine example of a city which enjoys the fruits of this liberty' (20:15), but he ironically wrote this sentence while he was living in Voorburg, banished from his own Sephardic community in Amsterdam at the age of 23, and seeking quieter waters and employment. He had witnessed the imprisonment and subsequent death of his friend Adriaan Koerbagh who, a few years before the publication of the *Theological-Political Treatise*, had published two treatises that provoked the wrath of the Calvinist clergy. Spinoza published the *Theological-Political Treatise* anonymously and although his authorship was an open secret in Europe, it remained a text that one could not admire openly, for its 'monstrous opinions'.

It is with particular fervour that Spinoza seeks to explain how 'this freedom [to think, judge and worship according to one's own mind] may not only be allowed without danger to piety and the stability of the republic but cannot be refused without destroying the peace of the republic and piety itself' (preface, 8). Not only is freedom of thought not a threat to peace and stability, but the active oppression of freedom of thought inevitably tends toward conflict and unrest. Freedom of thought is a right that people possess naturally. No one would accept being completely stripped of this right; it is a right that 'no one can give up' (18:6; 20:1; 20:4). It is simply impossible to have someone's mind completely under one's control. Although the power of governments can be great, it will never be so great that the rulers can do whatever they want (17:3). Governments that try to control people's thoughts will only rouse the anger of the people (18:6). Therefore, those who hold sovereign power 'can best retain their authority and fully conserve the state only by conceding that each individual is entitled both to think what he wishes and to say what he thinks' (preface, 14). A government that denies the people freedom to think would have to be a very violent one. The 'less people are accorded liberty of judgment, consequently, the further they are from the most natural condition and, hence, the more oppressive the regime' (20:14). A government that recognizes people's natural right to think and judge (although not act) as they see fit is a more moderate, more stable and more durable government.

Spinoza also affirms the social and political benefits of allowing freedom of thought and judgment. This liberty is essential to the advancement of the arts and sciences and will promote progress and prosperity (20:10). Freedom of thought is needed to cultivate knowledge that feeds into a sound foundation for government: 'that society will be safer, more stable and less vulnerable to fortune, which is for the most part founded and directed by wise and vigilant men' (3:5). Even though Spinoza insists on the natural and political equality of man, those very few who have a propensity to develop their reason have a role to play as well.

In terms of thinking about democracy, Spinoza challenges the reader to think about how and why democracy is the best form of government even when one shares Spinoza's assumption that most people are unlikely to become rational political agents committed to the public good. Furthermore,

Spinoza's argument that democracies are more stable compared to other regimes merits attention. Arguably, the influence of religion on the people was Spinoza's main concern at the time, and he seeks to explain in the *Theological-Political Treatise* how the negative impact of superstition on political stability can be dealt with. At the same time, one may wonder how modern democracies can deal with people's propensity to seek easy explanations for things that cause fear and anxiety. We wish Spinoza *were* still alive today; he would have made a fascinating companion in our conversation about the state of our democracies in the twenty-first century.

Notes

1. Baruch Spinoza, *Theological-Political Treatise*, trans. M. Silverthorne and J. Israel (Cambridge: Cambridge University Press), 16:8. Page references to this edition will be given in parenthesis throughout the text of this chapter.

2. In broad outline, we follow the main thesis of Jonathan Israel who, in his important article 'The Intellectual Origins of Modern Democratic Republicanism (1660–1720)', *European Journal of Political Theory* 3, no. 1 (2004): 7–36 argues that Spinoza is one of the main representatives of a particular brand of republicanism, namely Dutch republicanism, that is distinct from the British republican tradition on account of its more radical nature.

3. Spinoza's rejection of monarchy was a sensitive issue at the time. When the *Theological-Political Treatise* was published in 1670, the United Provinces had been under republican rule for twenty years after the death of the quasi-monarchical Stadholder William II of the House of Orange. However, monarchical forces remained strong and in 1671, the *Rampjaar* or 'Year of Disaster', an angry mob roused by monarchical and clerical forces murdered the brothers De Witt, who were the leaders of the United Provinces for most of its republican period and admired by Spinoza, in the streets of The Hague. The year marked the end of the republican period as William III, also known as William of Orange, was appointed as Stadholder of several of the provinces.

4. This point was made by Justin Steinberg, 'Benedict Spinoza: Epistemic Democrat', *History of Philosophy Quarterly* 27, no. 2 (2010): 145–64.

CHAPTER TEN

Thomas Paine and Democratic Contempt

Mario Feit

For all men being originally equals, no one by birth could have a right to set up his own family in perpetual preference to all others for ever, and though himself might deserve some decent degree of honors of his contemporaries, yet his descendants might be far too unworthy to inherit them. One of the strongest natural proofs of the folly of hereditary right in kings, is that nature disapproves it, otherwise she would not so frequently turn it into ridicule by giving mankind an ass for a lion.
Secondly, as no man at first could possess any other public honors than were bestowed upon him, so the givers of those honors could have no power to give away the right of posterity, and though they might say 'We choose you for our head', they could not without manifest injustice to their children say 'that your children and your children's children shall reign over ours for ever'. Because such an unwise, unjust, unnatural compact might (perhaps) in the next succession put them under the government of a rogue or a fool. Most wise men, in their private sentiments, have ever treated hereditary right with contempt; yet it is one of those evils, which when once established is not easily removed;

many submit from fear, others from superstition, and the more powerful part shares with the king the plunder of the rest. This is supposing the present race of kings in the world to have had an honourable origin; whereas it is more than probable, that could we take off the dark covering of antiquity, and trace them to their first rise, that we should find the first of them nothing better than the principal ruffian of some restless gang, whose savage manners or pre-eminence in subtilty obtained him the title of chief among plunderers; and who by increasing in power and extending his depredations, overawed the quiet and defenseless to purchase their safety by frequent contributions.[1]

Democracy has met with contempt from its inception. Plato bemoaned that democracy 'treats everyone as equal, whether or not they are'.[2] As a result, democracy's 'lifestyle has no rhyme or reason'.[3] Contempt for democracy by no means ends with Plato, nor with the disappearance of the ancient Greek form of democracy he ridiculed. In fact, contempt for democracy has even shaped modern experiments in democratic self-government. As Sheldon Wolin explains, modern '"constitutional democracy" is . . . an ideological construction designed not to realize democracy but to reconstitute it and, as a consequence, repress it'.[4] Modern democracies pay homage to the democratically self-governing people at the same time as they create obstacles to genuinely popular control of political life. Jacques Rancière would add that a 'new hatred of democracy can be succinctly put: there is only one good democracy, the one that represses the catastrophe of democratic civilization'.[5] In other words, contempt for democracy has both a long provenance and undermines even the contemporary pursuit of democracy.

Contrary to this tradition of contempt for democracy, Thomas Paine in *Common Sense* offers us a democratizing form of contempt – what I call democratic contempt, namely, contempt for non-democratic forms of government and social relations. Paine's democratic contempt provides crucial impetus for democratic revolutions and experiments. It makes possible the pursuit of democracy, as it channels our political affects and desires in a democratic direction. Intriguingly, Paine shows us how negative affects can be critical in the creation of affirmative, democratic ideals and practices. Democratic contempt, in other words, consists of more than a rejection of non-democracy; it generates a positive vision of democratic equality. Fleshing out Paine's democratic contempt does therefore more than improve our understanding of a frequently overlooked democratic theorist; it also helps us to push back against contemporary contempt for democracy, so that we can – inspired by Paine – generate further democratic moments.

Paine's call for democratic revolution in *Common Sense* rests on contempt for monarchy: 'Most wise men, in their private sentiments, have ever treated hereditary right *with contempt*; yet it is one of those evils, which when once established is not easily removed; many submit from fear, others from superstition and the more powerful part shares with the king the plunder of the rest.'[6] Paine here asserts an *unspoken* consensus, namely that hereditary forms of government are contempt-worthy. This is a bold claim, seeing that hereditary monarchy was the prevalent form of government in Paine's time. However, with his assertion Paine inverts the meaning of this historical fact: that monarchy prevails proves not its legitimacy but its illegitimacy, for it rests on the suppression of wise men's democratic contempt. Critically, Paine claims that the putative acceptance of monarchy stems in reality from fear, superstition or the narrow self-interests of those who unduly profit from it. The very fact that democratic contempt has had to be a *private* form of wisdom exacerbates hereditary monarchy's contempt-worthiness. Hereditary monarchy simply could not withstand any reason-based public challenge.

Paine's democratic contempt results from and facilitates reason. In particular, he uses reason to question the origins and legitimacy of hereditary monarchy. If one looks past the superstitions and myths formed around monarchy, one can see that this form of government proceeds from predatory forms of power. The first kings were 'nothing better than the principal ruffian of some restless gang, whose savage manners or pre-eminence in subtilty [sic] obtained him the title of chief among plunderers'.[7] Far from the image of divinely anointed protectors of their subjects, kings originally – and in essence always[8] – are shrewd and violent criminals. Indeed, these thugs, as Paine goes on to explain, set themselves up as rulers by preying on the weakness of their would-be subjects. They run a protection scheme, where the weak have to fund these thugs-cum-kings, which intensifies and cements the power differential that formed the real origin of monarchy. Paine's turn to reason leads him to develop a counter-history.

Although Paine could rest his case based this counter-history, he develops two additional objections, both of which concern monarchy's hereditary transmission. In doing so, Paine further demonstrates that rational analysis drives democratic contempt, for he even considers a hypothetical scenario – of one generation consenting to be ruled by a monarch, and of that originally legitimate government being made hereditary – which he clearly rules out with his counter-history. Paine objects to two ways in which monarchy may have become hereditary: first, when a king makes political rule a form of property to be passed on to his descendants and second when a generation who consents to be governed by a monarch also grants the same rights to his descendants. Paine rejects both on grounds of equality. In both cases, natural human equality is violated in the effort to treat political rule as hereditary. The difference consists in who commits the injustice of depriving future generations of political equality: a king or a founding generation.

The intergenerational injustice of creating a hereditary title to rule to Paine ultimately rests on an intragenerational injustice, namely, to assume that there could be politically significant, natural hierarchies among humans.[9]

Paine turns to the historical record of hereditary monarchy to buttress his case for natural equality:

> One of the strongest *natural* proofs of the folly of hereditary right in Kings, is, that nature disapproves it, otherwise she would not so frequently turn it into ridicule by giving mankind an *ass for a lion*. . . . Because such an unwise, unjust, unnatural compact might (perhaps) in the next succession put them under the government of a rogue or a fool.[10]

Political merit is not a natural trait that can be passed on. In fact, quite the opposite may be the case. Descendants may only poorly imitate their ancestors (donkeys pretending to be lions), may lack ethics ('rogue') or may be incompetent ('fool'). That putatively noble family trees include individuals who clearly are not superior to others demonstrates to Paine nature's contempt for hereditary rule. Nature, in other words, manifests democratic contempt with each hapless descendant of monarchic or aristocratic families. Paine, to be clear, does not take nature to merely make the case that political merit cannot be passed down biologically; he turns the impossibility of natural transmission of political merit into a sign that any given king's putative political merits were never grounded in nature. Nature affirms political equality; it never set any one individual, let alone any family tree, above others.[11] Accordingly, Paine has nothing but contempt for the thugs-cum-kings who pretend otherwise.

Many who share Paine's desire for democracy may be worried about unleashing negative affects, such as contempt, in the name of democracy. They may worry that democratic contempt could ultimately undermine democracy. For example, Paine's justified contempt (against monarchy and aristocracy) seems to also nurture potentially troubling contempt for ordinary individuals who are 'so weak as to . . . worship the ass and lion'.[12] Perhaps it is inevitable that in deriding a type of political regime Paine also becomes contemptuous of its – duped – supporters. Perhaps this division between dupes and democrats cannot be avoided if the goal is to empower the people as a whole. However, Paine's democratic contempt also channels other, troubling affects that cannot be defended. For example, he mobilizes his audience's anti-Catholicism by claiming that 'monarchy in all instance is the Popery of government'.[13] Moreover, he draws on anti-Islamic prejudices when he claims that the mythmaking around monarchy's origins are 'Mahomet like'.[14] It could be said that these troubling comments imperfectly anticipate aspects of Paine's *Age of Reason*, which he wrote seventeen years after *Common Sense*, and in which he dismisses *all* revealed religions as anti-democratic superstitions. However, in *Common Sense* Paine still invokes the authority of Christian scripture in building his case against monarchy, which leaves the impression that his version of democratic contempt rests on a partial, religious perspective.[15] Democratic contempt is therefore not without risks.

Paine can help us understand why democratic contempt's benefits may be worth any attending risks. Eschewing democratic contempt would be difficult, seeing that it is a logical response to subjecting monarchy and aristocracy – he dismisses the latter as 'No-ability'[16] – to rational analysis. Moreover, democratic contempt aids in adopting a rational understanding of non-democratic regimes. In particular, democracy faces steep obstacles; non-democratic regimes, after all, rely on the fact that 'a long habit of not thinking a thing *wrong*, gives it a superficial appearance of being *right*, and raises at first a formidable outcry in defense of custom'.[17] Elsewhere Paine adds: 'There is existing in man, a mass of sense lying in dormant state, and which, unless something excites it to action, will descend with him, in that condition, to the grave.'[18] In other words, reason alone may not suffice to the task of unmooring an undemocratic common sense. Anti-democratic ideologies are too entrenched. Affect, however, does have the potential of undoing the hold of anti-democratic beliefs and feelings. As democratic contempt encompasses both reason and affect, it will be more effective at mobilizing individuals.

Its mobilizing function distinguishes democratic contempt from other forms of reason. This, then, begs the question whether democratic contempt should be treated mostly as a rhetorical strategy rather than, as I have, as a constitutive part of Paine's democratic reason. Certainly, as a text *Common Sense* is designed to rouse its readers. But any rhetorical motivations and maneuvers should not prevent us from treating Paine's democratic contempt as a form of reason, for otherwise we would dismiss much of his oeuvre as 'mere' political pamphleteering. Paine develops theoretical conclusions about politics – in short, a political theory – precisely because he writes to an audience that he seeks to rile up in a democratizing manner. Indeed, I would claim that a democratic political theory more likely emerges from a fusion of affect, rhetoric and reason. For a democratic theory that takes ordinary people seriously as they are would be suspicious of a rigid distinction between reason on the one and affect as well as rhetoric on the other hand; indeed, these kinds of distinctions can undermine progress towards democratic ideals even today, as Iris Marion Young has shown, as preferences for putatively non-rhetorical or dispassionate speech tend to favor elites to the detriment of those pushing for more democratic equality.[19] Democratic contempt, then, must not be dismissed as a rhetorical device; it facilitates thinking about and arguing for democracy in a democratic manner.

To some, Paine's democratic contempt may appear dated – critical for an age of democratic revolutions, but irrelevant for our age, when few countries are governed by monarchs or aristocrats, and when even non-democratic regimes pretend to democratic legitimacy. However, Paine's democratic contempt remains relevant today. Not only does Paine help steel us against popular culture's occasional bouts of nostalgia for kings and queens; more importantly, he challenges us to resist structural forms of inequality that undermine present-day democracies. Paine's democratic contempt militates against economic inequality, especially when poverty and wealth are inherited. Paine, in other words, demands that we do not rest on the laurels of having democratic political processes and institutions; we must also democratize our way of life.

Paine's democratic contempt is timely because it commits us to democratizing our way of life by pursuing economic justice. The 'banditti of ruffians' that made themselves kings not only rob their peoples of political self-determination, but also impoverish them by creating 'a continual system of war and extortion'.[20] Indeed, non-democratic regimes create inherited poverty, and refuse to come to the aid of the poor: 'the resources of a country are lavished upon kings, upon courts, upon hirelings, imposters and prostitutes; and even the poor themselves, with all their wants upon them, are compelled to support the fraud that oppresses them'.[21] Paine cites the House of Lords as an example of unjust political privilege causing economic injustice: the privileged pass tax laws that benefit themselves; consequently, ordinary people experience hardship due to having to pay the lion's share of taxes.[22] Hereditary poverty and despair are, then, direct consequences of hereditary political privileges. Moreover, inherited poverty deepens the already existing political inequality: 'Despotic government supports itself by abject civilization, in which debasement of the human mind and wretchedness in the mass of the people, are the chief criterians [sic].'[23] That is, hereditary economic inequality is not simply an effect of but also a cause of political inequality.

Democratic revolutions should ipso facto diminish the likelihood that governments are structured to create, intensify or entrench poverty. However, Paine does not think that the establishment of representative democracy by itself guarantees economic justice. He therefore calls for a welfare state that actively redresses non-democratic regimes' abiding legacy of poverty.[24] Democratic contempt cannot stop at securing political emancipation; it must simultaneously result in economic emancipation:

> A revolution in the state of civilization, is the necessary companion of revolutions in the system of government. . . . But when a system of government, shall be so organized, that not a man or woman born in the republic, but shall inherit some means of beginning the world, and see before them the certainty of escaping the miseries that under other governments accompany old age, the revolution of France will have an advocate and ally in the heart of all nations.[25]

Democratic contempt issues both in a democratic revolution *and* in the creation of economic *rights* that are designed to overcome poverty.[26]

Paine calls on us to ensure that individuals inherit economic and political structures that enable their agency.

In *Agrarian Justice* Paine provides a second strand from which to argue against inherited economic injustice. This argument expands the concept of democratic contempt beyond its original context, namely, the critique of monarchy and aristocracy. As Paine claims, originally and in essence still all land is collective property. Those who 'own' land – and have been passing it to their descendants – are strictly speaking renters, who moreover do not pay their fair share of what they owe to the community, especially to those who have been deprived of 'their natural inheritance'.[27] Paine could treat those who enjoy private property in land with the same contempt as the thugs-cum-kings – all engage in institutionalized theft, and thereby create and benefit from economic injustice. Yet, Paine holds off on contempt in this instance, to an extent: 'The fault, however, is not in the present possessors. No complaint is intended, or ought to be alleged against them, *unless they adopt the crime by opposing justice.*'[28] Paine reserves democratic contempt only for those property owners who resist efforts to create economic justice by recompensing those who were disinherited. Additionally, he warns them that aside from being unjust they are also unwise, for they may inadvertently unleash a kind of contempt that would destroy even legitimate, private property rights.[29] Democratic contempt is thus more moderate than other forms of contempt that may be generated by abiding economic injustice – for it respects both the rights of those who have and those who lack private property.

Paine's democratic contempt is timely for several reasons. First, economic justice has not been achieved. Far from it, those who benefit from economic injustice are using our democratic institutions and processes to obstruct a collective pursuit of democratic justice. Second, we need to reinvigorate our democratic contempt, so that we react with suspicion to oligarchs presenting themselves as public saviors. These modern-day analogues to the once venerated thugs-cum-kings threaten our precarious democratic institutions and norms from within. Finally, as contempt seems to be coursing through our contemporary political life, Paine reminds us that we should resist the siren song of anti-democratic contempt. Instead, we should embrace democratic contempt to overcome anti-democratic traditions and vestiges, and to more boldly enact the democratic vision of life as equals.

Notes

1 Thomas Paine, 'Common Sense', in *Rights of Man, Common Sense, and Other Political Writings*, ed. Mark Philp (Oxford: Oxford University Press, 1998), 15. The author wishes to thank Char Miller, Doug Dow, Xavier Márquez, Colin Davis and John Morrow for their helpful suggestions.

2 Plato, *Republic*, trans. Robin Waterfield (Oxford: Oxford University Press, 1998), l. 558c.

3   Plato, *Republic*, l. 561d.
4   Sheldon Wolin, 'Norm and Form: The Constitutionalization of Democracy', in *Athenian Political Thought and the Reconstruction of American Democracy*, ed. J. Peter Euben, John R. Wallach, and Josiah Ober (Cornell University Press, 1994), 32.
5   Jacques Rancière, *Hatred of Democracy*, trans. Steve Corcoran (London: Verso, 2006), 4.
6   Paine, 'Common Sense', 15 – emphasis added.
7   Ibid., 15.
8   Thomas Paine, 'Rights of Man: Part the Second. Combining Principle and Practice', in *Rights of Man, Common Sense, and Other Political Writings*, ed. Mark Philp (Oxford: Oxford University Press, 1998), 220–1.
9   For more on Paine's commitment to intra- and intergenerational justice see my 'For the Living: Thomas Paine and Generational Democracy', *Polity* 48, no. 1 (January 2016): 55–81.
10 Paine, 'Common Sense', 15.
11 Ibid.
12 Ibid., 16.
13 Ibid., 15.
14 Ibid., 16.
15 Ibid., 11–14.
16 Thomas Paine, 'Rights of Man: Being an Answer to Mr Burke's Attack on the French Revolution', in *Rights of Man, Common Sense, and Other Political Writings*, ed. Mark Philp (Oxford: Oxford University Press, 1998), 158.
17 Paine, 'Common Sense', 3.
18 Paine, 'Rights of Man: Part the Second', 228–9.
19 Iris Marion Young, *Inclusion and Democracy* (Oxford: Oxford University Press, 2000), chapter 2.
20 Paine, 'Rights of Man: Part the Second', 220–1, 264.
21 Ibid., 271.
22 Ibid., 277, 279.
23 Thomas Paine, 'Agrarian Justice', in *Rights of Man, Common Sense, and Other Political Writings*, ed. Mark Philp (Oxford: Oxford University Press, 1998), 430.
24 Paine, 'Rights of Man: Part the Second', 294–304.
25 Paine, 'Agrarian Justice', 429–30.
26 Ibid., 419.
27 Ibid., 417–19.
28 Ibid., 420.
29 Ibid., 429.

CHAPTER ELEVEN

Alexander Radishchev's *Journey from St. Petersburg to Moscow*: The Defence of Natural Rights and the Right to Self-defence

Andrew Kahn

In a firm voice and ringing pronunciation I finally declaimed the following.
Each person is born into this world the equal of any other. We all have similar limbs, we all have reason and will. Man considered, therefore, outside society is a being dependent on nobody else for his own deeds. But he puts a limit on these, consents not to subordinate himself to the general will alone, becomes obedient to the commands of other human beings, in a word becomes a citizen. For the sake of what cause does he restrain his desires? For what purpose does he set a power over himself? Unlimited in the exercise of his will-power, why does he limit it through the condition of obedience? 'For his own sake', says reason. 'For his own sake', says an inner voice. 'For his own sake', says wise legislation. It follows therefore that whoever wants to deprive him of the advantage of being a citizen is his enemy. He seeks in the law defence and retribution against his

enemy. If the law either does not have the power to defend him or does not wish to do so, or lacks the power to help him immediately in his present woe, then the citizen uses his natural right of defence, preservation, welfare. For the citizen . . . the first duty arising from his organism is defence, preservation, welfare. The Assessor murdered by the peasants violated with his bestial actions their rights as citizens. At that moment when he condoned the violence of his sons, when to the heartache of the betrothed he added rape, when he threatened murder because they dared to resist his hellish domination, at that moment the law intended to protect the citizen was distant and its power was imperceptible. That was when the law of nature awakened and the power of the insulted citizen, inseparable from the law concerning injury, came into force. The peasants who killed the bestial Assessor are innocent before the law. . . . The citizen, no matter the station of life into which he was fated to have been born, is and always will be a person.[1]

Alexander Radishchev, a Westernized Russian civil servant and legal theorist, is best remembered as the author of the *Journey from St. Petersburg to Moscow* (1790), a work of travel literature that takes a narrator through the landscape of late Enlightenment Russia.[2] Radishchev had first-hand experience of Russia's judicial and taxation systems, and offers a biting critique of the state of the empire filtered through stories of exploitation and frustrated reform. Although the book cleared the censor, Catherine the Great reacted furiously, ordering the confiscation and destruction of the entire print-run of more than 600 copies. An initial death sentence was commuted to exile in Siberia. Socialist revolutionaries, including the Bolsheviks, regarded him as a hero and forerunner in radical politics.[3]

Eighteenth-century Russia was an absolutist state. It did not, however, lack the rule of law.[4] Catherine promulgated a new legal code in 1767. While much of this document was cribbed from the works of Montesquieu and Beccaria, the package looked progressive.[5] In the event, only a few parts of the code were implemented. The *Journey* poses an enquiry into whether the basis of a better society lay in alternative forms of government; in administrative reform and a less corrupt civil service and judiciary; or in changes to moral expectations that would benefit the common good and potentially educate the ruling class. Radishchev tended to avoid explicit terminology that would have been instantly objectionable to an absolute ruler. He uses the Russian word for democracy only once in all his writings, but frequently substitutes equivalent expressions in writing about the interest, the condition and rights of the people.

This context underpins the creation of a democratic moment in the seventh chapter ('Zaitsovo') of the *Journey*. The *Journey* mounts more of a pragmatic than theoretical critique of absolutism at a moment late in Catherine's reign when it had been seen to have deteriorated into despotism and rampant cronyism. In the preceding chapter, called 'Novgorod' after the legendary city-state and republic destroyed by Ivan the Terrible in the sixteenth century, the speaker asks, 'What is popular right?' Drawing on Rousseau's myth of the state of nature, he equates popular right and the general will. In the chapter that concerns us, he addresses the meaning of citizens' rights. The vehicle for political statement is a speech made in a law court, ending a tale of injustice. 'Zaitsovo' narrates how the son of a landowner exercised his *droit de seigneur* and violently raped a young peasant girl. Her fiancé and his brothers came to her rescue, a melee ensued, the landowner and his sons were killed and the peasants brought to trial. This passage comes from a speech made by one of the judges who defends the right of the serfs to self-defence and identifies popular violence as a democratic instrument. The passage employs the concepts of egalitarianism, citizenship and the rights of resistance. In explicitly treating the conditions under which the population might overturn a state of economic obedience, the chapter gives an implicit definition of the political arrangements to which 'democracy' may refer as an ideal or possible alternative.

The speech begins with a declaration of egalitarian principle in order to establish the idea that each individual has a right to liberty. This is a remarkably progressive statement in its Russian context. In the absence of economic liberty, Radishchev asks whether liberty can be exercised through collective action to protect individuals or a group when the social contract has been broken: popular action might stop wrongdoing and in the longer term might realign norms of conduct with a concept of the natural order he supposed to be free. Arguments on the basis of natural justice were not routine in Russian thought and writing of the period. The only precedent for state sanction of popular action was a traditional idea of 'collective responsibility', seen as a more passive way to meet certain requirements imposed on the peasantry like tax or conscription levels.[6] Moreover, the principle of the general will mooted here would also have been provocative, since Catherine the Great's objections to Rousseau were well-known.

Democracy as represented in the dramatic story told in the chapter involves the direct participation of the members of a group who use collective action when the masters to whom they have historically ceded autonomy no longer rule adequately. Underlying this view is the idea that the exercise of power of one person over another cannot be justified if it grievously violates the interest of the subjected person. This egalitarian defence of democracy presumes that a society, defined by class structures whose economic interests are paramount, ought at least to guarantee the safety of a subordinate class. Within that framework, reason must be applied in the judgment and punishment of crimes in order to ensure the safety of all. When these conditions are violated, however, he envisages, as happens here, a democratic process in which even serfs become citizens and the people rise up: democracy here is people power in its basic sense. Citizenship is construed from a moral standpoint according to which obedience to an elite or state lapses when their authority has been compromised by violation of those basic rights. Democracy does not extend to the political realm through representation or a franchise, and it only involves an element of self-determination when the self faces considerable danger. It is under these conditions that even serfs, who must always be recognized as human, can become temporary citizens.

This speech constitutes a democratic moment because it creates a speaker who is an ardent defender of the people's interests. In practice, as the *Journey* demonstrates repeatedly, liberty entitles one to live without the threat of bodily harm, but does not imply that any individual is the master of his or her life. This is not a vision of the equal advancement of the interest of individuals' within a pluralistic society. His idea of equality is not relational since Radishchev (who never freed his own serfs) nowhere argues that all are equal in political rights; or that the equal opportunity to pursue social equality should be a norm. But the speech envisages the possibility that there are conditions in which a champion of the people, like an elected representative or perhaps like the Gracchi in ancient Rome, will arise if democratic action can spearhead a permanent change to social conditions. Radishchev's views on government were positioned between the reality of Russian history and his knowledge of influential European accounts. He followed Montesquieu in accepting that many factors influenced the types of government best suited to nations, and in that respect theoretically accepts the view that absolutism and oligarchy were the natural shape of the Russian state.

If Radishchev concedes that historically republicanism has been extinguished in Russia, he does not accept that there will either be no more republicans or that other principles of democratic association cannot come into play. Multiple inspirations may account for the justification of popular rebellion, and they would include Locke, Diderot's essay on 'Natural Right' ('Le droit naturel') in the *Encyclopédie*, Rousseau as the author of the first and second discourses, the abbé Raynal's *History of the Two Indies* (1777), especially for its accounts of slave rebellion and the Spartacus *noir*, and the French *Declaration of the Rights of Man and the Citizen* (1789). Few Russians knew John Locke's writings, but Radishchev seems well aware of his *Two Treatises*. He may be following Locke in suggesting that there are rights not dependent on the exercise of the franchise that may not be violated because one may not consent to their violation. He does not deny that landowners are economically superior. But he does deny any assumption that they might be inherently superior. The defence of the accused brothers rests on the grounds that they could not be expected to relinquish their minimal liberty based on the egalitarian principle that all human persons share a fundamental moral status.

In the fragment 'Discourse on Political Economy' Rousseau asks, 'is not the body of the nation committed to provide as conscientiously for the preservation of the least of its members as for that of all the others? and is the safety of a single citizen any less the common cause than the safety of the entire state?'[7] In Radishchev's depiction, the answer to the rhetorical question is that the preservation of the economic interests of the elite has been the sole function of the peasantry. But the story of rape and violence acknowledges that the economic security of one class has jeopardized the physical safety of a larger class. The point of the speech in 'Zaitsovo' is to draw conclusions from the violence. One is that such episodes lay bare a system of coercion on a national scale out of which new moral requirements become relevant. Clearly the speaker believes that there is a moral equivalence between serfs and masters consistent with Locke's view that everyone has equal natural rights, and that what is morally required must also be enacted in justice. Each person has a right not to be harmed by others, and in this case Radischev argues the landowners forfeited their rights by misconduct that provoked the murder. Landowners must now be obliged to acknowledge the rights of their serfs in the future, and to cultivate relations of community, if not for the sake of equality, then at a minimum for the sake of their own self-protection.

But the stringent compulsion to avoid coercive practices, already sanctioned in the law codes of Catherine's regime but not widely taken up, places on a socio-economic group a restraint and standard of minimum decent behaviour. The case for acquittal looks controversial to the landowners because it adopts an egalitarian premise that was alien to them as members of a socio-economic group whose privileges had been unchecked. In the essay 'On Jurisprudence' (1801–2), Radishchev employs the language of human rights to indicate that there are mandatory duties and protections that must be respected as a good in themselves. The speech in 'Zaitsovo' does not make its claim mainly on behalf of human rights, since his egalitarianism is chiefly instrumental and aimed at the cessation of violence and the signalling of a need to change because a democratic sanction is a latent force of correction against evil.

Despite the later Soviet tradition of reading Radishchev as a proto-Bolshevik, the *Journey* does not provide a blueprint for overhauling Russia's political economy in the age of Catherine the Great. The critique does suggest, however, that any attempts at reform may come from the threat of social unrest. In order to avert rebellion, the government and the nobles will have to reconsider their practices and exercise a common humanity. Readers might suspect that a non-instrumental belief in Lockean natural rights and a strict moral duty to respect them would be his true feeling and that there is a background idea here that all people are equal in their fundamental worth. He shows awareness that few Russians would have understood this as a substantive view, a point illustrated by the reaction of the elite peers who resent the speech and read it as a justification of murder rather than advice to moderate their actions consistent with a minimal definition of rights and liberty. The chapter goes on to make a lesser case for moral conduct on grounds of self-interest. While short of ideal this is still a better outcome because reasonable conduct will promote safety on both sides.

The assumption of the *Journey* is that the class hierarchy of Russia, guaranteed by its authoritarian political system, would not change although it might be amenable to reform. This idea of human rights basically comes down to the 'lower limits on tolerable human conduct'.[8] Even securing the acknowledgement of principles such as egalitarianism and rights underlying democracy in the basic sense of group self-protection would be a major shift. The chapter on Novgorod concludes that republicanism as a form of government was only a blip in Russia's history and not to be revived. That does not exclude the value of republicanism or the promise of more radical forms of direct democracy implied in the justification of collective action and popular rights.

Does this speech reflect a pessimism or optimism on the part of the author that democracy of some kind might last longer than a moment in Russia? Historical theories of liberty, popular sovereignty and a democratic right to justice had no grounding in eighteenth-century Russia. In practice, the principles of social contract and natural law adopted by Catherine in 1767 did not restructure property relations; nor did the reform of the justice system eradicate widespread corruption. As a man of the Enlightenment, and a translator of the historical work of Mably, Radishchev believed that nations went through cycles of progress and decline determined by factors like economic circumstances, international standing and leadership models. Radishchev's own positions on the forms of constitution shifted between enlightened absolutism to radical republicanism, tempered toward the end of his life by a hope for a parliamentary monarch under the young Tsar Alexander I.[9] The Roman Republic was brought down by agrarian conflicts, and the Novgorod Republic could not withstand invasion. The age of the French Revolution held out a live example of what might happen when economic exploitation and political ferment reached a point of no return. It occurred at a moment when some Russian thinkers, like Radishchev and like his speaker, had the conceptual language needed to explain why the inhumanity represented in local acts of tyranny was incompatible with the survival of absolutism.

The self-destruction of absolutism promised positive reform or the usurpation of sovereign power by the people, a scenario he could not fully explore. Radishchev pinned his hopes on a class of educated elite and meritocratic civil servants who knew better. The art of the democratic moment here is to supply a model of conduct that might stabilize the life of the two estates as a medium-term expedient by eliciting compromise – or might justify on the basis of self-defence a transfer of sovereignty to the people. That shift from violence to a new social system might be thought to re-enact the transition Rousseau portrays at the end of Book I of the *Social Contract* in which a fundamental pact 'rather than destroying natural equality, on the contrary substitutes a moral and legitimate equality'.[10] In using this language, in the shadow of the French Revolution and its threat of mob violence he sought to put the Empress on notice of a choice between an incremental transition to a just oligarchy or a brutal shift to people power.[11]

Notes

1. Alexander Radishchev, *Puteshestvie iz Peterburga v Moskvu*, ed. V. A. Zapadov (Leningrad: Nauka, 1992), 42–3. All translations are my own. No complete or adequate translation of Radishchev's *Journey* is available in English yet. A translation by Andrew Kahn and Irina Reyfman of the entire *Journey from St. Petersburg to Moscow* is forthcoming in The Russian Library series, published by Columbia University Press.
2. For accessible introduction, see David Marshall Lang, *The First Russian Radical: Alexander Radishchev, 1749–1802* (London: Allen & Unwin, 1959), much of which has been summarized in Jonathan Israel, *Democratic Enlightenment* (Oxford: Oxford University Press, 2011), 626–30.
3. See, for an example of this ideological thrust, the introductory essay in A. N. Radishchev, *Polnoe sobranie sochinenii*, ed. A. K. Borozdin, I. I. Lapshin, and P. E. Shchegolev (St Petersburg: M.I. Akinfiev, 1907), vol. 1, vii–xxxviii.
4. On the eighteenth-century origin of Russian civil rights, see Isabel de Madariaga, *Politics and Culture in Eighteenth-Century Russia* (London: Longman, 1998), 92–7.
5. Isabel de Madariaga, *Russia in the Age of Catherine the Great* (London: Yale University Press, 1981).
6. Michael Confino, *Domaines et seigneurs en Russie vers la fin du XVIII-e siècle. Étude de structures agraires et de mentalités économiques* (Paris: Institut d'études Slaves, 1963), 96.
7. See Jean-Jacques Rousseau, http://www.rousseauonline.ch/Text/discours-sur-l-economie-politique.php [accessed 14/7/17].
8. Henry Shue, *Basic Rights* (Princeton: Princeton University Press, 1996), 48.
9. See Franco Venturi, *Europe des Lumières. Recherches sur le 18e siècle* (Paris: EHESS, 1971), 283–4.
10. On context, with only passing remarks on Radishchev, see Thomas Barron, *Russia Reads Rousseau, 1762–1825* (Evanston, Illinois: Northwestern University Press, 2002), 255–6. Monika Baár, 'Echoes of the *Social Contract*

in Central and Eastern European Europe, 1770–1825)', in *Engaging with Rousseau: Reaction and Interpretation from the Eighteenth Century to the Present*, ed. Avi Lifschitz (Cambridge: Cambridge University Press, 2016), 95–114 ends with comments on the Russian reception that cannot be endorsed.

11 See Dan Edelstein, *The Terror of Natural Right. Republicanism, the Cult of Nature and the French Revolution* (Chicago: University of Chicago Press, 2009), 127–70 ('Off with their Heads').

CHAPTER TWELVE

Of Postmen and Democracy: Sieyès's Theory of Representation

Lucia Rubinelli

More than two years ago, I undertook to demonstrate that the representative system will bring us to the highest levels of liberty and prosperity possible in our present situation. The 'friends of the people' at the time prevented me from printing this work after having read only its first page. In their crass ignorance, they think that the representative system is incompatible with democracy . . . I wanted to prove that the people will only benefit from delegating to representatives all types of power that comprise the public order and from reserving for itself only the power to entrust with office, each year, known and sensible men . . . But at the time, as much as today, there was a widespread and largely detrimental mistake: that the people should only delegate the powers it cannot directly exercise itself . . . This is tantamount to saying to those who want to write letters to Bordeaux that, for instance, they would better preserve their freedom by protecting their right to bring the letters themselves . . . it is evident and rational to say that to be represented in as many things as possible is

to increase one's liberty, in as much as to accumulate too many representations on the same person is to decrease it.[1]
A constitution requires a constituent power. All public powers are subject to laws, rules and forms that they are not authorized to change. Since they did not create them, they cannot change their constitution; similarly, they cannot change each other's constitution. The constituent power can do everything. It is never submitted to any given constitution. The Nation that thus exercises the largest and most important power, must be, in doing so, free from all constraints and forms, other than those it freely chooses to adopt. But it is not necessary for the members of society to directly and individually exercise the constituent power; they can entrust representatives who will assemble only for this specific object, and are not authorised to exercise any constituted power. Among numerous peoples, this delegation is required by the very nature of things.[2]

In 1789, weeks before the beginning of the Revolution, Sieyès wrote the following words: 'France is not, and cannot be, a Democracy.'[3] It might seem surprising to start a chapter on Sieyès's theory of democracy with such an affirmation. The Abbé Sieyès is universally considered one of the most influential theorists of democracy and yet, in 1789 he explicitly rejected the possibility of establishing a democratic regime in France. Understanding this apparent contradiction will help clarify Sieyès's peculiar contribution to the theory and practice of modern democracy. In order to explore it further, it is however necessary to start by contextualizing his startling affirmation. This exercise will shed light on what Sieyès meant by the term democracy, what he disliked about it and what he proposed as an alternative.

Born in 1748 in the south of France, Sieyès began reflecting on the people's political power long before the Revolution got under way. Nonetheless, he gained notoriety only in 1788–9, due to a series of pamphlets, including the most famous of all, *What is the third estate?* In this work he claimed that political authority, far from belonging to the monarch, lay with the productive portion of society, the 'Third Estate'. The latter comprised all citizens who did not belong to the first two Estates, the nobility and the clergy, and who actively contributed to the economic life of the country. Once elected as representative of the Third Estate in 1789, Sieyès urged the transformation of the Estates General into the National Constituent Assembly. Soon after his re-election to the National Convention, he was forced to flee Paris to avoid execution. Recalled after the Terror, he drafted the constitution of year III (1795) and was appointed to the *Directoire* where he allegedly helped to organize the *coup d'état* of 18 Brumaire, 9 November 1799. He lived the last years of his life in Brussels and died in 1836.

One of the most active figures in the revolutionary decade, Sieyès occupied a very distinctive position in the intellectual and political landscape of the time. Although he was personally close to many figures in the moderate liberal camp – both Girondins and monarchists – he never fully identified with any of the political factions active during the Revolution. Rather, he argued for the autonomous character of his political project. This was grounded on a series of sociological and economic insights into the composition and workings of modern European states. Referring to Adam Smith's economic thought, he argued that the most distinctive feature of the historical time he was living in was the division of labour among individuals in society. In contrast to ancient times, the modern social condition was characterized by high levels of labour specialization. It was an evident fact of modern life that individuals specialized in particular activities and utilized all their resources to become experts in that particular field. When they did so, however, they were left with neither enough time nor enough knowledge to pursue all the other activities that are necessary to the everyday life in society. As a consequence, they devolved the completion of these activities to other people who were, in turn, expert in their specific fields.[4]

This point can be explained with an example similar to one Sieyès had used. Let's assume I am a baker and I want to send a letter to Bordeaux: I will not carry the letter to Bordeaux myself, because I would have to close my bakery for several days. Instead, I will hire a postman, who is an expert in the field of dispatching letters around France, to do the job for me. At the same time, however, the postman will not bake his own bread while in Bordeaux. Most likely, he will buy it from my or someone else's bakery. This, in Sieyès's view, is the core of the division of labour. The system of reciprocal devolution of tasks was not only a social fact observable in the everyday life, but also a precondition for the expansion and development of commerce and the arts. Sieyès called it 'representation'. 'Wherever labour is divided, everything is representation',[5] which entails that representation 'is everywhere in the private sphere as well as in the public order: it is the mother of productive industry and commerce, as well as of liberal and political progress. I can say even more; it is mixed up with the very essence of social life.'[6]

Sieyès's understanding of the role of representation in society had far reaching consequences for his political theory. Accordingly, he maintained that in ancient times democracy was a widespread and well regarded system of government because citizens had both enough time and enough knowledge to take part in the day-to-day running of the *polis*. This was due to the absence of the division of labour which, in turn, depended on the small size of ancient cities and on the presence of slaves, who carried out most of the tasks needed in the everyday life of the citizens. This was not, however, the case in modern societies, where the population was organized according to the principles of the division of labour. As a result, French citizens had no time to focus on the day-to-day business of politics, and they also lacked the competences to understand the complexities of modern political decisions. Sieyès saw politics as just one amongst other activities to be devolved to representatives. As in all other cases of representation in society, political activities had to be delegated to the experts in the field and this meant that democracy had to be excluded from the range of political regimes that could be established in France in the eighteenth century.

However, some clarification is needed at this point. When Sieyès wrote that France could not be a democracy, he meant the form of democracy normally associated with ancient practices of direct self-rule in Greek city states. Anachronistically, these models were hugely popular during the Revolution, when Girondin and Jacobin leaders pledged to establish mechanisms meant to directly involve the people in the decision-making process. These forms of popular participation were, in Sieyès's view, unrealizable and ill-suited for large states like modern France. Not only were they inconsistent with the division of labour, but they would have also fragmented France into a myriad of federated councils unable to work together as a national whole. Several times during the course of the Revolution, he expressed his disapproval of what was *then* considered to be 'democracy', i.e. direct or semi-direct popular rule. Yet, he did not disapprove of the principle of popular political authority per se, which is what we *now* consider to be the founding principle of all democratic regimes. Quite the contrary. When, in 1788, he started writing '*What is the third estate?*', he meant it to be a manifesto for the affirmation of the people's political authority. He claimed that political power should only belong to the productive part of society, the vast majority of the population, so as to exclude all hierarchical distinctions based upon aristocratic or clerical privileges. Acknowledging that political authority was lodged in the people was, in Sieyès's view, the only way of enforcing and protecting the principle of liberty, 'for the fulfilment of which everything is done'.[7]

More specifically, at the root of Sieyès's understanding of the principle of popular power and its institutional implications lay a double definition of liberty. First, Sieyès conceived of liberty as independence. By this he meant the capacity to act according to one's will without subjection to any form of domination. In his words, 'a free man is he who obeys only his own will. In order to be binding, his commitments must have been free, must have been the consequence of his own decisions.'[8] Consequently, Sieyès provided a first definition of liberty as absence of impediments to the achievement of personal goals and as absence of domination by other men. When transferred to the political domain, this definition of liberty meant that citizens are bound to the legal and political system only as long as they have freely agreed to submit to its rules. In relation to this basic principle, Sieyès argued before the National Assembly that since all citizens 'like all of you are bound to obey the law, they must also, like you, participate in its formation. This contribution must be equal.'[9] In arguing so, Sieyès presented popular participation in the law-making process as a fundamental principle of modern politics. This is, *a priori*, consistent with the ancient understanding of democracy as direct popular rule.

However, Sieyès added a caveat: a second definition of liberty. The latter entails the empowerment of men to overcome the obstacles they face in order to obtain what they have independently set as their goals: 'man needs to be free not to be fruitlessly free, but to exercise or employ his power and to progressively increase it'.[10] Considering that 'power' in this context indicates the individual capacity to successfully realize one's personal goals, it follows that liberty is only guaranteed when individuals have the time and resources necessary to pursue their aims. In a society where labour is divided this requirement can only be achieved through representation. As discussed above, representation frees individuals from having to deal with the necessities of life on their own, increasing their ability to pursue their goals and exercise their freedom. In Sieyès's terms 'it is clear that being represented in as many things as possible is a way to increase your liberty'.[11] It follows that it is preferable, for the individual, to 'make others do',[12] to delegate power, including political power, to representatives. In saying so, Sieyès established the second fundamental principle at the basis of his theory of politics: although citizens are the ultimate holders of the political power, they exercise it only indirectly, through temporarily elected representatives. In contrast with the previous principle, this marks a fundamental difference with ancient understandings of democracy as well as with practices of direct popular rule proposed during the Revolution by members of the Girondin and Jacobin clubs. Rejecting the idea that individual liberty could only be realized through people's direct participation in the law-making process, he argued that it was better enforced through practices of representation.

But how is it possible to make sure that representatives act in the interest of people's independence and do not abuse their power? Sieyès put forward a distinctive answer. He theorized the distinction between the people's constituent power and the constituted powers of the representatives. In order to guarantee the first principle of liberty in modern states, he maintained that the people should directly authorize the creation of the political order. More specifically, each individual should contribute to the creation of the constitution. This contribution needed to be completely free and unconstrained, because the nation as a whole recognized no superior authority and its will could not be limited by previous legal provisions. In Sieyès's words: the people's 'Constituent power can do everything. . . . The nation that thus exercises the largest, the most important of its powers, must be, in the exercise of this function, free from all constraints and forms, other than those it freely chooses to adopt.'[13] However, the people cannot directly take part in the process of writing the constitution. This would be practically impossible. Consequently, Sieyès argued that their contribution should be limited to the *authorization* of the constitutional text. This could happen ex-ante or ex-post. If ex-ante, the people would elect representatives to the constituent assembly on the basis of their political views and, in so doing, delegate to them their power to write the constitution. Once the writing process was completed, the text would immediately enter into force because it would be pre-authorized by the popular election of the members of the constituent assembly. By contrast, the authorization ex-post consisted in a popular vote on the text of the constitution, drafted either by elected representatives or by experts. It would thus amount to the authorization of the specific content of the text, as opposed to the previous case, in which the people authorize the writing of the text, but not the details of its content. Both options were, in Sieyès's view, possible, but he had a strong preference for the first. In any case, they were both sufficient to guarantee the respect of the first definition of liberty as independence: whether ex ante or ex post, the people had a say in the process of drafting the state's constitution.

The second principle of liberty was guaranteed by the constituted powers of the political order. Once the nation has authorized the constitution and the political system entered into force, the people are no longer directly involved in day-to-day politics, or in participating in the law-making process. If they were, the second principle of liberty, people's empowerment to achieve the goals they have independently set for themselves, would be violated. People would be forced to use their time and knowledge to run the political system and thus contradict the principle of the division of labour. As a consequence, the people confer the ordinary working of the political system to the 'constituted order'. The latter is a combination of delegated powers run by representatives. These can only act in accordance with the people's will as directly expressed in the constitution and 'can change nothing in the conditions of their delegation'[14] because 'the powers of the public establishment are submitted to the law, to rules and forms that they are not authorized to change'.[15] Moreover, they are submitted to popular scrutiny at regular intervals, through elections. To sum up, the constituted order derives its authority from the constituent power of the nation, but can only exercise it inside a series of pre-established limits.

The fundamental difference between the constituent power and the constituted order is therefore the conceptual instrument that allowed Sieyès to defend and implement his political project. While people's liberty (independence from unauthorized powers) finds its inalienable expression in the nation's constituent power, its actual exercise is delegated to the constituted order, leaving room to the implementation of people's free initiative beyond the impediment of having to deal with everyday politics (liberty as empowerment). Moreover, the hierarchical distinction between the constituent power and the constituted order prevents confusion between the two levels of political authority: the people, holding the original constituent power, exercise it only indirectly while the delegates, holding a derivative-constituted power, exercise it only within limits. The outcome of this theoretical construction is a constitutional representative government that, deriving its legitimacy from people's initial authorization, is ultimately subject to the limits the constituent authority drew for its representatives when framing the constitution. As such, it entails a practice of popular power that is different from both ancient understandings of direct democracy and Jacobin or Girondin reinterpretations of the latter as popular self-rule. Yet it substantially contributed to the systematization of what we now consider to be modern representative democracy.

Notes

1. Emmanuel Sieyès, 'Opinion de Sieyès sur plusieurs articles des titres IV et V du projet de constitution', *Oeuvres de Sieyès*, ed. M. Dorigny (Paris: EDHIS, 1989), 5. The only English translation of Sieyès is E. Sieyès, *Sieyès Political Writings: Including the Debate between Sieyes and Tom Paine*, ed. M. Sonenscher (London: Hackett, 2003). It contains only four texts, and where relevant I quote them. Otherwise all other translations into English are mine.
2. Sieyès, 'Préliminaire de la Constitution', *Oeuvres de Sieyès*, 35–6.
3. Emmanuel Sieyès, 'Sieyès, Instructions donnée par S. A. S. Monseigneur le Duc d'Orléans à ses représentants aux baillages 1989', *Oevures de Sieyès*, 68. Some passages of what follows overlap with my article 'Thinking Beyond Sovereignty: On Sieyès and Constituent Power', *European Journal of Political Theory* in April 2016.
4. Emmanuel Sieyès, 'Observations sur le rapport du Comité de constitution concernant la nouvelle organisation de la France', in *Oeuvres de Sieyès*, 35.
5. Emmanuel Sieyès, *AP* 5-1/2, Dossier 284 in E. Sieyès, *Manuscrits de Sieyès*, ed. C. Fauré (Paris: Honoré Champion, 1999), 59.
6. Emmanuel Sieyès, 'Dire de l'Abbé Sieyès sur la question du veto royal, à la séance du 7 septembre 1789', in *Oeuvres de Sieyès*, 13–14.
7. Sieyès, *Manuscrits de Sieyès*, 467.
8. Ibid., 473.
9. Sieyès, 'Dire de l'Abbè Sieyès sur la question du veto royal, à la séance du 7 semptembre 1789', 13–14.
10. Emmanuel Sieyès, 'Journal d'instruction sociale par les citoyens Condorcet, Sieyès et Duhamel, 8 Juin 1793', in *Oeuvres de Sieyès*, 35.
11. Sieyès, 'Dire de l'Abbè Sieyès sur la question du veto royal, à la séance du 7 septembre 1789', 6.
12. Sieyès, *Manuscrits de Sieyès*, 460.
13. Ibid., 35.
14. Emmanuel Sieyès, *Qu'est-ce que le tiers etat?* (Paris: Flammarion, 1988), 128.
15. Sieyès, 'Préliminaire de la constitution', 35.

CHAPTER THIRTEEN

'Morals and Enlightenment': Bolívar's Virtuous Democracy in the Angostura Address

Guillermo Aveledo

Love of country, love of the law, love of leaders, are the noble passions that must exclusively occupy the soul of a republican. . . . If country, law, and the authorities are not held as sacred, society is a morass, an abyss, hand-to-hand combat between individuals and groups.
To extricate our nascent republic from this chaos, not even the full weight of our moral faculties will suffice unless we can unify our country: its governmental structure, its legislative body, and its national spirit. Unity, unity, unity – that must be our motto. If the blood of our citizens is diverse, let us make it one. If our constitution has divided the powers, let us unify them. If our laws are moribund relics of every ancient and modern despotism, let us tear down this monstrous edifice and, obliterating even its ruins, build a temple of justice in whose sacred precincts we can dictate a Venezuelan code of law. If we need to consult monuments and models of legislation, Great Britain, France, and North America will offer us theirs.

Popular education should be the highest concern of paternal love for our congress. Morals and enlightenment are the poles of a republic. Morals and enlightenment are our first necessities.[1]

How best to establish a popular government with a corrupted and stillborn citizenry? Which institutions would serve better the purpose of creating a state both democratic and stable? Such are pressing questions for any revolutionary statesman, but more so for general Simón Bolívar, as he addressed the inauguration of the Constitutional Congress in Angostura, on a hot and humid day of February, 1819, during the South American wars of independence.

Simón Bolívar (1783–1830) remains a towering figure among the many leaders that witnessed the breakdown of society during that era. To this day, he is a vivid icon within Latin America, to the extent that his extensive written works, long-winded and prolific as befit his peculiar political career, are used by politicians and commentators from all sides of the ideological spectrum. Bolívar sits at the crux of the region's optimism about its future and pessimism regarding its own character, inciting strong emotions from different misreadings.

The myriad of unsuccessful attempts to install a durable and legitimate form of government in Venezuela triggered the most violent civil conflict of the Spanish American wars of independence during the 1810s,[2] and brought Bolívar to the forefront of revolutionary politics, where he displayed both his revolutionary zeal and military outlook in political affairs.[3] Bolívar's political thought crystallized under the strength of this experience: while the installation of a democratic republic was the sole legitimate pursuit in a revolutionary war, liberal institutions were too weak, and the people of Spanish America were unprepared to live under a democratic constitution, prone as they were to fanaticism and servitude.[4] Bolívar also learned specific lessons from his wide but unsystematic reading of the political theory of his day. From Montesquieu's *Spirit of the Laws*, Bolívar took to heart the warnings against creating political institutions out of tune with the specific spirit – culture, morals religion, climate – of a particular nation, as well as the warning that the guiding principles of any republican government, be it aristocratic or democratic, were the prevailing virtues of its leaders and citizens, especially moderation and love of country. And he further agreed with Rousseau's assertion in *The Social Contract* that the only source of legitimacy and stability for a just government was the elimination of particular interests in favour of the General Will.

To create a lasting and virtuous government from warring factions and races after the cataclysmic upheaval of the wars of independence, Bolívar proposed a redefinition of popular government among Colombia's citizens. In 1819, the Angostura provisional Colombian government was not the product of a creole-only elite, but the result of a completely new army, which had among its officer class and active troops members of all the racial castes. It is to this audience that Bolívar presented his dire views on the possibilities and needs of democratic self-rule in his famous Angostura Address. Since political corruption had been the cause of both the failure to institutionalize a democratic republic and of the civil war that ensued, Bolívar proposed an institutional framework that would shape the nation's virtues and take advantage of those citizens who, emerging among the warring factions and races, had proved sufficiently enlightened and virtuous so as to have survived not merely 'some new political tempest, or bloody war, or even an outburst of popular anarchy, but the spectacle of every disruptive force'.[5]

In Bolívar's view, legislators had previously tried to conjure patriotism out of thin air, but the influence of Spanish conquest had bequeathed a population unfit for self-rule, morally weak, easily duped into acquiescing to despotism, and inept at understanding its natural freedoms:

> our lot has always been purely passive and politically insignificant [. . .] we have always occupied a station lower than that of servants [. . .] Enslaved by the triple yoke of ignorance, tyranny, and vice, we Americans have never experienced knowledge, power, or virtue [. . .] We've been ruled more by treachery than force and corrupted more by vice than by superstition.[6]

Bolívar was repeating the common trope of the Spanish black legend: the Iberian nation was described as the most backward, ferocious and fanatical of all the European powers, with faulty institutions and declining influence in the new, civilized world. This insistence served the purpose of belittling his main political antagonist, but Bolívar dispensed with the delusion of copying a 'foreign' polity more akin to a virtuous commonwealth such as that of the United States. An 'absolute democracy', still longed for by many of the Angostura congressmen, was out of the question.

Nevertheless, Bolívar was unyielding on the need to abolish aristocratic rule: 'A republican government has always been, still is, and must ever be that of Venezuela. It must be founded upon the sovereignty of the people, the division of powers, civil liberty, the proscription against slavery, the abolition of monarchy and privileged classes.'[7] To reverse course would be to render the sacrifices endured by thousands of patriotic citizens fruitless, and it was imperative that the conflict's hardships should bring about freedom's fruits, even if they were 'succulent . . . but hard to digest'.[8] Bolívar aspired to popular rule but he feared the people were not immediately ready for 'untrammelled freedom, absolute democracy'. How could a democratic republic be thus established? The answer was twofold: find the model for future citizens among those individuals who had sacrificed the most, and build the new institutions around them, checking relative present freedoms in order to secure their future liberty.

For Bolívar, the revolutions in Colombia had been a trial, before which no single caste would have been prepared to establish a legitimate form of rule. The war itself became the evidence of such impossibility, but it also created a new kind of citizen: the military man. Alas, if the new Republic should only rest upon its armed citizens, how could an oligarchical entrenchment be prevented? The answer lay in Bolívar's redefinition of the people itself, by upending the prescription of a representative government of laws made by the people. Countering Enlightenment tropes, he argued that the patriots and citizens needed in order to uphold popular self-rule did not require property or education, but merely virtue, defined as the capacity of individuals to look beyond particular factional interests. Virtue could – and should – be instilled, but in the meantime, a popular government had to be construed from 'the people' at hand, all the while promoting the necessary measures so as to ensure that both property and education spread among the potential future citizens now freed by the might of the actual citizens. The normative ideal was a democratic republic; the practical reality was that the different divisive forces in play during the civil wars – ideology, race, geographical distance, economic inequality – needed to be harmonized.

For Bolívar, thus, 'the people' was not an extensive concept, deriving from the whole of the free population, and not even from its richest or most enlightened persons, as the creole republic of 1811 had advocated, and the war had cruelly decimated. The war had brought forward a new kind of citizen, from which society's betters had effectively emerged: the soldiers of the republican forces, '[m]en who have sacrificed all the pleasures and wealth they formerly possessed as a result of their virtues and talents; men who have experienced the pits of cruelty in a horrid war [. . .], men who deserve so much from their country demand the attention of the government.'[9] Bolívar could be accused of being disingenuous, as he was addressing an audience of military officers, among whom many caudillos were present, and of whose personal ambition he knew. But beyond offering compensation for their sacrifices, Bolívar was upholding them as 'Liberators of the Republic', as the core element of the nation's active citizenry.[10]

Ultimately, this was an egalitarian argument: only the army upheld the reality of racial equality and the dissolution of the old caste system, just as his proposed absolute abolition of the slave trade would, given that both the troops and officers of the republican armies were not only from the minority white creole former elite, but also from the popular castes of African descendants, native peoples and *mestizos*.[11] Natural and physical inequality were openly acknowledged by Bolívar, yet that inequality should not hinder 'the right of every citizen to contribute to the framing of laws, as member of the sovereign', though only within representative institutions among the virtuous, and not in 'popular gatherings, always tumultuous'. And in any case extreme equality would run counter to the 'order, tranquillity, circumspection, prudence and wisdom' demanded by strong institutions.[12]

Consequently, the basis of the new citizenry was to be moral, rather than racial or economic. The people would participate insofar as their capacities would allow them to do so without endangering the common good. A moderate republic, more attuned to the wisdom of Britain than that of the overtly democratic United States, was in order. Not only would it have a restricted electorate, 'the first dam against popular license', it would also discriminate between the powers of its representative bodies: a Chamber of Representatives, which would provide space for the discussion of current affairs among its factions, and a hereditary Senate, which would protect the lasting interests of the Republic, being 'above the fray of partisan politics'.[13] The lower house would elect the first generation of Senators among its more deserving citizens ('this race of virtuous, prudent, bold men who [. . .] have laid the foundation of the republic at the cost of the most heroic sacrifices'), but its continuity would rest upon the establishment of a school for legislators, where the future representatives 'would learn [. . .] the knowledge needed to adorn the mind of a public servant, [. . .] the career to which they are destined by Providence, and [. . .] would prepare their spirits for the dignity that awaits them'.[14] The natural virtues of the current leadership, which had shown enough evidence of patriotism and reason, would be polished by political education.

Bolívar also defended the institution of a unitary executive, while disparaging federalism as the amorphous chaos of fractious and semi-sovereign little provinces. While the judiciary appears underdeveloped in the address, the role of preserver of legal and moral rectitude is found in the proposal of an 'audacious invention': a 'Moral Power' that, similar to Athens' Areopagus or Roman censors, was to serve as moral check against executive impropriety, and to oversee all matters regarding the education of children, patriotism, honesty and any fault against public morals, imposing severe 'moral chastisements' instead of corporal punishments.[15] In this regard, the concern over public education and the moral shortfalls of the general population prevails in Bolívar over any qualms about the abuse of power. To foster 'love of country' and 'love of the law', Bolívar's political virtues, it would be necessary to have 'love of leaders', and that would only happen if the people could restrain their own base impulses, which would only be possible in due time. In effect, the establishment of a democratic republic was postponed until an active citizenry was in place, when power could again be fully redistributed. But the checks on the representatives' power, as well as the measures to instil virtue and reason among the people, had to be put into effect immediately.

Ultimately, Bolívar's model for an ideal polity to 'regenerate the character and customs imposed on us by tyranny and war'[16] stems from an unremitting pessimism concerning the current virtues of the people, while harbouring an unbridled optimism regarding the formative effects of political institutions in transforming their character, and a deep-seated personal trust about the patriotism and wisdom of the citizens born out of war. Neither the legislators of Angostura, nor most of the new statesmen of the nascent Republic of Colombia, fully shared his inclinations, dismissing the most controlling elements of the *Libertador*'s proposal[17] and eventually opposing his authority and political influence as illiberal, all the while dismantling his more progressive measures regarding slavery and the rights of non-propertied officers. During the last decade of Bolívar's life and political career, his project for a unified Colombian republic unravelled and he was more frequently accused of being a petty tyrant. But this dissension would not change his ambiguous evaluation of democracy, to which his Angostura Address remains the most lasting testament.

It would be unfair to chastise Bolívar regarding his views about the perils of democracy, conceived as the direct rule of the people, a common fear at that time. But Bolívar's expectations of political virtue came from his conviction that the attributes of popular military heroes would help them fulfil their duties as mentors of the new citizenry, a belief derived from his vexing formative years and his own martial ethos. Alienated and impatient about the deliberations of parliaments, and desperate for the end of a dire social catastrophe, sacrifices in the battlefield seemed to verify the mettle of the emerging elite to which he belonged. While this view may have proved itself politically inadequate for the aftermath of the independence wars, since neither order, liberty nor equality prevailed, perhaps his pessimism was not completely unwarranted.

Notes

1 'Discurso pronunciado por el Libertador ante el Congreso de Angostura el 15 de febrero de 1819, día de su instalación', in Simón Bolívar, *Obras Completas* (México: Editorial Cumbre, 1976), vol. VI (book VIII), document 83, 255–6. Translations from the Spanish are my own. A standard English translation can be found in Simón Bolívar, Frederick H. Fornoff, trans., and David Bushnell, ed., *El Libertador: writings of Simón Bolívar* (Oxford: Oxford University Press, 2003).

2 John Lynch, *The Spanish American Revolutions, 1808–1826* (New York: W.W. Norton & Co., 1973), 189–217.

3 Fernando Falcón, *El Cadete de los valles de Aragua: el pensamiento político y militar de la Ilustración y los conceptos de guerra y política en Simón Bolívar, 1797–1814* (Caracas: Universidad Central de Venezuela, 2006), 29–94.

4 For Bolívar the war had 'confirmed that perfectly representative institutions are not appropriate to our character, our customs, and our current level of knowledge and experience ... Unfortunately, the acquisition of these qualities to the necessary level would seem to be very remote from us; on the contrary, we are dominated by the vices contracted under the rule of a nation like Spain, which has shown itself to excel only in pride, ambition, vengeance, and greed.' Simón

Bolívar, Carta de Jamaica (Caracas: Ediciones de la Presidencia de la República, 1972), 166.
5   'Discurso . . .' Bolívar, *Obras Completas*, vol. VI, document 83, 237.
6   Ibid., 239.
7   Ibid., 247.
8   Ibid., 240.
9   Ibid., 259.
10 In a revealing letter to general Santander, regarding continuing legislative opposition to his constitutional ideas, Bolívar quipped:

> These gentlemen think that the will of the people is their will, forgetting that in Colombia the people is in the army, because it really is there, and because it has conquered its rights as a people from the very hands of its former tyrants; because it also is the people who wants, the people who does and the people who can; all the rest are folks that merely loaf around with more or less malignancy, more or less patriotism, but all of them with no more right to be anything but passive citizens . . .

> Letter from Simón Bolívar to Francisco de Paula Santander, San Carlos, 16 June 1821, in Bolívar, *Obras Completas*, vol II, document 493, 75.

11 There is a problem with the word 'slavery' as used in the Angostura address. According to the tropes of Enlightenment political thought, slavery was often used to mean political servitude under absolute or despotic rule. But chattel slavery was rarely confronted head-on by thinkers who might have even profited from the trade (Bolívar himself sought the support of British slave-owners in 1815). 'Slavery' is used in that political and not economic sense in all but one mention in the address, but Bolívar had set free his own slaves in 1814, and decreed the freedom of former slaves who joined the republican forces in 1816, as well as in multiple decrees abolishing the slave trade and ordering the emancipation of slaves issued during his Southern campaign. The Angostura Congress postponed any emancipatory measures, and the matter was only settled in Colombia and Venezuela in the 1850s.
12 Proyecto de Constitución de 1819 (Title I, 1st Section, Article 15), in Pedro Grases (comp.), *El Libertador y la constitución de Angostura de 1819* (Caracas: Banco Hipotecario de Crédito Urbano, 1970), 115.
13 'Discurso . . .' Bolívar, *Obras Completas*, vol. VI, document 83, 250.
14 Ibid., 250–1.
15 Ibid., 256. Bolívar's Project for a Constitution of Bolivia clarified the jurisdiction of the Moral Power, as censoring and vigilant authority over 'the sciences, the arts, education, and the press' ('Discurso del Libertador al Congreso Constituyente de Bolivia', Ibid., 402).
16 Ibid., 257.
17 Caracciolo Parra Pérez, *Bolívar: contribución al estudio de sus ideas políticas* (Caracas: Academia Nacional de la Historia, Fundación Bancaribe para la Ciencia y la Cultura, 2015), 105–6.

CHAPTER FOURTEEN

The Puzzle of Political Leadership in Tocqueville's *Democracy in America*

Ryan K. Balot and Zhichao Tong

The universality of citizens names the legislature of each state, and the federal constitution, transforming each of these legislatures in their turn into an electoral body, draws the members of the Senate from them. Therefore the senators express, however indirectly, the result of universal suffrage; for the legislature that names the senators is not an aristocratic or privileged body that draws its electoral right from itself; it depends essentially on the universality of citizens; it is generally elected by them every year, and they can always direct its choices by filling it with new members. But it suffices that the popular will pass through this chosen assembly for it to be worked over in some way, and it comes out reclothed in more noble and more beautiful forms. The men so elected, therefore, always represent exactly the majority of the nation that governs; but they represent only the elevated thoughts that are current in the midst of it, the generous instincts that animate it, and not the small passions that often agitate it and the vices that dishonor it. It is easy to perceive a moment in the future when the American republics will be forced to multiply [the use of] two stages in their electoral system under penalty of being miserably lost on the shoals of democracy.[1]

This passage reveals the ambivalence of Tocqueville – similar to that of most canonical thinkers, ancient or modern – toward democratic self-government. On the one hand, Tocqueville holds that a democratic society requires the guidance of men who can be trusted to improve upon popular sentiment.[2] On the other hand, however, he is like the American Founders in adamantly insisting that the root of all legitimate political authority in America lies in popular consent. Whatever political power is not ultimately traceable or accountable to the people is illegitimate. In this sense, at least, the mixed regime of classical political philosophy was abandoned at Tocqueville's democratic moment. Because of the transformation observed by Tocqueville, democracy could now only be moderated by, but not mixed or replaced with, aristocratic features. As many contemporary readers have appreciated, Tocqueville's representation of America as a robustly self-governing democracy now comes to sight as a lost (and almost utopian) ideal, rather than as an accurate reflection of current American political norms, institutions and practices.

To bridge the gap between popular legitimacy and the improvement of popular sentiment, Tocqueville insisted on the need for democratic leadership. He maintained that such leadership could be secured through the adoption of indirect representation via multiple electoral stages. Yet the Senate became one of the Union's most corrupt political institutions by the time of the Gilded Age (1870–1900), and the early procedure of indirect election was eliminated by the Seventeenth Amendment. Despite Tocqueville's misguided prediction, however, his chain of reasoning gives rise to an interesting puzzle, one that is still relevant today: why did the multiplication of electoral stages fail to produce the ideal political leadership envisioned by Tocqueville? Exploring that question will uncover both lasting questions about democracy as a political regime and, more specifically, significant challenges faced by democracies in their modern, representative forms.

Why does a democratic society need political leadership? Although Tocqueville does not raise this question explicitly, or imagine a society without political leaders, it is useful to explore the aims that, in Tocqueville's view, democratic leaders ought to pursue. Tocqueville is less inclined than many thinkers to impugn the citizenry's capacity to govern itself, or to assume that people-power will inevitably degenerate into an irrational decision-making process. True, he does not admire the people's untutored intelligence: universal suffrage, he says, rarely constitutes 'a guarantee of the goodness of choices' (I.2.5, pp. 188, 190). Yet Tocqueville also acknowledges that democracy's possible epistemic inferiority is more than compensated for by the educational impact of democratic institutions. Through political participation, ordinary citizens in America fashioned themselves into a people of public spirit and cultivated intelligence (I.2.6).

Tocqueville's deepest concern is the very ethos of the democratic social state: materialism and individualism. Democratic society requires leadership, according to Tocqueville, because an unrestrained democratic culture will, in the long term, undermine democracy itself (I.2.5, p. 192). Hence democratic leaders, at least ideally, must have internalized an ethical outlook that both appreciates and perceptively regulates the psychology of the people.

For Tocqueville, the pursuit of wealth is 'essentially a middle-class passion' that grows and spreads within a democratic people 'who are excited and limited by the obscurity of their origin or the mediocrity of their fortune' (I.2.5, p. 192). Since all individuals in a democratic society are expected to 'pass through the same filter', 'great ambitions breathe uneasily' and most people become satisfied with their 'small and coarse pleasures' (II.3.19, pp. 602–3).[3] The apparently harmless democratic indulgence in material enjoyment could nevertheless lead to dangerous consequences. A man who immerses himself solely in permitted pleasures will not only 'lose the use of his most sublime faculties', but also preoccupy himself with 'public tranquility', which 'naturally disposes citizens constantly to give the central power new rights, or to allow it to take them' (519, 643–4). The pursuit of private, materialistic satisfactions thus tends to undermine the cultivation of political independence and civic-mindedness – those virtues, that is, that make a self-governing regime healthy and keep it sound. His concern that materialistic acquisitiveness erodes political virtue links him to the longstanding republican critique of *luxuria* (luxury) on these grounds, but Tocqueville places this critique in a newly populist register by refusing to gesture toward the traditionally republican 'mixed regime' as a solution.

The democratic tendency toward what Tocqueville calls 'individualism' significantly compounds the problem. After the disappearance of the fixed social order of aristocracy, people are no longer 'bound in a tight manner to something that is placed outside of them' (II.2.2, p. 483). There then arises 'a reflective and peaceable sentiment', which encourages each individual to withdraw completely to the private sphere in order to attend exclusively to his own affairs (482). The general apathy among citizens works to the advantage of political despotism since tyrants prosper when citizens abandon public engagement. As a result, self-absorbed individuals are considered by despots to be attractively docile subjects, as their public indifference is transformed, perhaps counterintuitively, into 'a sort of public virtue' (p. 482).

Good political leaders must therefore make continuous efforts to combat the excessive development of those two democratic instincts. Instead of putting 'citizens to sleep in a happiness too even and peaceful', they are encouraged to 'give them difficult and perilous affairs' so as 'to elevate ambition and to open a theater for it' (II.3.20, p. 604). Moreover, they ought to foster a social environment friendly to religious belief so that 'a taste for the infinite, a sentiment of greatness, and a love of immaterial pleasures' could spread within the society and counter the dangerous tendencies of materialism (II.2.15, p. 519). It is striking that, from our current vantage point, both suggestions sound potentially harmful rather than helpful to civic flourishing, particularly because of their militaristic, and even millenarian, overtones.

Against the public passivity bred by individualism, leaders should promote a participatory political culture that maximizes citizens' concern for public affairs. The purpose of democratic government thus does not stop at giving 'the nation as a whole a representation of itself' (II.2.4, p. 486). What is also needed is to 'give political life to each portion of the territory' in order to 'multiply infinitely the occasions for citizens to act together and to make them feel every day that they depend on one another' (487). The common bond among individuals, something 'naturally' dissolved after the abolishment of the aristocratic social order, could then be 'artificially' recreated through a rich associational life. Solidarity, in Tocqueville's presentation, cooperates with political independence to produce an engaged but never tyrannical or faction-ridden citizenry.

Paradoxically, perhaps, a strong and visionary democratic leader will check the democratic ethos precisely with a view to fostering enlightened democratic instincts, habits and ideas. In Tocqueville's own words, a democratic people needs to be enlightened so as turn the imprudently narrow pursuit of individual well-being into 'the doctrine of self-interest well understood' (II.2.8, p. 500). The ideal candidate would best carry out his responsibilities by remaining detached from, yet not despised or feared by, the democratic majority. Consequently, Tocqueville praises the role of lawyers in America.[4] Not only do they characteristically draw from their work 'the habits of order ... which naturally render them strongly opposed to the revolutionary spirit and unreflective passions of democracy', but with their legal knowledge they also come to form 'a sort of privileged class' whom 'the people do not distrust' (I.2.8, pp. 252, 257). Those who choose the law as their profession thus constitute 'the sole aristocratic body' in a democratic society 'that can moderate the movements of the people' (263). This aristocracy further 'finds the principal sources of its power' in 'the institution of the civil jury' – which Tocqueville describes as 'a school, free of charge and always open', where citizens temper their 'individual selfishness' through being involved in 'something other than their own affairs' (262–3). Through their public-spirited involvement in juries, citizens unexpectedly learn the habits of ordered judgment that serve them well in their own private, commercial and familial activities.

The Senators encountered by Tocqueville during his visit were also supposed to be men of aristocratic character. On the one hand, coming from the background of 'eloquent attorneys, distinguished generals, skillful magistrates, or well-known statesmen', they represented the intellectual elite of America whose words on the Senate floor 'would do honor to the greatest parliamentary debates in Europe' (I.2.5, p. 191). On the other hand, they held office as a 'result of universal suffrage' and hence were not demonized as 'the enemy of popular interests' (192).

Tocqueville could, in fact, find only one key distinction between the enlightened Senate and the mediocre House of Representatives: the former was indirectly elected (192). Citizens chose only the legislature of each state, which in turn named members of the Senate. 'The popular will' was first 'worked over in some way' by a 'chosen assembly' and then came out 'reclothed in more noble and beautiful forms' (192). Senators so elected represented 'the elevated thought' of the majority rather than 'the small passions that often agitate it and the vices that dishonor it' (192). Hence, Tocqueville strongly recommends the layering involved in a double electoral process and considered it central to extending political freedom to all citizens, whether elite or ordinary.

Historically speaking, however, the American Senate did not live up to Tocqueville's idealistic presentation. Instead of providing political leadership, the indirectly elected Senate gradually became a place of legislative corruption and electoral gridlock. Calls for the direct election of the Senate gathered force in the late nineteenth century when its members were increasingly perceived to be controlled by Gilded Age monopolies. The ratification of the Seventeenth Amendment in 1913 finally changed both the process of electing Senators and the way vacancies would be filled, turning the Senate into another political institution based directly on the popular vote.

Why was the electoral process transformed in this unanticipated way? It is Tocqueville's great merit that he provides the resources with which we might plausibly rethink, and even disagree with, his own conclusions. One relevant analysis can be found in Chapter 20, Part Two, Volume II of *Democracy*, where Tocqueville discusses 'the path by which industry ... could well lead men back to aristocracy' (530). Despite its privileged position, Tocqueville argued, the new industrial class cannot bear the task of political leadership, since its economic pursuits tend to debase workers, or ordinary citizens, and to become an all-consuming end for the 'masters'. Tocqueville's analysis illustrates the distinctiveness of the modern elite and helps to explain why a modern political meritocracy, such as the one envisioned by many theorists in China and elsewhere, would likely turn out to be antithetical to sound democratic leadership. 'The particular enlightenment' of the governmental power may well unite itself all too effectively with 'the ignorance and democratic weakness of the subjects', resulting in an ethically repulsive political community in which democratic freedom is undermined and despotism reigns (II.4.4, pp. 648–9).

Tocqueville identifies several differences between a traditional aristocracy and a manufacturing aristocracy. Although both depend on inequality between rich and poor, they are governed by two entirely different mentalities. 'The territorial aristocracy of past centuries', while considering itself to be naturally superior, did not care solely about itself (II.2.20, p. 532). Instead, it 'was obliged by law or . . . mores to come to the aid of its servants and to relieve their miseries' (II.2.20, p. 532). Masters and servants were always bound together through 'the same families' that had been 'settled for several generations' (II.3.5, p. 548). By contrast, the 'manufacturing aristocracy of our days' sees 'no genuine association' between itself and the workers it hires (II.2.20, p. 532). 'After having impoverished and brutalized the men whom it uses', it only 'leaves them to be nourished by public charity in times of crisis' (II.2.20, p. 532). The hierarchical relationship between employers and employees turns out to be purely instrumental, since it depends solely on the 'faithful and rigorous execution of contract' (II.3.5, p. 551). The instrumentalizing of human relationships – prototypically exemplified by the exploitative practices of a manufacturing elite – foreshadows, for Tocqueville, one of democracy's worst potentialities.

At the heart of the new manufacturing aristocracy is nevertheless a self-defeating paradox: although industrialists aspire to unequal conditions, their fortunes are entirely dependent on the democratic social state. Only when conditions become somewhat 'equalized in the body of the nation' can there arise a general 'need for manufactured objects' (II.2.20, p. 531). Those who specialize in 'the cheapness that puts these objects within the reach of mediocre fortunes' can succeed precisely because a democratic people will always have 'new desires' which can be satisfied through 'opening great workshops and . . . dividing work strictly' (II.2.20, p. 531). Mass commerce both wears down ordinary workers and dulls the citizens' sensitivity to beauty and fine craftsmanship, producing a neglect even of prized objects (not to mention other individuals) that are worthy of admiration for their own sake (II.1.11).

Writing in the 1830s, before America's rapid industrialization, Tocqueville himself did not worry much about the danger posed by this new aristocracy. He regarded it as merely 'an exception . . . in the entirety of the social state' that applied 'only to industry and to some of the industrial professions' (II.2.20, p. 531). Therefore, in spite of all its brutalities, the manufacturing aristocracy was still considered to be 'one of the most restrained and least dangerous' (532).

Tocqueville's stance was more reasonable in his own day than in ours, because America was, at that time, only just making a transition from a predominantly agricultural society to a more industrialized one in which disparities of wealth and the instrumentalities of relationships would become ever more prominent. The two-stage electoral system, while making the Senate less attached to unreflective popular passions, also turned it into an institution that could be more readily captured by business interests. Political reforms that empowered ordinary citizens were proposed by American Progressives between 1890 and 1917 because they feared that the manufacturing aristocracy had come to control both the means of production and the democratic political system. Woodrow Wilson offered an articulate expression of the Progressives' concerns in his New Freedom speech delivered during the 1912 presidential campaign:

> There is a power somewhere so organized, so subtle, so watchful, so interlocked, so complete, so pervasive, that they had better not speak above their breath when they speak in condemnation of it. . . . They know that somewhere, by somebody, the development of industry is being controlled. . . . The masters of the government of the United States are the combined capitalists and manufacturers of the United States. . . . The government of the United States at present is a foster-child of the special interests.[5]

In recent years, given the success of lobbying groups and wealthy donors, the top one percent once again plays a disproportionate role in American politics, thereby justifying Rogers Smith's view that 'in twenty-first-century America . . . Tocqueville's secondary worry concerning an industrial and commercial aristocracy or oligarchy seems more apt'.[6]

As Tocqueville foresaw, the manufacturing (and now technological and financial) aristocracy has helped to erode the basis of civic solidarity and failed to offer any solid basis for political leadership along Tocquevillian lines. Instead of guiding people to prize the intrinsic goodness of civic friendships and associational activities, the predominant industrial and financial system encourages a narrow love of well-being; indeed, its own existence depends on a consumerist culture that persistently creates new demand for 'goods' that take us ever farther from Tocqueville's ideals. Based on Tocqueville's writings, it is hard to avoid the inference that a society founded on unchecked materialism and individualism – the quintessentially democratic threat to democracy itself – will also be the one where a manufacturing aristocracy is most likely to prosper.

Understandably, Tocqueville worried most poignantly about the soft despotism that arises in states where citizens lack independence and feel satisfied by an anesthetizing range of simple pleasures. Acting primarily as consumers in a market society, citizens may well become 'an innumerable crowd of like and equal men who resolve themselves without repose, procuring the small and vulgar pleasures with which they fill their souls' (II.4.6, p. 663). A technocratic political leader, watching from above and representing the industrial class, will then enjoy an open field in which to dominate the citizenry by ministering to it: instead of encouraging 'reflective patriotism' and active engagement, the soft tyrant 'provides for their security, foresees and secures their needs' (225, 663). The drift toward self-dwarfing is one that all democratic citizens should, in Tocqueville's presentation, be especially wary of.

If Tocqueville provides no clear solution to the conundrum of democratic political leadership, he at least vividly analyses the potential dangers associated with calls for a 'meritocratic' political system of technocratic management and limited participation.[7] Nor can we reduce the question of good political order to the proper balance between the technical expertise of the few and the voice of the many.[8] Instead, democratic statesmen will always face the formidable challenges of both cultivating the civic-mindedness of ordinary people and fostering the emergence of political leaders with sound ethical characters, independence of materialistic interests, and concern for the 'sublime pleasures' of political freedom (II.2.1, p. 481).

Notes

1 *Democracy in America* I.2.5. All references to Tocqueville are to this edition: Alexis de Tocqueville, *Democracy in America,* trans. Harvey C. Mansfield and Delba Winthrop (Chicago: University of Chicago Press, 2000).

2 For Tocqueville, the democratic 'social state' refers chiefly to the non-existence of aristocratic hierarchy rather than to any particular configuration of democratic politics. Hence, the 'democratic society' here could be exemplified by the societies found in most modern national states, including those under the rule of non-democratic governments.

3 This applies to the offspring of the few opulent citizens as well since they are now also expected to prove that they deserve their wealth through their business skills rather than mere family inheritance.

4 An interesting question, of course, is whether today's legal professionals occupy, or can occupy, the role that Tocqueville ascribes to them, ideally, in the present passage.

5 Woodrow Wilson, *The New Freedom* (London: Dent, 1916), 57–8.

6 Rogers Smith, 'Oligarchies in America: Reflections on Tocqueville's Fears', *Journal of Classical Sociology* 10, no. 3 (2010): 189–200, 196.

7 See Daniel Bell, *The China Model: Political Meritocracy and the Limits of Democracy* (Princeton: Princeton University Press, 2015).

8 See Josiah Ober, 'Democracy's Wisdom: An Aristotelian Middle Way for Collective Judgment', *American Political Science Review* 107, no. 1 (2013): 104–22.

CHAPTER FIFTEEN

'Family Selfishness' and the Corruption of Public Virtue: Harriet Taylor Mill's *Enfranchisement of Women*

Katherine Smits

With respect to the influence personally exercised by women over men, it, no doubt, renders them less harsh and brutal; in ruder times, it was often the only softening influence to which they were accessible. But the assertion, that the wife's influence renders the man less selfish, contains, as things now are, fully as much error as truth. Selfishness towards the wife herself, and towards those in whom she is interested, the children, though favoured by their dependence, the wife's influence, no doubt, tends to counteract. But the general effect on him of her character, so long as her interests are concentrated in the family, tends but to substitute for individual selfishness a family selfishness, wearing an amiable guise, and putting on the mask of duty. How rarely is the wife's influence on the side of public virtue: how rarely does it do otherwise than discourage any effort of principle by which the private interests or worldly vanities of the family can be expected to suffer. Public spirit, sense of duty

> *towards the public good, is of all virtues, as women are now educated and situated, the most rarely to be found among them; they have seldom even, what in men is often a partial substitute for public spirit, a sense of personal honour connected with any public duty. Many a man, whom no money or personal flattery would have bought, has bartered his political opinions against a title or invitations for his wife; and a still greater number are made mere hunters after the puerile vanities of society, because their wives value them.*[1]

In 1850, before any national organization and activism by supporters of women's suffrage in Britain, the first National Woman's Rights Convention met in Worcester, Massachusetts, to discuss women's rights – encompassing equal pay, better education and access to careers, but focussing centrally on the right to vote. Women's activism in the United States had been propelled by the Abolition and Temperance movements, both of which had provided opportunities for women to speak in public and organize, and which, in the case of Abolition, rested on arguments for equal civil and political rights that could obviously be extended to women. The Abolitionist leader William Lloyd Garrison had been the first to sign a petition for women's suffrage sent to the Massachusetts legislature the previous year. Over 1,000 people attended the Worcester Convention, the ideas and goals of which were publicized in a series of tracts which were read widely in the United States and in Britain. They had a powerful effect in driving activism for women's suffrage in both countries. The first political association supporting votes for women in Britain was formed in Sheffield in 1851 and presented a petition to the House of Lords.

Equality for women had enjoyed some support in Radical circles in Britain in the late eighteenth century. Jeremy Bentham advocated women's suffrage first in 1789, and continued to develop his arguments in his more general essays on parliamentary reform – although in later essays, including his unfinished Constitutional Code, he asserted that the cause was so unpopular that it could not then be pursued.[2] In her *Vindication of the Rights of Woman* published in 1792, Mary Wollstonecraft attacked the ways in which women were socialized and educated under patriarchy, and asserted their rationality and moral equality with men. Wollstonecraft did not demand the right to vote, although she makes a brief reference to the right of women, as well as men, to be represented in government.[3] In 1825, socialists William Thompson and Anna Wheeler published their *Appeal to One Half of the Human Race,* demanding political and civil rights for women,[4] but the idea of women's suffrage was dismissed even by Radical supporters of extending the suffrage for men, on the grounds that women were dependent on men who represented their interests, and that they were likely to use their votes as directed by men. As the Chartist movement gathered strength and support amongst progressives in the early nineteenth century, the issue of women's representation was largely set aside in favour of the more widely supported case for extending manhood suffrage.

Interest in women's education and moral equality continued, however, in Unitarian intellectual circles in which Mary Wollstonecraft had moved. In 1850, this community included Harriet Taylor, then forty-three years old and a passionate advocate of progressive political causes, including women's rights and socialism. Taylor was at this point an intellectual collaborator with her long-term companion and future husband John Stuart Mill, also well-known for his commitment to the social and political equality of women.[5] In 1851, Harriet Taylor Mill published, anonymously, her polemical essay 'Enfranchisement of Women'. 'Enfranchisement' takes the Worcester Convention's proceedings and platform as its frame, and goes on to make an impassioned argument for women's political and civil rights, education and access to the professions and to public life, equality in marriage and the right to vote. The impact of this essay on emerging feminist thinking has been largely eclipsed by John Stuart Mill's better-known *The Subjection of Women,* published in 1869, after Taylor Mill's death. The essays make some similar arguments,[6] and indeed for some time 'Enfranchisement' was assumed to be an early version by Mill himself of his *Subjection.*[7] Critics have more recently concluded that it is most likely that they worked on 'Enfranchisement' together.[8]

As I show here, Taylor Mill's 'Enfranchisement' makes its case for women's civil, political and economic equality with men, drawing not, as Mill did in *The Subjection*, on utilitarian reasons of human happiness, but rather upon natural rights and justice, and on republican conceptions of freedom, independence and the value of political participation. Taylor Mill argues that women have an inherent right to political participation and representation, which it is unjust and oppressive to deny (397). But she also ties women's exclusion from the suffrage to their economic and social dependence, and argues that their lack of political power produces in women the 'vices of artifice', and in men the 'vices of power' (410). The denial of political rights to women prevents them from developing and enlarging their interests and perspectives, encouraging them instead to press selfish family concerns upon men, thus corrupting the public good. The extract at the beginning of this chapter describes Taylor Mill's dark vision of the society that is produced by denying women their right to the vote: beset by corruption and hostile to public virtue. Women ought to be entitled to full political rights, Taylor Mill argues, primarily because it is just – both as a matter of principle in treating people equally, and because their exclusion renders a just polity practically unsustainable.

Like contemporaneous political claims against slavery and for civil and political equality for black Americans, to which it refers, 'Enfranchisement' relates the right to political representation to broader civil and economic rights. But Taylor Mill's arguments for votes for women go further, challenging the distinction between the public and private spheres central to liberalism, by critically analysing the operation of patriarchal power in both. (Here she presages Second Wave feminism's central argument that 'the personal is political'.) Taylor Mill assumes that the subordination of women in the home, as well as in public life, is essentially political – in both its enforcement of tyrannical relations of domination and subordination in the home, and in its corrupting effects upon public life. The power of men over the women in their families is analogous to the power of kings over subjects – it has 'reached the stage which the power of kings had arrived at, when opinion did not yet question the rightfulness of arbitrary power' (407) and thus is susceptible to the same critique of aristocratic power that characterized eighteenth and nineteenth century democratic thinking. Wollstonecraft had argued similarly in the *Vindication of the Rights of Woman* that 'unconditional obedience, is the catchword of tyrants of every description . . . and one kind of despotism supports another'.[9]

Like Wollstonecraft, Taylor Mill sees the effects of women's subject status as vicious. Because they are denied political participation, they are incapable of perceiving the public good. What is crucial here is the effect that exercising the right to vote has upon the understanding and perspective of voters. Like Mill, Taylor acknowledged the concern that women, like working class men, were insufficiently educated to exercise political judgement. But both believed that granting suffrage to uneducated men and to women would encourage them to consider issues in a broader light and to take into account the public good, rather than merely their own selfish interests. As she asks rhetorically in an earlier essay written with Mill: 'Are votes given as a means of fostering the intelligence of voters, and enlarging their feelings by directing them to a wider class of interests? This would be as beneficial to women as to men.'[10] The stunted perspectives and opinions of women have broader effects: the moral nature of men also suffers as a result of women's subordination and their consequent inferiority as intimate companions, producing 'a progressive deterioration among men in what had hitherto been considered the masculine excellences'. Men are, Taylor Mill writes, 'falling into the feebleness which they have so long cultivated in their companions' (408). In sum: 'the position is equally corrupting to both; in the one it produces the vices of power, in the other, those of artifice' (410). We might note here that domination infects all social relations: paradoxically, although women are dominated by men, in the familial sphere they attempt a counter-dominance by way of influence, thus spreading to men their own corruption.

But the damaging effects of patriarchy are felt beyond individuals: its corruptive force operates not only upon women themselves and the men associated with them, but also upon public life. Taylor Mill asserts that confinement of women to the domestic sphere and to familial concerns leads them to dedicate themselves to the advancement of their families and familial interests, and to attempt to press men to advance 'selfish' family interests in the public sphere. Thus the public sphere becomes the arena of competing private interests, and is undermined by lack of commitment to the public good. This suspicion of the role of family interests in derogating from the public good originates in the classical world; we might think here of Plato's rejection of family ties for the Guardian class in *The Republic*, and Pericles's injunction to the parents of Athens to place the honour of the city above their selfish love for their sons, in the Funeral Oration recorded by Thucydides. But for Enlightenment civic republicans such as Rousseau and Wollstonecraft, the 'selfishness' of women, whether innate, as Rousseau argued, or inculcated, as Wollstonecraft held, and their influence over men, constitutes a particular threat to public virtue, above that of familial ties. Women promote the interests of families over the common good, but also prefer, in their supposed materialism, superficiality and concern with appearances, what Taylor Mill refers to as 'the puerile vanities of society' over the public good.

Like Wollstonecraft, Taylor Mill argues that this selfishness is the product of the socialization and subordination of women. What will prevent it is the establishment of democratic participation on the basis of equality – both in public government and in private and familial life. In this, Taylor Mill, like Mill in 'The Subjection', imagines the family as a 'miniature polis'.[11] Equality in the family will help to develop 'masculine' citizen virtues in both men and women, based around commitment to the common good. Here she echoes Wollstonecraft's view about the relationship between equality of the sexes and citizenly virtues; Taylor Mill points out in addition that women are subject already to the duties of citizenship, such as paying taxes and facing the judicial system, and thus should also be entitled to 'the rights of citizenship' (398).

Taylor Mill's arguments about the evil effects of systematic subordination reflect a republican view of liberty as independence – as freedom from subjection to the arbitrary power of others. This understanding of liberty, sometimes contrasted with the 'negative liberty' that denotes freedom from external restraints, involves the assertion of the self against attempted domination. It is demonstrated as well as reinforced by independent action in the civic sphere. 'Enfranchisement' addresses the theme of independence in several ways: early in the essay, Taylor Mill comments that the movement in the United States is notable because it is 'not merely for women, but by them' (395) – the president of the Convention and numerous speakers were women. For Taylor Mill, this is the assertion of a civic and social independence – but also crucial in her view was economic independence. In this, Taylor Mill goes beyond Mill in *The Subjection*. In that essay, Mill argues for the right of women to work and participate in public life, but asserts that for most married women, managing the home and family would constitute their occupation. There would, he allowed, no doubt with his late wife in mind, be exceptions. By contrast, 'Enfranchisement' endorses the

Convention's demand for 'partnership in the labours and gains, risks and remunerations of productive industry'. Taylor Mill argues:

> Even if every woman, as matters now stand, had a claim on some man for support, how infinitely preferable it is that part of the income should be of the woman's earning, even if the aggregate sum were but little increased by it, rather than that she should be compelled to stand aside in order that men may be the sole earners, and the sole dispensers of what is earned. (403)

It is women's rights to participate in labour and production, and to earn their own incomes, which distinguishes them from children who are 'necessarily dependent, and under the power of others' (404). Taylor Mill saw economic independence as part of an 'active life' (401) which also included the exercise of political rights. The right to vote was the fundamental requirement for freedom from domination, for both men and women.

Taylor Mill's twin arguments for women's equality, inherent rights and republican independence, reflect the complexities of liberal discourse in this period. In the late eighteenth century, both Lockean natural rights and neoclassical civic republicanism had shaped the discourse of the American revolutionaries; later, de Tocqueville emphasized the role of active participation in civil society, in sustaining the republican political structures of the new American republic. Mill was an enthusiastic advocate of de Tocqueville's work, and develops his argument that civic and democratic participation foster a commitment to the public good, by enlarging the perspective of citizens from their narrow private interests. Mill combines elements of republican and liberal discourse in *The Subjection* and also *On Liberty,* and the relative influence upon his thinking of republicanism has been the subject of some scholarly debate.[12] It seems likely that Mill influenced Taylor Mill here, although she would also have been familiar with Mary Wollstonecraft's deployment of civic republican arguments for women's equality in the second *Vindication*.

It would be mistaken to assume that Taylor Mill's civic republican arguments concerning the public good dominate 'Enfranchisement'; rather the essay reflects intertwined republican and liberal ideas. Taylor Mill claims civil and economic rights for women as individuals: 'Each individual will prove his or her capacities, in the only way in which capacities can be proved – by trial' (400). Her purpose is polemical rather than philosophical, and her analysis of the corruption caused by the subordination of women, and the lack of commitment to the public good is followed by a more recognizably Radical political critique of the power of the Catholic Church over its female adherents, and then the association of women's influence with illiberal and Conservative political opinions. She concludes her essay returning to the Women's Rights Convention, in a polemical endorsement of the rationalism of women's claims, and a rejection of sentimentality. She praises the speeches at the Convention generally, but with exceptions: 'things to which it is impossible to attach any rational meaning, have found their way into the resolutions' (415). Here she refers to the demand for 'social and spiritual union', which she describes as 'verbiage, serving only to mar the simplicity and rationality of the other demands' (415). 'What is wanted for women', Taylor Mill writes, 'is equal rights, equal admission to all social privileges; not a position apart, a sort of sentimental priesthood' (415). In this she attacks the view common among opponents of women's suffrage that the world of politics was too dirty and harsh for women, who should instead remain apart and above it, as moral exemplars for men (404–5).

Although Taylor Mill ends her essay with the prediction that 'the example of America will be followed on this side of the Atlantic' (415) and a hopeful reference to the Sheffield petition, it would be some time after 'Enfranchisement of Women', indeed after 'The Subjection', that the movement for the vote for women in Britain would make a real political impact. 'Enfranchisement' was separately published after it first appeared in *The Westminster Review,* and bought by thousands, but the Women's Social and Political Union, which led the suffrage campaign, was not formed by Emmeline Pankhurst and her supporters until 1903, and suffrage was not granted to women (over 30) until 1918. However 'Enfranchisement' was also read with enthusiasm by American women mobilizing for the vote in the late nineteenth century, including Susan B. Anthony, and became one of the best-selling tracts in the American women's rights movement.[13] Its influence here ranks with Wollstonecraft's second *Vindication,* also often cited by American women's suffrage activists. The political influence of Taylor Mill's essay – the purpose for which it was undoubtedly intended – is clear; ironically, given its passionate defence of women's independent action, its status as an early feminist argument amongst critics and scholars has been obscured and diminished by the assumption that it was merely a forerunner to Mill's *Subjection.*

Notes

1 Harriet Taylor Mill, 'Enfranchisement of Women', in John Stuart Mill, *The Collected Works of John Stuart Mill, Volume XXI, Essays on Equality, Law and Education,* ed. John M. Robson, Intr. Stefan Collini (Toronto: University of Toronto Press, 1984), 411–12. (http://oll.libertyfund.org/titles/mill-the-collected-works-of-john-stuart-mill-volume-xxi-essays-on-equality-law-and-education). Page numbers to this edition will be given in parentheses throughout the text of this chapter. Originally published in *The Westminster and Foreign Quarterly Review* LV (July, 1851): 289–311.

2 Lea Campos Boralevi, *Bentham and the Oppressed* (New York: W. de Gruyter, 1984), 16–17.

3   Mary Wollstonecraft, 'A Vindication of the Rights of Woman', in *The Vindications*, eds. D. L. Macdonald and Kathleen Scherf (Peterborough, ON: Broadview, 1997), 285.
4   See Jim Jose, 'Giving Voice to Feminist Political Theory: The Radical Discourse of Anna Doyle Wheeler and William Thompson', in *Feminist Moments: Reading Feminist Texts*, ed. Susan Bruce and Katherine Smits (London: Bloomsbury Academic, 2016), 59–66.
5   For an excellent summary study of Mill's and Taylor's intellectual relationship and the different strands of progressive and democratic thinking they brought together, see Alice S. Rossi, 'Sentiment and Intellect: The Story of John Stuart Mill and Harriet Taylor Mill', in *Essays on Sex Equality*, ed. Alice S. Rossi (Chicago: University of Chicago Press, 1970), 1–63.
6   For Mill's concerns about women's lack of commitment to the public good, see John Stuart Mill, 'The Subjection of Women', in *The Collected Works of John Stuart Mill*, vol. XXI, 329.
7   For a spirited critique of the reception of Harriet Taylor Mill's ideas by critics, see Jo Ellen Jacobs, '"The Lot of Gifted Ladies is Hard": A Study of Harriet Taylor Mill Criticism', *Hypatia* 9, no. 3 (1994): 132–62.
8   Susan Moller Okin, 'John Stuart Mill's Feminism', in *Mill's 'The Subjection of Women'* ed. Maria H. Morales (Lanham: Rowman and Littlefield, 2005), 30.
9   Wollstonecraft, 'Vindication of the Rights of Woman', 289.
10 Harriet Taylor and John Stuart Mill, 'Papers on Women's Rights (1847–50)', in *Collected Works of John Stuart Mill*, vol. XXI, 386.
11 Nadia Urbinati, *Mill on Democracy: From the Athenian Polis to Representative Government* (Chicago: University of Chicago Press, 2002), 182.
12 Discussed in Urbinati, *Mill on Democracy,* 147–9. See also D. E. Miller, 'John Stuart Mill's Civic Liberalism', *History of Political Thought* 21, no. 1 (2000): 88–113.
13 Evelyn L. Pugh, 'John Stuart Mill, Harriet Taylor and Women's Rights in America, 1850–1873', *Canadian Journal of History* 13 (1978): 425. Cited in Jo Ellen Jacobs, *The Voice of Harriet Taylor Mill* (Bloomington: Indiana University Press, 2002), 219.

CHAPTER SIXTEEN

Lenin: Soviet Democracy in 1917

Paul Blackledge

Apparently the chief question of the revolution both in Germany and Austria now is: Constituent Assembly or Soviet government? . . . The [social democrats] speak about 'pure democracy' and 'democracy' in general for the purpose of deceiving the people and concealing from them the bourgeois character of present-day democracy. Let the bourgeoisie continue to keep the entire apparatus of state power in their hands, let a handful of exploiters continue to use the former, bourgeois, state machine! Elections held in such circumstances are lauded by the bourgeoisie, for very good reasons, as being 'free', 'equal', 'democratic' and 'universal'. These words are designed to conceal the truth, to conceal the fact that the means of production and political power remain in the hands of the exploiters, and that therefore real freedom and real equality for the exploited, that is, for the vast majority of the population, are out of the question. . . . It is sheer mockery of the working and exploited people to speak of pure democracy, . . . This is tantamount to trampling on the basic truths of Marxism which has taught the workers: you must take advantage of bourgeois democracy which, compared with feudalism, represents a great historical advance, but not for one minute must you forget the bourgeois character of this

> 'democracy', its historically conditional and limited character.
> . . . The bourgeoisie are compelled to be hypocritical and to describe as 'popular government', democracy in general, or pure democracy, the (bourgeois) democratic republic which is, in practice, the dictatorship of the bourgeoisie, the dictatorship of the exploiters over the working people. . . . But Marxists, Communists, expose this hypocrisy, and tell the workers and the working people in general this frank and straightforward truth: the democratic republic, the Constituent Assembly, general elections, etc., are, in practice, the dictatorship of the bourgeoisie, and for the emancipation of labour from the yoke of capital there is no other way but to replace this dictatorship with the dictatorship of the proletariat. . . . and establish democracy for the poor.[1]

So dominant is the modern tendency to reduce the meaning of democracy to its liberal form that the phrase 'Marxist democracy' is all too often dismissed as an 'oxymoron'.[2] This dismissive posture betrays a fundamental misreading of Marx's and Lenin's politics that functions to obscure the power of their critique of liberal democracy. Pivoting on the claim that Marx's critique of capitalism culminated in Stalin's dictatorship, Cold War liberals posited their worldview as the free alternative to 'totalitarian' Marxism. Ironically enough, beneath the bluster of ideological opposition, Communists agreed that Marxism and Leninism led to Stalinism, differing from liberals by their embrace rather than rejection of this movement.

However, by agreeing that Stalin was Marx's legitimate heir, the Communists necessarily broke with the content of Marx's critique of capitalism.[3] More specifically, the claim that Leninism led to Stalinism involves a very significant elision over Leon Trotsky's critique of Stalinism. In 1937 Trotsky wrote that just as a socialist revolution was essential for the triumph of freedom in the West, socialism in Russia could only be realized through a new 'revolution' against the Stalinist 'bureaucracy'. Trotsky believed that the aim of this new Russian Revolution should be not merely to substitute 'one ruling clique for another', but to change 'the very methods of administering the economy and guiding the culture of the country. Bureaucratic autocracy must give place to Soviet democracy. A restoration of the right of criticism, and a genuine freedom of elections, are necessary conditions for the further development of the country.' This powerful critique of Stalinism is important not merely because it was made by the organizer of the October Revolution and Lenin's closest collaborator in 1917, but also because it was rooted in a deep understanding of Marx's and Lenin's democratic model of socialism.[4] The true oxymoron from this perspective is the concept of 'liberal democracy', against which 'Marxist democracy' is conceived as the really revolutionary alternative that, *mutatis mutandis*, harks back to classical Athens as its precursor.[5]

According to Lenin, workers' councils or soviets emerged in Russia in 1905 and again in 1917 as 'universal mass organisations of precisely those classes that are oppressed under capitalism'.[6] Soviets, by contrast with bourgeois parliaments, function as the living embodiment of a real democratic movement that marked the culmination of a process Marx had first recognized in the 1840s. As Lenin wrote in his 1917 *Letters on Tactics*: 'I am deeply convinced that the Soviets will make the independent activity of the *masses* a reality more quickly and effectively than will a parliamentary republic.'[7]

This claim was theoretically underpinned by Lenin's retrieval of Marx and Engels's analysis of the state and parliamentary forms in his *The State and Revolution*.[8] The key insight that Lenin took from Marx was that socialism could only come through a revolution which would not only smash the old state but replace it with a new truly democratic form.

In the 1840s, Marx's 'discovery' of the proletariat coincided with his critique of the state form. For Marx, whereas the state was a form of alienation in its various constitutional guises, the proletariat offered the potential to overcome alienation by reabsorbing the functions of the state into society in a way that harked back to, but was deeper than, the Athenian democratic form. Communism in this sense marks the *Aufhebung* (simultaneously the abolition, transcendence and preservation) of the state and civil society in a new framework in which socialist revolution and democracy are conceived not as radical alternatives but as two sides of the same coin.[9] If this point tends to be obscured by superficial and usually anachronistic interpretations of Marx's deployment of the concept of the 'dictatorship of the proletariat', once we recognize that this concept was intended to illuminate the class content of political power rather than its supposed undemocratic form we can begin to see how Engels could write that 'the democratic republic . . . is even the specific form of the dictatorship of the proletariat'.[10]

Marx and Engels came to this conclusion through a profound critique of state theory as mediated through their analyses of nineteenth-century revolutions.[11] In 1859, Marx claimed that it was through his 1843 *Critique of Hegel's Doctrine of the State* that he first realized that 'legal relations as well as forms of state are to be grasped neither from themselves nor from the so-called general development of the human mind, but rather have their roots in material conditions of life'.[12] In this youthful essay, Marx extended Feuerbach's criticism of religion to a critique of Hegel's analysis of the state form. He argued that just as Feuerbach had shown Christianity to be the essence of religion that pointed to the possibility and indeed necessity of overcoming religion, so democracy, that is socialized humanity (our very nature), was the essence of all political constitutions and this social content pointed to the potential transcendence of these constitutions; that is to the transcendence of the state as an alien power over people.[13]

According to Marx, whereas the social nature of humanity had heretofore been realized as an alien (state) power, democracy, or rather 'true democracy', potentially realizes our essence such that 'the political state disappears'.[14] Almost three decades later he described the Paris Commune in very similar terms: the Commune represented 'the reabsorption of the state power by society as its own living force instead of a force controlling and subduing it'.[15] He conceived the Commune as a concrete historical realization of the 'true democracy' he had first analysed in 1843 when he argued that, though all forms of state are in fact founded on the democracy (the common people), it is only through true democracy that the state can become the 'self-determination of the people'.[16] Consequently, it is through true democracy or communism that the state is simultaneously preserved, abolished and transcended.

This perspective underpins Marx's claim that American democracy was a 'swindle'. He argued that the Federalists intended to, and succeeded in, maintaining the liberal primacy of property relations in a context of burgeoning revolutionary democracy – they 'utilised democratic forms to frustrate genuine democratic control from below'.[17] They did so by creating something radically new: a liberal democracy in which the people relinquished all but nominal control over their representatives.[18] In liberal democracies formal democratic control over the political levers of power coexist with the real 'alienation of political power which was so foreign to the Greek conception of democracy'. By contrast with the Greeks, the Federalists created a constitution in which 'primary producers are subject to economic compulsions which are independent of their political status'.[19] This was anathema to Greek democracy in which, according to Aristotle, 'the free born and poor control the government . . . as distinct from oligarchy, in which, the rich and better born' are in the driving seat.[20] The modern democratic swindle is a swindle precisely because the rich maintain real control while the poor merely hold to the semblance of power.

This is not to say that Marx believed 'that democracy was just a bourgeois plot . . . to ensure that bankers could protect their assets from wolfish governments'.[21] On the contrary, he insisted that bourgeois democracy was 'a major step forward for humankind' as compared with feudal and absolutist states.[22] Lenin agreed: although 'Bourgeois democracy . . . always remains, and under capitalism is bound to remain, restricted, truncated, false and hypocritical' it nonetheless represented 'a great historical advance in comparison with medievalism'.[23]

Despite being a historical step forward from feudalism it remained a 'snare and deception' for the workers because parliamentary republics are both 'structurally interdependent' with capital while simultaneously having a social basis in an atomized population. If the bourgeois state's structural interdependence with capital sets the parameters of what is politically possible within bourgeois democracies, the atomization of voters at the ballot box reproduces those forms of general alienation and powerlessness that ensure that these parameters are seldom challenged by the demos.[24] So whereas the Athenian democratic form ensured the people exercised real power, bourgeois democracies combine *de jure* formal equality with *de facto* 'domination of the capitalist exploiters'.[25]

Soviet democracy, by contrast, exceeded even the democratic pretentions of the Paris Commune. Whereas the Commune was based upon territorial units, because soviets were rooted in the democratic control at work they could begin to overcome the separation of economics and politics characteristic of the bourgeois democratic swindle: 'by making the economic, industrial unit (factory) and not the territorial division the primary electoral unit' soviet democracy was a 'higher level of democracy' than the parliamentary form.[26] Soviet democracy thus acts as the concrete form of Marx's communism: 'an association, in which the free development of each is the condition for the free development of all'.[27]

Clearly the experience of Stalinism presents a profound problem for the Marxist claim that the soviet model amounted to an 'extension of democracy' by contrast with bourgeois parliaments.[28] One response to this problem has been to reject outright the model of the October Revolution because Leninism supposedly undermined sovietism. The weakness of this critique of Lenin's politics is that it posits a too one-sided opposition between soviets and revolutionary parties. Of course these are distinct entities, but they are best understood not as alternatives but as complementary forms: the historical record suggests that socialists must be organized within soviets to ensure the democratic potential of these organs of workers' power is realized.[29]

If the October Revolution was won through soviets led by Bolsheviks, this victory was itself predicated upon mass collective action on the part of the working class. As Lenin put it: 'For the first time in world history, the revolutionary struggle attained such a high stage of development and such an impetus that an armed uprising was combined with that specifically proletarian weapon – the mass strike.'[30] A decade earlier, Rosa Luxemburg argued that it was through mass strikes that the working class could begin to overcome its normally fragmented state to make possible workers' power that overcame the bourgeois separation between politics and economics.[31] Lenin's view was that while the mass strike created the possibility of workers' power, soviet power acted as the concrete realization of this potential.

The opposition between soviets and parliaments came to a head in 1917. Though the Bolsheviks had long demanded the election of a parliamentary Constituent Assembly, and though they continued to make this demand throughout 1917, after April 1917 they did so while simultaneously demanding 'all power to the soviets'. The consequences of this contradictory perspective became apparent immediate upon the elections to the Constituent Assembly: whereas the Bolsheviks were a majority in the All Russian Congress of Soviets, they held only 25 percent of the seats in the Constituent Assembly – which was dominated by the Socialist Revolutionary Party. This result was not as clear cut as it first appears: because the election was held prior to a split between Left and Right SRs, the Right SRs were over-represented in the Assembly while the Left SRs, who were then the Bolshevik's coalition partners, were massively under-represented. Nonetheless, in essence the election reflected the fact that while the Bolsheviks were a majority amongst the urban proletariat, they remained a minority amongst the peasantry.

The question facing the Bolsheviks in January 1918 was whether or not they should succumb to this new power. Beyond the fact that in a deeply polarized context defeat for soviet power would have seen the Constituent Assembly replaced by a military dictatorship, for the soviets to succumb to the Constituent Assembly would have meant bowing before a less democratic form of representation. As Lenin argued, 'In relation to the provisional government the Constituent Assembly represented, or might have represented, progress; in relation to the regime of the Soviets, and with the existing electoral lists, it will inevitably mean retrogression.'[32] The logic of this situation was simple: when posed with a choice between soviets and Constituent Assembly, the Bolshevik chose soviets – and they did so for very democratic reasons.[33]

In the ensuing civil war the Constituent Assembly became the beacon for counter-revolution. Though the Bolsheviks triumphed militarily, the civil war was a social catastrophe for Soviet Russia. By 1920 the value of industrial production had declined to about 13 percent of its 1913 level, while between 1913 and 1921–2 the number of waged workers dropped from 11 million to 6.5 million with the number of industrial workers being more than halved.[34] This incredibly harsh context meant that sheer physical survival became the primary goal both for ordinary Russians and for the new revolutionary regime. Far from Russian totalitarianism being a consequence of Lenin's anti-democratic project, 'the "objective" social circumstances of Russia's revolution and civil war contain sufficient conditions for the collapse of the mass revolutionary wave, without recourse to causal factors stemming from the "subjective" deficiencies of Lenin's early formulations'.[35] This meant that the objective basis for soviet power – an organized and militant working class – largely disappeared in the years immediately following the Revolution. If soviets were the 'universal mass organizations of precisely those classes that are oppressed under capitalism', with the decimation of the proletariat the soviets became empty shells. This process was the precondition of Stalin's rise to power, and his victory was consummated through the liquidation of the last vestiges of the Bolshevik Party.[36]

Unfortunately, attempts to conflate soviet democracy with Stalinism fit the ideological need to limit democracy to its castrated bourgeois form. By contrast, Marxist democracy stands in the tradition of, first, Marx's critiques of the state and parliamentary forms, second, his celebration of the Paris Commune as a deepening of the parameters of democracy and, finally, Lenin's and Trotsky's analysis of the experience of the soviets or workers councils as a further deepening of the democratic form.

For a brief moment in 1917 the victory of the soviets against the Provisional Government meant that the Russians were the 'freest people in the world'.[37] The soviet state expanded democracy to become, as Lenin put it, 'for the first time . . . democracy for the poor, democracy for the people, and not democracy for the money-bags'.[38] Soviet Russia in 1917, like the Commune half-a-century earlier, had a radical democratic form whose social content was 'the rule of labour over capital'. It was to this social content that Marx and Lenin referred when they spoke of the dictatorship of the proletariat, and though civil war, famine and the isolation of the revolution led to the transformation of the social content of this dictatorship under Stalin we should not forget the real hope for 'true democracy' or communism that was briefly glanced through the Russian soviets in 1917.

Notes

1. Vladimir Lenin, '"Democracy" and Dictatorship', December 1918, in Lenin, *Collected Works*, vol. 28, 368.
2. Joseph Femia, *Marxism and Democracy* (Oxford: Oxford University Press, 1993), 1.
3. Herbert Marcuse, *Soviet Marxism* (New York: Columbia University Press, 1958).
4. Leon Trotsky, *The Revolution Betrayed* (New York: Pathfinder, 1972), 288–9: 49–52.
5. Richard Hunt, *The Politics of Marx and Engels Volume 1* (London: MacMillan, 1974), 255; Richard Hunt, *The Politics of Marx and Engels Volume 2* (Pittsburgh: University of Pittsburgh Press, 1984), 84.
6. Vladimir Lenin, 'Draft Programme of the Russian Communist Party (Bolshevik)', in *Collected Works*, vol. 29, 99–140, 106.
7. Vladimir Lenin, 'Letters on Tactics' in *Collected Works*, vol. 24, 53.
8. Ralph Miliband, *Class Power and State Power* (London: Verso, 1983), 154–66.
9. Shlomo Avineri, *The Social and Political Thought of Karl Marx* (Cambridge: Cambridge University Press, 1968), 37.
10. Hal Draper, *The 'Dictatorship of the Proletariat' from Marx to Lenin* (New York: Monthly Review Press, 1987), 11–41, 37.
11. Vladimir Lenin, 'A Contribution to the History of the Question of the Dictatorship', in *Collected Works*, vol. 31, 340–61, 340.
12. Karl Marx, Preface to *A Contribution to the Critique of Political Economy* (London: Lawrence and Wishart, 1970), 20.
13. Avineri, *Marx*, 35–6.
14. Karl Marx, 'Critique of Hegel's Doctrine of the State', in *Early Writings*, ed. Karl Marx (London: Penguin, 1975), 88.

15 Karl Marx, 'The First draft of The Civil War in France', in *The First International and After*, ed. David Fernbach (London: Penguin, 1974), 246.
16 Marx, 'Critique of Hegel', 89.
17 Hal Draper, *Karl Marx's Theory of Revolution*, vol. 1 (New York: Monthly Review Press, 1977), 306.
18 Ellen Meiksins Wood, *Democracy against Capitalism* (Cambridge: Cambridge University Press, 1995), 213.
19 Wood, *Democracy against Capitalism*, 217, 201.
20 Ibid., 220.
21 John Keane, *The Life and Death of Democracy* (London: Simon & Schuster, 2009), 86.
22 Brian Roper, *The History of Democracy* (London: Pluto Press, 2013), 217.
23 Vladimir Lenin, 'The Proletarian Revolution and the Renegade Kautsky', *Collected Works*, vol. 28, 229–325, 243.
24 Paul Blackledge, 'Left Reformism, The State and the Problem of Socialist Politics Today', *International Socialism* 2, no. 139 (2013): 25–56.
25 Lenin, 'Draft Programme of the Russian Communist Party (Bolshevik)', *Collected Works*, vol. 29, 99–140, 107.
26 Lenin, 'Draft Programme of the Russian Communist Party', 108; cf. Alex Callinicos, *The Revenge of History* (Cambridge: Polity, 1991), 111.
27 Karl Marx and Frederick Engels, *Manifesto of the Communist Party,* in Marx *The Revolutions of 1848* (London: Penguin, 1973), 62–98, 87.
28 Alex Callinicos, 'Socialism and Democracy' in *Prospects for Democracy*, ed. David Held (Cambridge: Polity, 1993), 200–12, 201.
29 Leon Trotsky, *The Lessons of October* (London: Bookmarks, 1987), 69–77; Donny Gluckstein, *The Western Soviets* (London: Bookmarks, 1985), 235.
30 Lenin, 'Question of the Dictatorship', 341.
31 Rosa Luxemburg, *The Mass Strike* (London: Bookmarks, 1986), 73.
32 Tony Cliff, *Lenin: The Revolution Besieged* (London: Pluto Press, 1978), 31.
33 And so too did Rosa Luxemburg, despite her earlier criticisms of the Bolshevik policy on this issue (Rosa Luxemburg 1918, 'The National Assembly' in *Rosa Luxemburg: Selected Political Writings,* ed. Robert Looker (London: Jonathan Cape, 1972), 262–5.
34 Alec Nove, *An Economic History of the USSR: 1917–1991* (London: Penguin, 1992), 89–110.
35 Peter Sedgwick, 'Introduction', *Year One of the Russian Revolution*, ed. Victor Serge (London: Pluto Press, 1992), 13.
36 Nigel Harris, *The Mandate of Heaven* (London: Quartet Books, 1978), 272.
37 Mike Haynes, *Russia: Class and Power, 1917–2000* (London: Bookmarks, 2002), 21.
38 Lenin, 'The State and Revolution', *Collected Works*, vol. 25, 461.

CHAPTER SEVENTEEN

Democracy in the Revolutionary Thought of Rosa Luxemburg

Rosemary H. T. O'Kane

Experience demonstrates . . . that the living fluid of the popular mood continuously flows around the representative bodies, penetrates them, guides them. . . . And is this ever-living influence of the mood and degree of political ripeness of the masses upon the elected bodies to be renounced in favour of a rigid scheme of party emblems and tickets in the midst of revolution? Quite the contrary! It is precisely the revolution which creates by its glowing heat that delicate, vibrant, sensitive political atmosphere in which the waves of popular feeling, the pulse of popular life, work for the moment on the representative bodies in the most wonderful fashion. . . . All this shows that the 'cumbersome mechanism of democratic institutions' possesses a powerful corrective – namely, the living movement of the masses, their unending pressure. . . . [T]he remedy which Trotsky and Lenin have found, the elimination of democracy as such, is worse than the disease it is supposed to cure; for it stops up the very living source from which alone can come the correction of all the innate shortcomings of social institutions. That source is the active, untrammelled, energetic political life of the broadest masses of the people. . . .

[I]t is a well-known and indisputable fact that without a free and untrammelled press, without the unlimited right of association and assemblage, the rule of the broad mass of the people is entirely unthinkable.[1]

This passage is from *The Russian Revolution*, which Rosa Luxemburg wrote in her prison cell in Germany in 1918. Her radical speeches and writings had led to previous prison sentences; her opposition to the First World War resulted in her imprisonment without trial until November 1918. Though Polish by birth, Rosa Luxemburg lived in Germany for most of her adult life; on arrival, in 1898, she became a highly active member of the German Social Democratic Party (SPD), a Marxist party. In 1915, she described German social democracy as having been 'generally acknowledged to be the purest incarnation of Marxian socialism'.[2] The party's programme (the Erfurt Programme of 1891) stated the 'principles' of the SPD as: 'the abolition of class rule and of classes themselves'; 'equal rights and equal obligations for all, without distinction of sex or birth'; and the end of 'not only the exploitation and oppression of wage earners in society today, but every manner of exploitation and oppression, whether directed against a class, party, sex, or race'.[3]

Following from the SPD's stated principles the party programme also made policy 'demands'. These included: equality between the sexes in both public and private laws; the abolition of all laws that prevented full freedoms of expression, opinion, association, assembly and religion; free schools and free school meals for all boys and girls; free administration of justice; free medical care; and taxes no longer to benefit the 'privileged few'. The programme also made specific demands for the protection of the working class, including: a maximum eight hour normal working day; a minimum working age of fourteen; the rights of trade unions, to be safeguarded through the 'freedom of association'; and pensions, unemployment and sick pay under a state system of workers' insurance. Crucially, too, the programme set out political demands for universal suffrage, for all men and women over the age of twenty; free and fair elections; proportional representation; and referendums. The SPD was also pacifist and, so, another demand was for a militia in place of the standing army with the elected parliament ('popular assembly') to deal with 'international disputes' through arbitration.

Rosa Luxemburg stayed true to all these principles and demands of social democracy throughout her life but, in 1917, she left the SPD and joined the newly founded Independent Social Democratic Party, USPD, along with the other members of the radical wing of the SPD, the International Group (the Spartacus Group), which she, with others, had founded in 1916. She left the SPD because of the party's patriotic support for the war. After the war ended, in November 1918, the International Group first changed its name to Spartacus League and then broke from the USPD to form the German

Communist Party, KPD. As one of the leaders of the uprising that began on 6 January 1919 and lasted six days, Rosa Luxemburg was murdered, on 15 January, by Volunteer Corp (Freikorps) soldiers.

Luxemburg's roles as one of the founding members of the German Communist Party and as a leader in the January Uprising make *The Russian Revolution* of special significance. She wrote it in critical reaction to the news of events taking place in Russia following the Bolshevik takeover in the October Revolution, 1917, which she pieced together from the accounts in Russian and German newspapers and other publications that were smuggled into her prison cell and from news brought by visitors. Specifically, the selected passage on democracy was written in reaction to the Bolsheviks' decision to dissolve the Constituent Assembly, which they did in January 1918 just one day after it had met for the first time, and to their failure to uphold the essential guarantees of democracy of universal suffrage, freedom of the press and the right of association and assembly for opponents and not just supporters of the regime.[4]

In spite of the work being smuggled out of the prison in 1918 *The Russian Revolution* was not published until 1922, three years after Luxemburg's death and after the Bolsheviks had become the victors in the Civil War. Her criticisms of Bolshevik actions and methods made the work highly controversial within communist circles. Unsurprisingly, they gave rise to the claim that while in prison she had been unable to obtain all the facts and that after she had been released from prison she had changed her mind about Bolshevik tactics.[5] But wider consideration of her works shows clearly that her views of democracy were consistent over time and central to her thought. Furthermore, in her strong rejection of Trotsky's argument for dissolving the Constituent Assembly and criticisms of the Bolsheviks' failure to ensure essential democratic guarantees, Rosa Luxemburg offers far more than a defence of democracy. Through focussing on the dictatorship of the proletariat, the revolutionary turning point in Marxist theory between the capitalist and the communist modes of production, the passage draws out the essence of her view of democracy in both its 'bourgeois' (liberal) and socialist forms and highlights what is distinctive about her view: the crucial importance of the active participation of the broad masses of the people as the lifeblood of democracy.

Trotsky explained the Bolsheviks' justification for the dissolution of the Constituent Assembly in *October to Brest-Litovsk*.[6] It is from this pamphlet that, in the passage, Rosa Luxemburg quotes the phrase 'cumbersome mechanism of democratic institutions', to which she takes such exception. She rejects Trotsky's argument that workers' experience in the revolutionary struggle resulted in such rapid political development that the democratic process could not keep pace, so rendering representation meaningless. She also goes against the commonly held position that bourgeois democracy is nothing more than the election of representatives every set number of years by championing the relationship between parliamentary representatives and those outside parliament whom they, theoretically, represent. She argues that far from that relationship only being present at election time and quickly becoming irrelevant, the relationship is carried forward as 'the living fluid of the popular mood continuously flows around the representative bodies, penetrates them, guides them'.

As evidence of the effect of 'the popular mood', Luxemburg pokes fun at conservative social democratic parliamentary representatives 'suddenly finding revolutionary tones in their breasts . . . whenever there is rumbling in factories and workshops and on the streets' (61) and she also points to the transformation brought in 'the first stages of every revolution', giving examples ranging from the Long Parliament in England, from 1642 to 1649, to the Fourth Russian Duma, from 1909 to February 1917. She argues, furthermore, that such examples demonstrate not only how representatives could be stirred on by active public political participation but also why during the immediate stage after the proletarian revolution – the dictatorship of the proletariat, in which Lenin and Trotsky were engaged in the October Revolution – it was crucial that 'the entire mass of the people', through political training and education, had every opportunity to develop and practice their democratic skills: 'for the proletarian dictatorship that is the life element, the very air without which it is not able to exist' (68). The proletarian dictatorship could not be rushed through and particularly in Russia where, unlike in Germany, experience of bourgeois democracy had been so limited. Indeed, in Russia she saw 'giant tasks' ahead for which 'the most intensive political training of the masses and the accumulation of experience' (68–9) were essential.

It is critical to Luxemburg's understanding of democracy that she insisted that political training and accumulation of experience for the masses could not be achieved if the government consisted only of one party and freedom of action and opposition had been suppressed:

> Freedom only for the supporters of the government, only for the members of one party – however numerous they may be – is no freedom at all. Freedom is always and exclusively freedom for the one who thinks differently. (69)

There was no 'ready-made formula' for socialist transformation 'in the pocket of the revolutionary party' (69), she argued. Furthermore, 'the whole mass of the people must take part' in order to prevent not only dictatorship but also corruption: 'The only way to a rebirth is the school of public life itself, the most unlimited, the broadest democracy and public opinion' (70–1). This 'rebirth' was the socialist society that developed out of the transitional stage of Marx's proletarian dictatorship. That was not the kind of dictatorship in which Lenin and Trotsky were engaged, she explained, but, rather, 'a dictatorship of the *class*, not of a party or of a clique' and she made her meaning clear: 'dictatorship of the class, that means in the broadest public form on the basis of the most active, unlimited participation of the mass of the people, of unlimited democracy' (76–7).

Rosa Luxemburg's opposition to the Bolsheviks' top-down tactics was not simply something that she had written in the heat of the moment in her prison cell in 1918. In 1904, she had expressed precisely the same view in *Organisational Questions of the Russian Social Democracy*, where she described the Bolshevik position, as set out by Lenin in *One Step Forward, Two Steps Back*, as 'pitiless centralism' and emphasized the advantages that Germany had in having a 'bourgeois-democratic setup' under which workers' organizations consisting of local groups and clubs moved, over time, to the 'unity of a large, national body, suitable for concerted political action'.[7] In this earlier work she had also emphasized the crucial role played by 'the direct, independent action of the masses' throughout the history of the Social Democratic movement and had gone on to elaborate on 'the living spirit carried into the organization by the membership'.[8] She had then expanded on 'the natural pulsation of a living organism', which makes mistakes but, crucially, also learns valuable lessons through the mistakes made and concluded: 'Historically, the errors committed by a truly revolutionary movement are infinitely more fruitful than the infallibility of the cleverest Central Committee.'[9]

What Luxemburg criticized in bourgeois democracy were not the political structures and institutions designed to make democracy work in practice – the representative parliament, the multi-party elections, the freedom of the press and the freedoms of associations and assembly – for these all offered opportunities for the masses to gain training and experience in democratic processes. Though liberal democracy serves the interests of the bourgeoisie, the system also provides the means through which workers' organizations, not least the workers' social democratic movement, are able to grow. What she criticized in bourgeois democracy were the conditions that the formal structures of democracy concealed: the inequalities and injustices of a society that operated to the benefit of the class who owned the means of production. In line with her position on 'bourgeois parliamentarism', in *Reform and Revolution*, published back in 1900, that 'it is necessary to extract the kernel of socialist society from its capitalist shell',[10] Luxemburg now rejected Trotsky's dismissive remark that 'As Marxists we have never been idol worshippers of formal democracy' to argue:

> We have always revealed the hard kernel of social inequality and lack of freedom hidden under the sweet shell of formal equality and freedom – not in order to reject the latter but to spur the working class into not being satisfied with the shell, but rather, by conquering political power, to create a socialist democracy to replace bourgeois democracy – not to eliminate democracy altogether. (77)

Like other Marxists, Rosa Luxemburg has been criticized for not giving details of what the institutions and practices would be like in socialist democracy.[11] In the SDKPiL (Social Democracy of the Kingdom of Poland and Lithuania) programme, which she wrote in early 1906, she did, however, describe the democratic institutions and practices for the outset of socialist democracy in 'all-Russia', in the transitional stage of proletarian dictatorship.[12] The programme is similar to that of the SPD for Germany but her design for a highly pluralistic system with protections for minorities reflects the special history of Poland and Russia with their plural languages and cultures. But whether, for example, in the single class socialist society there would be multiple political parties, or even whether competing representatives would be organized in ways that resemble the political parties in bourgeois democracy, is not made clear. In a pamphlet published by the SDKPiL in 1905, however, Luxemburg does make clear that there would be 'freedom of conscience for every individual and the widest possible toleration for every faith and every opinion'.[13]

Luxemburg had good reason for not giving details of what the institutions and practices would be like in socialist democracy for it was crucial to her thought that socialist democracy must be formed through the active consent of the masses. As she argues in *The Russian Revolution*: 'Socialist democracy must proceed step by step out of the active participation of the masses; it must be under their direct influence, subjected to the control of complete public activity, it must arise out of the growing, political training of the mass of the people' (78). The kind of active participation that the population would have in socialist democracy is active involvement in decision-making, with power flowing not from the top down but from the bottom up, just as in the history of the social democratic movement. Socialist democracy is a pluralist, mass participatory, democracy; its institutions and structures taking time to develop and remaining responsive to change. In socialist democracy active participation would not be confined, as in bourgeois democracy, to voting and joining associations. Mass participation would be concerted political action that, crucially, would include spontaneous coming together with leadership responding to that spontaneous action.[14]

Rosa Luxemburg had developed her thoughts on the importance of spontaneous mass action and the role of political leadership in *The Mass Strike, the Political Party and the Trade Unions*, which she had written in 1906 after the failure of the 1905 Russian Revolution. From January 1906, she had played an active part in the revolution in the Kingdom of Poland, a part of the Russian Empire. The pamphlet had begun as an analysis of the 1905 Russian Revolution but had expanded into drawing lessons applicable to German trade unions with lessons also for the SPD. She argued that the spontaneity of workers' actions in Germany were being stultified by the leadership of the trade unions and made the case for mass strikes to be political strikes and not only economic strikes. It followed, she argued, that the role of the social democrat in the revolution is not to take care of the 'technical side, with the mechanism of the mass strike', but to 'assume *political* leadership in the midst of the revolutionary period'.[15] It was through this political leadership that, she argued, the 'feeling of security, self-confidence and desire for struggle', which the workers need, could be maintained alongside their spontaneity.[16] As Nye explains, 'a Luxemburgian leader speaks for others without dictating, makes clear what their actions mean in the aggregate and how they might be organized, coordinated, and carried forward'.[17]

In Rosa Luxemburg's thought, democracy is not a set of institutions, structures and policies imposed by government on society; democracy is active, not passive and is kept alive through the activity that flows through society. The form that society takes, its material conditions at its stage of history, sets the limits on the kind of democracy that can be achieved. Bourgeois democracy, being within the capitalist system, serves the interests of the bourgeoisie and concerted action for workers' rights and better economic conditions takes place through social democratic parties and trade union organizations. But, whether through their participation in mass strikes, or helping a party or casting a vote in an election, or reading about or taking part in debates and discussions on political, social and economic affairs, workers must be involved actively. This is why, for Luxemburg, in bourgeois/liberal democracies, workers' parties must be not just vote-getting but revolutionary parties: not organizing, managing and controlling on behalf of workers but being ever responsive to mass action.

Socialist democracy, likewise, is not something that is done by government on behalf of the mass of workers: it is the activity of the masses that gives life to socialist democracy. It is the dynamic process through which both the necessary material conditions for socialist democracy and the socialist democracy itself are realized. As Luxemburg explains, 'The socialist system of society should only be, and can only be, an historical product, born in the course of its realization, as a result of the developments of living history' (70). The right material conditions are those in which the working class is no longer subordinated to the capitalist owners of the means of production through the wage system and threat of unemployment. Conditions in which poverty, ill health, long hours of work and poor education do not sap energy and enthusiasm and where willingness to participate and ability to do so are enriched through training in and experience of democratic structures and institutions, including a free press and the freedom to form associations and to protest. In such a society, the greatest political freedoms are, through one's own reasoning, to think, to form groups and to engage in concerted political action. As she wrote in the Spartacus League programme, just one month before she was killed: 'The essence of socialist society is that the great working mass ceases to be a ruled mass and instead lives and controls its own political and economic life in conscious and free self-determination.'[18]

Notes

1. Rosa Luxemburg, 'The Russian Revolution', in *The Russian Revolution and Leninism or Marxism?*, by Rosa Luxemburg (Ann Arbor: Ann Arbor Paperbacks, University of Michigan Press, 1967), 60–2, 66–7. Page references to this edition will be given in parentheses throughout the text of this essay.
2. Rosa Luxemburg, 'The Junius Pamphlet: The Crisis in the German Social Democracy', in *Rosa Luxemburg Speaks*, ed. Mary-Alice Waters (New York: Pathfinder Press, 1994), 153–218, 263. Written in 1915, the pamphlet was first published in 1916.
3. The Erfurt Programme 1891, 'The Erfurt Program', 3, http://www.marxists.org/history/international/social-democracy/1891/erfurt-program.htm [accessed 14/7/17].
4. Luxemburg objected to the Bolsheviks' suffrage law, which limited suffrage to those who labour, for thereby disenfranchising those in middle-class jobs and the unemployed and those between jobs, from all classes. Ibid., 63–6.
5. See Nettl, *Rosa Luxemburg* (London: Oxford University Press, 1969), 445–6.
6. See Luxemburg, *The Russian Revolution*, 57.
7. Rosa Luxemburg, 'Organisational Questions of Russian Social Democracy', in *Socialism or Barbarism: The Selected Writings of Rosa Luxemburg*, ed. Paul Le Blanc and Helen C. Scott (London and New York: Pluto Press, 2010), 81–102, 84.
8. Luxemburg, 'Organisational Questions of Russian Social Democracy', 86, 93.
9. Ibid., 101, 102.
10. Rosa Luxemburg, *Reform and Revolution* (New York: Pathfinder Press, 1973), 52.
11. See Andrea Nye, *Philosophia: The Thought of Rosa Luxemburg, Simone Weil and Hannah Arendt* (New York: Routledge, 1994), 48; Nettl, *Rosa Luxemburg*, 168–70.
12. See Nettl, *Rosa Luxemburg*, 229–33.
13. Rosa Luxemburg, *Socialism and The Churches*, 1905 (London: Merlin Press, 1972), 25.
14. For consideration of the possible problems that might arise, in practice, in such a democracy, see Rosemary H. T. O'Kane, *Rosa Luxemburg in Action: For Revolution and Democracy* (New York and London: Routledge, 2015), 139–47.
15. Rosa Luxemburg, 'The Mass Strike, the Political Party and the Trade Unions', in *Rosa Luxemburg Speaks*, ed. Mary-Alice Waters (New York: Pathfinder Press, 1994), 153–218, 189.
16. Luxemburg, 'The Mass Strike, the Political Party and the Trade Unions', 190.
17. Nye, *Philosophia*, 48.
18. Rosa Luxemburg, 'What Does The Spartakusbund Want?', in *Rosa Luxemburg: Selected Political Writings*, ed. Robert Looker (London: Jonathan Cape, 1972), 275–86, 277.

CHAPTER EIGHTEEN

Max Weber's Charismatic Democracy

Xavier Márquez

Ever since the advent of the constitutional state, and even more so since the advent of democracy, the typical political leader in the West is the 'demagogue'. The unpleasant overtones of the word should not make us forget that it was Pericles, not Cleon, who first bore this title. Lacking an office, or rather being charged with the office of the leading strategist (the only office to be filled by election, in contrast to the others which, in ancient democracy, were filled by casting lots) Pericles led the sovereign ekklesia *of the* demos *of Athens. Actually, modern demagogy, too, employs the spoken word, and does so to an enormous extent, if one considers the electoral speeches a modern candidate has to make. . . . When plebiscitary leaders are in charge of parties, this means a 'loss of soul' . . . for the following, what one might call their spiritual proletarianisation. In order to be a useful apparatus in the leader's hands, the following has to obey blindly . . . But the only choice lies between a leadership democracy with a 'machine' and democracy without a leader, which means rule by the 'professional politician' who has no vocation, the type of man who lacks precisely those inner, charismatic qualities which make a leader.*[1]

Delivered in Munich in the chaotic period immediately after Germany's defeat in the First World War, Max Weber's famous lecture on 'The Profession and Vocation of Politics' comes across as a bracing dose of realism. From its opening definition of the modern state as the organization that 'lays claim to the monopoly of legitimate physical violence' (310), the lecture stresses that politics is about power and struggle; and though state power is more than mere violence – it requires, as Weber repeatedly notes, legitimation – the political leader who uses it is always making a 'pact with diabolical powers' (362). The lecture thus argues that political leaders need an ethics of *responsibility*: not just a cause that they believe in and feel called upon to fight for, but a concern with the intended and unintended consequences of political action in their struggle for this cause, and a clear-headed understanding of these consequences.

Both the German defeat and the revolutionary politics of the time, with their utopian tinge (the Bavarian revolution had taken place in November 1918), gave urgency to Weber's call for an ethics of responsibility. He had repeatedly stressed in his wartime writings that the key problem with the German Reich under Kaiser Wilhelm II was that it did not nurture responsible political leaders, both in the institutional sense of 'accountable leaders' and in the ethical sense of leaders willing to take responsibility for their actions.[2] 'The Profession and Vocation of Politics' was simultaneously a diagnosis of the causes of this failure, and an argument for a certain kind of democratic leadership. Loosely speaking, for Weber the key problem of modern politics (in Germany as elsewhere) was its general tendency towards *bureaucratization* (its 'professionalization'); and his solution was to embrace a more *political* democracy, a democracy that does not shun partisan struggle, trusts its leaders with genuine power, and accepts and even celebrates the inevitability of 'demagogy' as the key means through which leaders gain the confidence of the people.

Scholars have long noted that although Weber was a consistent supporter of both universal suffrage and the parliamentarization of politics in Germany in the late 1910s, he did not argue for the intrinsic value of democracy.[3] In his view, the ideal of 'self-government' in the modern state was a fiction.[4] Modern mass democracy was at best a form of oligarchy, where small groups made all important decisions, and ordinary citizens were dominated by political leaders and the state bureaucracy. As the opening extract for this chapter puts it, voters in mass democracies were for Weber little more than 'spiritual proletarians', blindly following the powerful emotional appeals of charismatic politicians. From this perspective, Weber's views fit into a long history of thinking about democracy that discounts the capacity of the many to escape the rule of the few; one thinks here of Thucydides' claim that Periclean Athens, though 'nominally a democracy' was in reality 'government by the first citizen' (2.65.9), the first demagogue.

But if democracy did not empower ordinary people in any important sense, Weber nevertheless thought it the best system, under modern social conditions, for the selection of leaders capable of articulating genuinely national interests and effectively using the state to pursue them. His instrumental defence of democracy as a more *efficient* means for producing leaders under modern social conditions than other forms of government was both original and enormously influential on contemporary views of the limits of self-government.[5] More strikingly, Weber even attempted to rehabilitate the ambiguous figure of the charismatic demagogue as a responsible political leader. This move is obviously troubling in light of the tragedy of German politics in the 1930s; yet at a time when populist leaders appear to threaten Western democracies again, Weber's defence of a certain kind of democratic charismatic leadership is worth examining in some detail.

Weber argued that genuine democratic self-rule was possible only in relatively simple social conditions. The ideal-type of democracy could only develop wherever small numbers of people were equal in status and administrative tasks were simple enough that no enduring differentiation between state officials and the members of the community emerged, as in the Swiss *Landesgemeinden* (cantonal governments) or some American townships.[6] But like most theorists of democracy since the nineteenth century, he thought that modern social conditions had rendered such forms of direct self-rule effectively impossible, since even small differences in the amount of time citizens can devote to politics tend to result in enduring distinctions between rulers and ruled, and in particular in the appropriation of political power by the rich: 'wherever it exists, direct democratic administration is unstable. With every development of economic differentiation arises the probability that administration will fall into the hands of the wealthy.'[7] Increases in population size, the division of labour and the need for continuous administration thus all inevitably result in the development of relationships of domination that displace or hollow out all forms of direct democracy.[8] From this point of view, the soviets of the Russian and Bavarian revolutions were a costly fantasy, easily rendered irrelevant by bureaucratic organizations.

Nevertheless, Weber, like Tocqueville before him, thought that the modern age had been decisively democratized, in the sense that the old status distinctions that structured aristocratic societies had been swept away with the emergence of the modern state. 'It is no mere coincidence', he wrote in a pamphlet on 'Suffrage and Democracy in Germany' published in 1917, that 'equal "numbers suffrage" is on the advance everywhere, for the mechanical nature of *equal* voting rights corresponds to the essential nature of today's state'.[9] The modern state considers the person not in terms of their particular social position (their 'estate', as in the *Ständestaat* of the medieval period), but simply as a citizen, the equal of all other citizens under the law. Its development thus rendered justifications for restricted suffrage increasingly untenable. And this demand for equal voting rights became all the more pressing during the war; one could not decently deny the suffrage to men who had faced death for the sake of the state.[10] The problem, for Weber, was thus not whether demands for democratic participation should be heeded, but which form the emerging 'mass democracy' should take. And here the key considerations for him were not about the consent of the people or the representation of their interests but about their *leadership*.

To be sure, Weber did not altogether discount the representative function of democratic institutions. As he put it in his 1917 series of articles on 'Parliament and Government in Germany under a New Political Order':

> it is . . . a condition of the duration of any rule that it should enjoy a certain measure of inner assent from at least those sections of the ruled who carry weight in society. Today, parliaments are the means whereby this minimum of assent is made manifest.[11]

One of the virtues of democratic competition was that parties were formed to represent specific interests or world views, including the interests of the working class. And the need to get the votes of specific groups put some limits on the pursuit of policy by leaders, even if voters themselves remained generally passive. But for Weber *all* political institutions required a minimum of assent ('legitimacy', in his theoretical terminology). Democracy was not unique in its need for assent, only in the explicit manner in which this assent was expressed. And Weber worried that the more parties represented specific material interests (a tendency which he thought was strengthened by electoral systems using proportional representation, as in the Weimar republic), the less likely they were to produce responsible leaders. A parliament made up exclusively of representatives of economic interests would be a parliament of '*closed, philistine minds*'[12] rather than 'a place for free rational debates' about genuinely national policy.[13]

Genuine leaders, according to Weber, are people capable of articulating a vision for national and not just sectional interests, and of pursuing that vision responsibly, through the 'slow, strong drilling of hard boards' that constitutes politics (369). Such people not only make politics their profession but have a *vocation* for it, an 'inner calling' that pushes them to fight for their cause. But they could not come to the fore if positions of power are in the hands of people with a quite different mentality. In particular, the excessive dominance of bureaucracies in the state and the political parties tended to smother the emergence of the man with a vocation for politics and resulted in irresponsible decisions. Yet since the bureaucratization of the state and the development of bureaucratized political parties were not accidental features of modern life, but long-term historical trends that we cannot avoid short of a radical (and destructive) simplification of social life, Weber argued for strengthening the mechanisms for the selection of leaders whose authority depended, not on bureaucratic structures, but on the confidence of the people, and who could therefore impose their will over those bureaucratic structures: the paradoxical figure of the *responsible* charismatic 'demagogue'.

The problem of bureaucratic domination displays both an institutional and an ethical dimension. Institutionally, the problem concerned the degree to which a political leader was able to control the bureaucracy, setting the 'political goals' which the bureaucrat must implement. Weber noted that the bureaucratic official, with his technical expertise, has an advantage over the amateur politicians supposed to direct them, and may come to expropriate their power (326). The resulting over-dominance of the state bureaucracy, which he saw as a particular problem for the German state during the war, led to irresponsible decisions in the institutional sense: top bureaucrats could not easily be *held responsible* for their decisions when their position depended only on the confidence of the monarch (himself an amateur). From this point of view, the obvious solution was to ensure that the highest decision-makers were genuinely accountable either to parliament or to the people, and that parliament had a robust right of inquiry to check the administration, a position that Weber advocated consistently in his political writings from the late 1910s. Without accountability there could be no responsibility.

More importantly, however, Weber thought that the training and socialization of state bureaucrats resulted in a mentality averse to genuine responsibility. Because the 'honour' of the official consists in carrying out a political leader's instructions, not in taking responsibility for them, 'precisely those who are officials by nature and who, in this regard, are of high moral stature, are bad and, particularly in the political meaning of the word, irresponsible politicians' (331). One thinks here in particular of Ludendorff, who essentially ruled Germany as a military dictatorship during the last years of the war but did not want to take responsibility for Germany's defeat.[14] Moreover, the bureaucratic mentality fails to understand the *political* consequences of action, since the bureaucrat is not trained for partisan combat but for impartiality, and thus does not normally learn how to defend his vision of the national interest in the context of partisan struggle. But modern politics is unavoidably structured by partisan conflict; decisions that do not take this context into account are necessarily irresponsible.

The training ground for political leaders therefore could not be the bureaucracy with its emphasis on meritocratic promotion and impartiality. Instead, Weber argued, the highest offices of the state should be open to people whose leadership talents have been tested, not by civil service examinations, but by partisan combat in defence of their cause, political work in parliament, and their overall ability to gather a following. Access to accountable power was key; if parliamentary leaders were powerless *vis à vis* state bureaucrats, Weber thought they would tend to be concerned with minor patronage or sterile ideological polemics.[15] In his wartime writings he thus focused on strengthening parliamentary institutions *vis à vis* the monarch. But by the time Weber delivered the 'Vocation' lecture, the monarchy was gone, and he had come to believe that a parliament fragmented by proportional representation would be too easily captured by unaccountable economic interests to be able to produce genuine leaders. The top leadership of the state, Weber now suggested, should have a *plebiscitary* legitimation, coming not from parliament but from the people. Such an office would be both a natural outlet 'for the desire for leadership' (351), and a counterweight to the 'machine politicians' without a vocation that he expected would dominate the new *Reichstag*.[16]

Machine politicians were an inevitable outgrowth of the development of political parties. Insofar as political leaders must be *politicians* rather than bureaucrats, Weber took it for granted that they would emerge from within political parties. But like all large-scale organizations, political parties tended to bureaucratize, especially under the pressures of the competition for votes; politics tended to become a *profession*. The result was the emergence of a new figure, the political professional or machine politician, who lives not (just) *for* politics (to fight for a cause, or a set of values) but *from* politics. The American 'boss' was Weber's main example: a person who was not interested in power as a means to fight for a cause, but as a way of making his living, as well as for the 'subjective rewards' that power brought.

The profession and vocation of politics are not mutually exclusive; one can live both *from* politics and *for* politics. But Weber argued that only the party leader who lives primarily *for* politics is able to articulate national interests that rise above class struggles.[17] Socially, this means that a genuine political leader is likely to be a person of independent means, that is, a person who does not need to make a living *from* politics. The lawyer emerged as a key figure in this context, since the advocate was both likely to have the rhetorical skills that were needed to fight for a cause effectively, and also to be more available for politics than many other kinds of people, given his high income and the specific demands of his work. (The overwhelming number of lawyers in the US congress and other national parliaments suggests that Weber was not wrong about this, even if not all of them are the kinds of leaders Weber hoped for.)

By contrast, Weber explicitly stressed that the rich capitalist entrepreneur, who might seem to possess 'independent means', was too tied to the running of his business to either devote sufficient time to politics, or to have a sufficiently dispassionate view of the class struggle (318–19). Capitalist entrepreneurs may be natural leaders, but they could not represent truly national interests. Similarly, the political professional without a vocation – the party boss – was too tied to the bureaucratic structures of the party, and too concerned with mere power, to provide responsible leadership. His concern was to maximize votes, not to defend a particular conviction; the politics of party bosses was therefore a 'soulless' politics, capable at best of representing sectoral interests, and tending to supress new ideas and new men.[18]

But party bosses would subordinate themselves to the charismatic leader, that is, the leader who was able, through the force of his personality, to gather a personal following and prove they could win office: the 'dictator of the electoral battlefield' (342). Such a charismatic leader did not merely 'represent' some interest group. He fought for an 'inner cause', shaping the views of his followers through his demagogy more than they shaped his; the followers then became basically passive, even 'spiritually proletarianised'. But they still played an important democratic role; for charisma has to be *proven* by works, and a leader who could no longer prove his worth by accomplishing the things he set out to do would be abandoned by his followers. (Charisma, in Weber, was never merely a matter of pure demagogic technique.) And while demagogy was a characteristic of all modern political systems (including the authoritarian system in Germany during the war),[19] only the demagogic leader who has to submit himself to plebiscitary approval in the context of a serious competition for power could be held accountable.

Thus we end with the paradox of a *responsible* charismatic demagogue. Like Tocqueville, Weber was searching for a new aristocracy, a social stratum capable of providing genuine leadership in the new democratic conditions;[20] indeed, also like Tocqueville, if for interestingly different reasons, he also looked to the legal profession as a potential source for it. The bureaucratization attendant to all modern large-scale organizations threatens the possibility of such leadership. The democratization of politics, insofar as it rewards the ambitious and provides outlets for charismatic leadership, offers an escape from the bureaucratic cage. But the double-edged nature of charismatic leadership did not escape Weber; acknowledging that both Pericles and Cleon can play this role, he was consistent in his demand that democracy must make it possible to hold *both* accountable.

Notes

1 Max Weber, 'The Profession and Vocation of Politics', in *Political Writings*, ed. and trans. Peter Lassman and Donald Speirs (Cambridge: Cambridge University Press, 1994). The original lecture was delivered in Munich on 28 January 1919, and then revised and published as a brochure in the series 'Intellectual Work as a Vocation. Four Lectures to the Union of Free Students' in October 1919. The excerpts at the beginning of this chapter appear at pages 331 and 351 of the Lassman and Speirs translation. All citations to the lecture are to this edition.

2 See, in particular, 'Suffrage and Democracy in Germany' and 'Parliament and Government in Germany under a New Political Order', both published in 1917, and both collected in *Political Writings*.

3 See, for example, David Beetham, *Max Weber and the Theory of Modern Politics* (Cambridge: Polity Press, 1985), 102. Beetham cites a letter by Weber to Ehrenberg of 1917 where Weber notes that 'forms of government are for [him] technical means like any other machinery'.

4 Mommsen quotes a letter by Weber of 4 August 1908 to Robert Michels: 'Such notions as the "will of the people", the true will of the people, ceased to exist for me years ago; they are *fictions*.' See Wolfgang Mommsen, *Max Weber and*

German Politics, 1890–1920, 2nd edn (Chicago: the University of Chicago Press, 1984), 395.

5. Joseph Schumpeter, who articulated and defended the classic 'minimalist' conception of democracy, was greatly influenced by Weber. See Joseph A. Schumpeter, *Capitalism, Socialism, and Democracy*, 3rd edn (New York: Harper, 1950). An updated defence of the 'minimalist' view of democracy can be found today in Adam Przeworski, *Democracy and the Limits of Self-Government* (New York: Cambridge University Press, 2010).
6. Max Weber, *Economy and Society*, ed. and trans. Guenther Roth and Claus Wittich (Berkeley: University of California Press, 1978), vol. II, chapter X, 948–9.
7. Weber, *Economy and Society*, 949.
8. Ibid., 951–2; J. J. R. Thomas, 'Weber and Direct Democracy', *The British Journal of Sociology* 35, no. 2 (1984): 216–40, 229.
9. Max Weber, 'Suffrage and Democracy in Germany', 103.
10. Ibid., 106.
11. 'Parliament and Government in Germany under a New Political Order', 165.
12. Max Weber, 'The President of the Reich', in *Political Writings*, 306. Emphasis in the original.
13. Mommsen, *Max Weber and German Politics*, 398.
14. Marianne Weber reported a conversation between Weber and Ludendorff emphasizing precisely this point: Weber apparently believed Ludendorff should have at the very least resigned at the end of the war. See Beetham, *Max Weber and the Theory of Modern Politics*, 236.
15. 'Parliament and Government in Germany under a New Political Order', 166–7.
16. Weber argued at length for a directly elected president both when he advised Preuss on the drafting of the Weimar constitution (see Mommsen, *Max Weber and German Politics*, 364–6) and in his public writings of the period (see especially 'The President of the Reich').
17. Beetham, *Max Weber and the Theory of Modern Politics*, 226–40.
18. Cf. 'Parliament and Government in Germany', 228–9.
19. Ibid., 220.
20. 'Suffrage and Democracy in Germany', 108–9.

CHAPTER NINETEEN

An Alternative Democracy: Dissent in Gandhi's Great Trial of 1922

Anuradha Veeravalli

I have no personal ill-will against any single administrator, much less can I have any disaffection towards the King's person. But I hold it to be a virtue to be disaffected towards a Government which in its totality has done more harm to India than any previous system. India is less manly under the British rule than she ever was before. Holding such a belief, I consider it to be a sin to have affection for the system. And it has been a precious privilege for me to be able to write what I have in the various articles tendered in evidence against me.

In fact, I believe that I have rendered a service to India and England by showing in non-co-operation the way out of the unnatural state in which both are living. In my opinion, non-co-operation with evil is as much a duty as is co-operation with good. But in the past, non-co-operation has been deliberately expressed in violence to the evil-doer. I am endeavoring to show to my countrymen that violent non-co-operation only multiples evil, and that as evil can only be sustained by violence, withdrawal

> *of support of evil requires complete abstention from violence. Non-violence implies voluntary submission to the penalty for non-co-operation with evil. I am here, therefore, to invite and submit cheerfully to the highest penalty that can be inflicted upon me for what in law is deliberate crime, and what appears to me to be the highest duty of a citizen. The only course open to you, the Judge and the assessors, is either to resign your posts and thus dissociate yourselves from evil, if you feel that the law you are called upon to administer is an evil, and that in reality I am innocent, or to inflict on me the severest penalty, if you believe that the system and the law you are assisting to administer are good for the people of this country, and that my activity is, therefore, injurious to the common weal.*[1]

Paradoxically, the space for dissent in democracy is a foundational problem. Since it is tacitly assumed that democracies are governments by the people or, at least, based on the consent of the people, for the people, the argument is that to go against the state would be to go against the will of the people, against themselves, in a manner of speaking.[2] In an attempt to circumvent the problem of difference and disagreement within the theories of the social contract on which democratic governments are founded, some have suggested that to expect 'conformity' is legitimate[3] and some have suggested a principle of overlapping consensus.[4] More recent political theory has dwelt on the idea of deliberative democracy, which is founded on the argument that the legitimization of democracy and democratic processes can only take place with the active participation of the people through reasoned discussion, and public debate on government policy and law.[5]

The overriding concern, however, as is seen in the experience of the modern nation state, is that despite argument and debate, there must ultimately be conformity to norms set by the state and its presuppositions of universal reason, which define visions of development, the good life and knowledge itself. This system in principle therefore is founded in the separation of the 'enlightened' expert point of view from the lay point of view, and the presumed superiority of the former over the latter. The limits of dissent follow accordingly from the presupposition that, in the final analysis, sovereignty is an attribute of the state, which by definition, by the logic of its institutions, is constituted on indubitable universal, rational, expert knowledge. As Immanuel Kant famously said in his essay describing government in the age of enlightenment:

> only the man who is himself enlightened, who is not afraid of shadows, and who commands at the same time a well disciplined and numerous

army as guarantor of public peace – only he can say what [the sovereign of] a free state cannot dare to say: 'Argue as much as you like, and about what you like, but obey!'[6]

The sovereignty of the individual and entire communities driven by different rationalities stands compromised within this framework.

In contrast to this conception of democracy, Gandhi's defence in the Great Trial of 1922 brings dissent and 'uncompromising disaffection' with government as the highest duty of a citizen in a democracy centre stage.[7] For Gandhi it is the individual who is sovereign and it is civil society as constituted by a plurality of sovereignties that must ultimately regulate, though not supersede, the authority of the state. The sovereignty of the people here does not rest in the representatives they send to parliament but precisely in 'the acquisition of the capacity by all to resist authority when abused'. Gandhi maintains a clear distinction between debate, which is the stuff of parliaments, and dissent by civil disobedience, which represents the sovereignty of the individual and civil society against an unjust state.

The problem of the divide between the expert and the lay person, on which the democratic process of the nation-state functions, is addressed by Gandhi's constructive programme.[8] Anticipating the threat of modern centralized regimes of government, political economy and knowledge, it envisages village republics that would be sites of decentralized experiments in non-violent technologies of political economy and institutions of social reform, which would regenerate and encourage the hands-on, local use of intelligence and skill, while making them economically and politically independent, yet interdependent, each in the service of the other. This would lay the foundation for substantial peace time preparation for non-violent civil disobedience.

Gandhi thereby presents the conditions for the possibility of a theory and practice of democracy necessarily constituted by institutions of non-violent dissent of the people. This is fundamentally different from representative/ parliamentary democracy as practiced in the modern nation-state. The trial of 1922 is an early illustration of the systematic deployment of the political method of civil disobedience calling into question the very presuppositions of the system of government.

In the aftermath of the promulgation of the Rowlatt Act (The Anarchical and Revolutionary Crimes Act) in 1919 all political dissent in an already disarmed, emasculated and colonized nation had become impossible. Gandhi, along with the publisher, Shankerlal Ghelabhai Banker, was charged under the act of sedition (Article 124A) for the offence of creating and propagating disaffection against the state through his writings in the newspaper *Young India*. This occasioned the Great Trial of 1922. Both were undefended. Gandhi, of course, pleaded guilty to all charges, arguing that under the circumstances, it had been his 'precious privilege' to write what he did and that 'it was a virtue to be disaffected towards a government which in its totality had done more harm to India than any previous system'.

The defence is a systematic exercise in the principles of an alternate democracy. The first task Gandhi takes on is to establish that he does not speak from the biased view of a victim of the Raj/colonial rule but as a loyal citizen, with no ill-will towards the King or threat to his final authority as sovereign of the state. Right from the beginning, with the choice to remain undefended and to plead guilty, we see Gandhi taking charge of the political terms of debate at the trial, bringing to bear on it his deepest convictions on the principles of government and its duty to its people. He cites his service to the Empire earlier, in South Africa, during the Boer and Zulu revolts, then during the First World War in 1914, when he raised a voluntary Ambulance Corps, and later, in India, his ready response to Lord Chelmsford's call for help in the war effort. He had made an effort, as a good citizen should, to garner Indian support for and to be of service to the state in its hour of need. These instances of service to the Empire have usually been read as Gandhi's attempts at placating or sucking up to the Empire. The most recent epithet it has earned him is 'stretcher-bearer of Empire'.[9] The fact that he recounts these instances of service as part of his 1922 defence speaks otherwise. He is, in fact, consciously laying the political grounds for the legitimation of civil dissent. The right to dissent is founded not merely in a fine conscience but politically, necessarily within the bounds of citizenship. A good citizen by definition is one who not only abides by the laws of the state but is at the same time one who keeps vigil against abuse of authority by the state and offers non-violent resistance to it. Therefore dissent which involves deliberate civil disobedience and breach of a law that is seen to be unjust must be offered with a willingness to accept due punishment by the state.

Gandhi's mode of argument and method of dissent are Socratic. Rejecting the charge that he had been corrupting the youth of Athens by provoking them to question the authority of the state and religion through his speculations, Socrates too first establishes, in his defence, that he has served Athens well, been a dutiful citizen and taken all public office he had been assigned with utmost seriousness. He then submits to the law of the land and willingly faces trial as a 'private citizen',[10] without succumbing to the temptation of escaping trial and punishment. So also, Gandhi submits to trial based on the law of the land, pleads guilty to all 'crimes' that he has been charged with, and willingly serves his sentence. Like Socrates, he asks the presiding judge to apply his mind to the case and consider what his office calls upon him to do, before giving his ruling. This is that moment of democratic truth when the state and those who hold public office in it must take their call too. Gandhi suggests to the judge that he might consider relinquishing office rather than ignoring the truth and thereby participating in the injustice and evil that the state seeks to perpetuate through him.

In his famous essay 'What is Enlightenment?' Immanuel Kant explains that freedom to use public reason is all that is required for enlightenment.

He defines the private use of reason, however, as that reason a person uses in civic office in order not to let it interfere with the performance of his duty as required by the authority of the institutions that he serves, either of the church or the state. For Kant, enlightenment requires a clear separation of the public and private use of reason. He perceives, nevertheless, the difficulty of a person's conscience rearing its head in the event of being caught in the contradiction between the private use of reason and the public use of reason. In such a case the person would be compelled to resign from office, according to Kant. It is this quintessential moment of truth, not of the use of public reason as much as of the moment of reflection on the contradiction that lies between the public and private use of reason, this call of conscience, at once private and public by definition, that Gandhi captures in his challenge to the judge at the great trial.

Gandhi's innovation beyond Socrates' method was to envisage a non-violent people's civil-disobedience movement. The initial experiments failed miserably in so far as they turned violent as, for instance, in the Chauri Chaura incident where the protesting mob burnt down a police station. Gandhi called off the movement immediately and took full responsibility for the tragedy, seeing the incident as a warning from God that the people were not ready for the experiment. Later, he led other civil disobedience movements, including the well-known Salt Satyagraha where each member joined the non-violent 'army' of his own will and conscience and willingly bore blows from police forces and punishment for breaking the law, without retaliation. In fact, as the Congress drew the draft constitution for India, he appealed to them to establish a state with a non-violent army along the lines of the non-cooperation movement. Of course, the Congress by then was sufficiently sold to the British model to expect Gandhi's non-violent model of democracy to work for Independent India!

After having established his credentials as a loyal citizen of the Empire, he proceeds to establish that what he saw as aberrations of government were actually problems intrinsic to the system itself, rather than of the British as colonial rulers. One may recall here his scathing attack of the British parliamentary system made already in 1908, as part of his 'condemnation' of modern civilization in 'Hind Swaraj'.[11] He likened the British parliamentary system to a sterile woman because it had not done one good thing, 'of its own accord', for the people of England. It was 'a costly toy of the nation' where members debated much, achieving little, and where a vote, independent of the party position, was looked down upon. Thus Gandhi points out that the sovereignty/swaraj of parliamentarians is compromised under the party whip and the majority will, the system itself rendering it impossible for members to be true representatives of the people.

The second step of his defence establishes the legitimacy of his disaffection and dissent against the Government. He recounts how the British government had systematically robbed the Indian people of their freedom in every way, political, economic and cultural. Its remorseless forgetting of horrific acts of commission like the Jallianwallahbagh massacre, its broken promises to the people and finally, its exploitation and destruction of agriculture and spinning and other cottage industries of the villages of India, had rendered them helpless. The government had not only systematically drained the country of its resources and emasculated its people, it had, with draconian laws, subdued all dissent. Under the circumstances, writing the articles in Young India and educating people about how their government had been exploiting them, was a duty of every citizen. Reiterating, at once, his common and equal citizenship with the English people as a citizen of the Empire and arguing that the problem was fundamental rather than local, he says that:

> In fact, I believe that I have rendered a service to India and England by showing in non-co-operation the way out of the unnatural state in which both are living.

Deprived of the possibility of this moment, democracy degenerates into what Plato describes it to be in the Republic: 'an agreeable form of anarchy with plenty of variety and an equality of a peculiar kind for equals and unequals alike'. If the paradoxical yet heady mix of liberty and equality that democracy offers is not to be reduced to a chaos of conflicting and sectarian interests, on the one hand, and a great leveller of values and aspirations under the garb of equality, on the other, then (Gandhi argues) dissent must necessarily transcend the selfish or narrow interest of any particular individual, group or community:

> The very essence of democracy is that every person represents all the varied interests which compose the nation. It is true that it does not exclude and should not exclude special representation of special interests, but such representation is not its test. It is a sign of its imperfection.[12]

Since each person in his sovereignty sees truth differently, and so also each community, it cannot by definition be imposed or enforced by anyone on another. Thus non-violence, for Gandhi, is a necessary condition of democracy: 'Science of non-violence can alone lead one to pure democracy.'[13] And the constructive programme (as argued earlier) is a necessary institutional foundation for this science of non-violence if it is not to be confined merely to sporadic movements of dissent but is also to address the larger issue of centralized state enforcement of an universal rationality and idea of progress.

It is this union of truth and non-violence that establishes the possibility of a plurality of sovereignties. In so far as the principle of sovereignty/swaraj strives to represent the unique voice of each individual and the lone voice of conscience even from a position of weakness, it can be contrasted with solidarity and the majority, where conformity and a common cause are a source of power as well as hegemony. In the former, a voice seeks to be heard by those in authority even if it is outnumbered by the multitude, while the latter depends on the force of its numbers and its power to compel submission to its demands. In the former, it is the ability of the one, or each, to reflect the interests of all while in the latter it is congruence or uniformity of interests or an erasure of difference by allegiance to the norms of an established regime that is the basis of strength.

Mirroring the methods of the state, it is the principle of solidarity that acknowledges the authority of power and therefore, the power of authority. The principle of sovereignty of the individual, on the other hand, presupposes a plurality of view-points and is based on the realization that the power of authority is effective only to the extent and in direct proportion to the acknowledgement of its authority or submission to it. The presuppositions of the sovereignty of the individual are founded in those of civil society, in principles of non-violence, service and self-suffering – a position of weakness, in contrast with those of the state, laws, rights and enforcement. Gandhi's acute awareness of this fundamental distinction between the principles of solidarity and of the sovereignty of the people is evident from his final indictment of both the British and their Indian counterparts in administration who believe that they are in charge of one of the best and most progressive systems of government when in fact it is a 'system of terrorism' which 'induces' in an emasculated public 'the habit of simulation' and in the administrators, 'a form of self-deception'. They believe that they can enforce affection through laws like the one he is charged with. As Gandhi goes on to point out, 'Affection cannot be manufactured or regulated by Law.'[14]

Notes

1 M. K. Gandhi, 'Statement in the Great Trial of 1922', in *The Voice of Truth*, ed. S. Narayan (Ahmedabad: Navajivan Publishing House, 1969), 23–4.

2 Hobbes and Rousseau, despite differences in their conceptions of both the reasons for and the nature of the Social contract, are both agreed on this matter.

3 R. Nozick, *Anarchy, State, and Utopia* (New York: Basic Books, 1974).

4 John Rawls, *A Theory of Justice* (Cambridge, MA: Harvard University Press, 1971).

5 Urbinati, *Democracy Disfigured* (Cambridge, MA: Harvard University Press, 2014); J. Habermas, *The Theory of Communicative Action, Vol. I: Reason and Rationalization* (Boston: Beacon Press, 1984); A. Gutmann and D. Thompson, *Why Deliberative Democracy?* (Princeton: Princeton University Press, 2004); C. Taylor, 'The Politics of Recognition', in *New Contexts of Canadian Criticism*, ed. A. Heble, D. Palmateer Pennee, and J. R. Struthers (Peterborough, Ontario: Broadview Press, 1997) all address the problems of deliberative democracy from different perspectives of rationality, multiculturalism and dissent but the terms of the debate are set within the limits of the presuppositions of democratic institutions in the modern nation-state such as, for instance, the sanctity of constitutions or majority versus minority opinion.

6   I. Kant, *An Answer to the Question: What is Enlightenment?*, trans. M. C. Smith, http://www.columbia.edu/acis/ets/CCREAD/etscc/kant.html (1784).
7   Urbinati, 'Democracy and Dissent', *Reset – Dialogues on Civilizations* (2009, online at http://www.resetdoc.org/story/00000001270 (accessed on 19 October 2016)) has argued that dissent is a constitutive virtue of democracy.
8   M. K. Gandhi, *Constructive Programme* (Ahmedabad: Navajivan Publishing House, 1945).
9   A. Desai and G. Vahed, *The South African Gandhi: Stretcher-Bearer of Empire* (New Delhi: Navayana Publishing House, 2015).
10 Socrates argues that the fight for justice must be as a private citizen, not a political person. *Apology*, XIX.32, trans. F. J. Church (The Liberal Arts Press, Inc., 1956).
11 M. K. Gandhi, *Hind Swaraj*, ed. S. Narayan (Ahmedabad: Navajivan Publishing House, 1939).
12 M. K. Gandhi, *The Collected works of Mahatma Gandhi*, vol. 75 (New Delhi: Publications Division Government of India, 1998), 266.
13 Gandhi, *Voice of Truth*, 446.
14 Gandhi, 'Statement in the Great Trial of 1922', 24.

CHAPTER TWENTY

Sun Yat-sen: People's Democracy and Chinese Democracy

Theresa Man Ling Lee

[T]he aims of the Chinese Revolution are different from the aims in foreign revolutions, and the methods we use must also be different. Why, indeed, is China having a revolution? To put the answer directly, the aims of our revolutions are just opposite to the aims of the revolutions of Europe. Europeans rebelled and fought for liberty because they had had too little liberty. But we, because we have had too much liberty without any unity and resisting power, because we have become a sheet of loose sand and so have been invaded by foreign imperialism and oppressed by the economic control and trade wars of the Powers, without being able to resist, must break down individual liberty and become pressed into an unyielding body like a firm rock which is formed by the addition of cement to sand. [. . .]
I classified mankind into three groups. The first group are those who see and perceive first: they are the people of superior wisdom . . . , whose insight into the future and whose many achievements make the world advance and give mankind its civilization. . . . The second group includes those who see and

perceive later: their intelligence and ability are below the standard of the first group; they cannot create or discover but can only follow and imitate, learning from what the first group have already done. The third group are those who do not see or perceive: they have a still lower grade of intelligence and ability and do not understand even though one tries to teach them; they simply act. [. . .] The progress of the world depends on these three types, and not one type must be lacking. The nations of the world, as they begin to apply democracy and to reform the government, should give a part to every man – to the man who sees first, to the man who sees later, to the man who does not see. We must realize that political democracy is not given to us by nature; it is created by human effort. We must create democracy and then give it to the people, not wait to give it until people fight for it.[1]

All three of the passages cited above are taken from a set of lectures on 'The Principle of Democracy' delivered at the Canton University in China by Sun Yat-sen (1866–1925) in 1924. These lectures, along with two other sets – one on 'The Principle of Nationalism' and the other on 'The Principle of Livelihood' – were subsequently published as a book under the title *San Min Chu I* ('The Three Principles of the People').[2] Despite his remarkable stature as the founding father of modern China, straddling the deep-seated political divide between the People's Republic of China and Taiwan, Sun's international reputation is considerably less pronounced. Moreover, he was undoubtedly a man of action and Sun considered himself more a political actor than a thinker. It is therefore not surprising that Sun has yet to be taken seriously as a major thinker in Western scholarship on Chinese philosophy and thought, while Sun studies in both Taiwan and China tend to be more ideological than academic. Nonetheless, as Marie-Claire Bergère, a French historian who wrote the most recent major biography of Sun, said, *San Min Chu I* is 'a fundamental work' of much import as it 'crystallizes the questions, ambitions, and ideas that fueled the debates of the first quarter of this [twentieth] century'.[3] More specifically, as we shall see, Sun's theory of democracy embodies this crystallization.

To appreciate what was at stake for Sun and his contemporaries, one needs to place Sun's thought in its historical context. This is not a methodological question of choosing the historical approach over the philosophical in the study of political thought. Rather, Sun's thought and Chinese history are inextricably linked. The political reality of China at the time was what prompted Sun to think of a unique solution to Chinese problems by drawing from both Chinese and Western political ideas, while his place as a much revered political leader meant that thought for him must necessarily inspire and orchestrate concrete and goal-oriented action. In Sun's words, a principle is at once 'an idea, a faith, and a power' (3).

When Sun delivered these lectures on the 'principles' of nationalism, democracy and livelihood in 1924, China had been a republic for thirteen years, following the abolition of the imperial state during the Revolution of 1911. Yet the nascent republic was plagued by an aborted attempt to restore monarchy early on and power struggle among political factions from the very start while the country splintered under the rule of warlords (former imperial generals). The impact of this protracted political crisis was made worse as Western powers and Japan continued their imperialistic expansion by carving up China into pockets of colonial outposts. Having served the Chinese Republic briefly as its first provisional president, Sun founded the Kuomintang (Chinese Nationalist Party) in 1919 to save China from obliteration. By 1924, Sun was ready to take his plan to yet another stage, which was to form an alliance, known as the United Front, with the newly founded Chinese Communist Party (1921). This strategic alignment, brokered by the Comintern (1919–43), was deemed to be necessary if China were to be reunified as a sovereign state free from internal political strife and external territorial encroachment. But the alliance soon fell apart when Sun died of cancer in 1925. The struggle for power between the two parties that ensued only ended with the proclamation of the People's Republic of China in 1949 by the Communist Party under Mao Zedong while the Kuomintang under Chiang Kai-shek retreated to Taiwan as a government-in-exile of the Chinese Republic. What is remarkable is that despite their ideological differences, both the Communists and the Nationalists claimed that their party was the true bearer of Sun's vision for a new China. A new China in this context meant a centralized state presiding over a united and sovereign China that is on par with other countries in the world, along with a mandate to serve its people by improving their livelihood.

Against this historical background, *San Min Chu I* is at once an anti-colonial political treatise that affirms nationhood and a blueprint for postcolonial state-building. Democracy as such is the pathway to this new nationhood. Yet Sun noted that 'the Chinese people's ideas of political democracy have all come from the West' because 'Western civilization . . . is in every way more advanced than Chinese civilization' (280–1). In other words, for Sun Chinese nationalism was anti-imperialistic but not necessarily anti-Western.[4] Sun, however, withheld giving full credit to the West as the inventor of democracy by reminding his audience that both Confucius and Mencius 'had already considered the idea of democracy' as they 'spoke for people's rights', only to be ahead of their time (169–70). Now more than 2,000 years later, the time was finally right because humanity had reached the age of 'people's sovereignty', when the 'people', as a 'unified and organized body of men', are the bearer of sovereignty, defined as the 'power and authority extended to the area of the state' (151–2).

Why then did the Chinese lag behind their Western counterparts in reaching this critical historical juncture? Sun's explanation was that the Chinese people were simply not as oppressed as the Europeans, both politically and socially. First, in contrast to European despotism, China's autocracy was not as 'severe' (225). Second, feudalism was long abolished in China with the founding of the first imperial state in 221 BCE. Consequently, there were neither inherited social classes nor an entrenched nobility that stood above the rest of the population (223–5). Accordingly, the Chinese did not have the same intense longing for liberty and equality as the Europeans (209). This was why the aim of democratic revolution in China was different from the ones that took place in Europe, as noted in the first extract at the start of this chapter. Given that the Chinese people had too much freedom, so much so that the Chinese were 'a sheet of loose sand', democracy in China was not about enhancing individual freedom. Rather, 'personal freedom' had to be sacrificed in order 'to make the nation free' (213). In other words, the 'Principle of Democracy' works hand in hand with the 'Principle of Nationalism' in Sun's vision.

Along with this rejection of personal freedom in the name of nation-building is Sun's claim that a modern state works more effectively when its citizens are not just individuals stripped of other embedded bonds among them. According to Sun, in the West where 'the individual is the unit', the individual expands immediately into the state; between the individual and the state there is no common, firm, social unit' (114). In contrast, the relation between the Chinese state and its citizens is mediated, first and foremost, by the family. Sun noted, 'there must first be family loyalty, then clan loyalty, and finally national loyalty. Such a system, expanding step by step, will be orderly and well regulated and the relationship between the small and large social groups will be a real one' (115). This, in Sun's view, is superior to 'knitting together ... a huge number of separate units', as it would have been the case 'where the individual is the unit' (115).

Later in these lectures, Sun pointed out that not only was the aim for Chinese democracy different, its implementation would also be distinctive. According to Sun, the most notable achievement of Western democracy 'within the past century has been the right to elect and to be elected', that is, 'representative or parliamentary government' (276). But Western nations had yet to solve the 'problem of administering democracy' (289). Its citizens are afraid of 'an all-powerful government which they cannot control' and are therefore constantly on guard against its power, rendering the government weak and ineffectual (294).

Against this concern, Sun put forth what he regarded as a 'fundamental solution' to the challenge of administering democracy through 'a new discovery', the distinction between 'sovereignty and ability' (296–7). In the second extract, Sun identified three distinctive groups of people based on their respective levels of ability. While the distinction thus drawn does not necessarily undermine the legitimacy of popular sovereignty, it does mean that not everyone is qualified to rule. In Sun's words, 'The foundation of the government of a nation must be built upon the rights of the people, but administration of government must be intrusted to experts' (318). Accordingly, there are 'two forces in politics' – 'the political power of the people and the administrative power of the government' (342). The two must work hand in hand to build a strong modern state. To do so effectively without 'the confusions of Western democracy' (318) means that the real challenge lies in improving the control mechanism of the people's power should it become necessary rather than in limiting government power before it is warranted (345).

For the people to have an effective control mechanism over government power, direct rather than representative democracy is in order. The people should be entrusted with four powers, including suffrage, power of recall, initiative and referendum (350–1). The first two enable the people to elect and to exercise direct control over officials and their respective positions in government (350). The latter two ensure that the people have control over the laws that govern them by giving them the power to introduce new law as needed and to amend 'an old law' that is no longer 'beneficial to the people' or to 'do away with the old law' altogether (350–1).

As for government power, Sun was in full support of constitutionalism and the separation of power though he was critical of the tripartite division in Western constitutional state. Instead, Sun proposed the 'quintuple-power' or 'five-power constitution', which he first articulated in 1906 and noted that it was 'entirely a creation of my own'.[5] Under this scheme, added to the executive, legislative and judicial branches are two other branches – the censor and the civil service examination board. Sun was quick to point out that both of these branches were present in the old imperial state and were effective in preventing the Chinese emperor, though autocratic, from having a complete monopoly over political power (356–7). The 'imperial censor' had 'the power to impeach' officials and the imperial examination board put China ahead in the world by '[t]he selection of real talent and ability through examinations' to serve the government (356). Sun argued that both of these branches remain just as important as before in a constitutional state by ensuring that the state has built-in mechanism for self-correction and improvement. In short, the 'five-power constitution' brought together the best of both worlds – the old imperial state in China and the modern constitutional state in the West (357–8). Sun was convinced that '[w]hen the four political powers of the people control the five governing powers of the government, then we will have a completely democratic government organ, and the strength of the people and of the government will be well balanced' (354).[6]

Through a total of six extended lectures, Sun became the first person in China to provide a comprehensive vision of democracy. In his view, democracy is the only way for China to go forward as it enables 'a high-powered, strong government' to be in place (344). But one challenge remains as 'the majority of the people are without vision' and those 'who have prevision must lead them and guide them into the right way' (318). Indeed, getting those 'without vision' ready for democracy is a task to be taken just as seriously as ensuring that democracy works once it is in place. In Sun's words, 'If we insist on using democracy without careful preparation beforehand, we will find it extremely dangerous and liable to kill us' (349).

Yet in these lectures Sun did not elaborate on how the majority of people who are 'without vision' will be guided. It is in *The Fundamentals of National Reconstruction*, published in the same year, that Sun outlined the implementation of democracy as a three-stage process – 'first, the stage of military rule; second, the stage of political tutelage; third, the stage of constitutional government'.[7] During the first stage, 'the whole administrative system shall be placed under military rule' to restore order, but '[a]s soon as a province is completely restored to order, the stage of political tutelage shall commence and the military stage come to an end' (10). In Sun's words, 'Without military rule the destructive side of the revolution cannot be accomplished thoroughly; without political tutelage its constructive work cannot be pushed forward' (3). To carry out the constructive work, 'the government should send persons, trained and qualified through examinations, to various districts (*hsien*) to assist the people in the preparation of self-government' (10–11). This includes the election of a district magistrate as the chief executive and representatives to make laws. A district is deemed to have achieved self-government when it fulfils the following tasks: completing a census and land survey of the whole district, establishing police and 'local defense forces', building and repairing roads within its boundaries, consolidating tax revenue and developing natural resources (11–13). But perhaps most important of all is the task of training people 'in the exercise of the four powers [suffrage, recall, initiative and referendum]' and to 'fulfil their duties as citizens' and to 'carry out the revolutionary principles' (11). Once every district in a province has attained self-government, the province is ready to move on to the stage of constitutional government (13). Finally, when more than half of the provinces have reached the constitutional stage, the People's Congress shall be convened to decide on and promulgate the Constitution (15).

It is clear that the three-stage process of democratization represents a bottom-up approach that is nonetheless carefully orchestrated from top-down. More specifically, democracy is not spontaneous and as Sun astutely noted, democracy is far from natural. This is why leadership is vital to the implementation of democracy. It is also clear from these lectures that Sun did not provide a defence for democracy because of its intrinsic value. Rather, democracy is deemed to be a necessary pathway to post-colonial nation-building. This raises the question of whether Sun would be prepared to adopt another pathway should it be available. Of course, the same question has been asked as to whether the founders of the Chinese Communist Party – Chen Duxiu (1879–1942) and Li Dazhao (1888–1927) – were truly committed

Marxists or whether they embraced Marxism because for them, Marxism was the pathway to nation-building. There is no doubt that the educated elites in early twentieth-century China were consumed by the urgent need to find a way to rebuild the country after more than 2,000 years of autocratic rule and more than half a century of Western and Japanese imperialistic encroachment. For many, the debates over political ideas simply had to yield some concrete course of action. While the Chinese Communists continue to hold the view that Mao Zedong Thought incorporates the Three People's Principles, it is in Taiwan, where the Three People's Principles, including the five-power constitution, are enshrined in the Constitution of the Republic of China, that there was a peaceful evolution to a multi-party democracy in the 1990s that continues to thrive today.

Notes

1. Sun Yat-sen, *San Min Chu I* (The Three Principles of the People), ed. L. T. Chen, trans. Frank W. Price (Shanghai: China Committee, Institute of Pacific Relations, 1927). The extracts cited are at p. 210, p. 297, and p. 299, respectively. All subsequent citations of the text are from this edition without additional endnotes.

2. Sun first articulated these principles in 1905. A few years before these lectures were delivered, Sun had in fact started to write a major book on these principles. Unfortunately, all the notes and manuscripts were destroyed in a fire on 16 June 1922 when Sun's house was raided by his adversaries (xi).

3. Marie-Claire Bergère, *Sun Yat-sen*, trans. Janet Lloyd (Stanford: Stanford University Press, 1998), 354.

4. Sun's view was typical of the political discourse of intellectuals during the early years of republican China – that one could be both nationalistic and pro-Western based on the conviction that Western thought on politics and society could be used to transform China into a modern nation-state. This marked a significant departure from the previous generation of reformers under the Qing dynasty, who held the view that all that was lacking to rebuild China's power was Western technology. For an insightful study of the intellectual milieu of early republican China, see Tse-tung Chow, *The May Fourth Movement: Intellectual Revolution in China* (Cambridge, MA: Harvard University Press, 1960).

5. Sun, 'Five-Power Constitution' (Speech delivered at the Kuomintang Special Agent's Office, July 1921), appendix to *Fundamentals of National Reconstruction* (Taipei: China Cultural Service, 1953), 19–20.

6. Sun, 'Five-Power Constitution', 32.

7. Sun, *Fundamentals of National Reconstruction*, 10. Page numbers found in the rest of the paragraph refer to this text.

CHAPTER TWENTY-ONE

Hobson on Democracy and the Humanized Economy

Colin Tyler

Pacific internationalism, not merely in the sense of disarmament and political co-operation, but expressed in a growing solidarity of economic institutions, is not merely in the long run but even in the short run essential to the survival and revival of democracy within each State. This judgment does not, however, signify that we must wait for an international solidarity, which now seems remoter than in 1918, before attempting seriously such national planning as is needed to replace the fumbling wastes and failures of a capitalism which can no longer be operated so as to secure its prime object, profit.

A revival of democracy upon a reformed basis will need a simultaneous activity upon the national and international fronts. The planning of economic life must be taken out of the hands of dictators and placed in the hands of the freely elected representatives of the people. This conscious struggle for economic democracy, with its equality of opportunity and standard of living, must be fought out within each nation. For only within the national area is the democratic sentiment strong enough and the concrete gains of victory clearly envisaged. And yet the separatist policy of 'setting your own house in order

> *first' is not adequate to the solution. For we have seen that this sentiment and policy are weapons utilised by capitalists and their politicians for the defence of their economic dominance. Militarism and protectionism are the direct products of this nationalism, and the newly developed arts of propaganda are even more skilfully applied to the production of 'emergencies' which shall keep 'the people' under discipline. While, therefore, the areas of this democratic struggle are primarily national, the need for the wider appeal to constructive internationalism is very urgent.*[1]

These words appeared in 1934, in the book *Democracy and a Changing Civilisation* written by the New Liberal radical thinker and journalist John Atkinson Hobson (1858–1940). The civilization to which Hobson referred here was not merely changing however, it was struggling for survival. Europe was still attempting to recover from the First World War (which had killed approximately 17 million people) and the world was only gradually recovering from the 1918–19 influenza pandemic (which had killed between 50 million and 100 million people, 3 percent and 5 percent of the world's population). The global economy was failing to recover from the stock market crash of 1929, while the international system was witnessing the gradual collapse of the League of Nations. Finally, Europe was witnessing the rise of extremist regimes in the form of the Union of Soviet Socialist Republics (USSR) and the Fascists in Italy, and was just beginning to see Nazi Germany asserting itself against Britain, France and the lesser Powers. 'Change' was too small a word to describe these realignments. Rather, the period was, in Richard Overy's words, 'a morbid age' during which, like much of the rest of the world, 'British society ... wrestled sometimes fatalistically, sometimes with undisguised relish, with this idea of crisis'.[2]

Hobson was at the epicentre of this public debate and he was cited as a pivotal influence by politicians and writers as diverse as the American educationalist and philosopher John Dewey, the British economist John Maynard Keynes, the Russian revolutionary Vladimir Ilyich Lenin and the South African social reformer Olive Schreiner. Even today, Hobson is quoted with admiration by the likes of Jeremy Corbyn, the leader of the UK Labour Party and others on the liberal left such as the economist and journalist Will Hutton. Hobson's most tangible influence was as one of the intellectual driving forces behind the New Liberal governments of Sir Henry Campbell-Bannerman and H. H. Asquith which, between 1905 and 1916, passed various forms of social legislation in the United Kingdom, including old age pensions and unemployment benefits.

Even though Hobson wrote a huge amount for the educated general reader over nearly fifty years, he returned to certain themes throughout his career, all of which impacted on the relationship between democratic institutions and virtues on the one hand and the corrosive effects of wealth and power on the other. Hobson's most important recurring themes are encapsulated within the quotation from his 1934 book *Democracy and a Changing Civilisation* given above. They included the interlinking of social life, democracy and economic processes, the destructive tendencies of the current, materialistic forms of corporate capitalism, the need for planned state intervention to prevent and correct the damage caused by these corporations, a great scepticism regarding elite rule – even when the elite is well-intentioned – and the associated need for interventionist states to be moderated by effective liberal democratic institutions. Other very significant themes included the internationalization and militarization of economic life and the need for the creation of effective mechanisms by which to manage that internationalism and militarism. Some themes were critical because they highlighted problems, while others were constructive because they sought to reform the world. All of these aspects are explored below. The discussion begins with the critical themes as these are most obvious in the quoted passage.

Throughout the passage, Hobson was careful to emphasize the interconnectedness of the domestic level of sovereign states and the international level of global institutions and economic trade: 'A revival of democracy within each State' was possible only through economic planning, international peace and a strong sense of economic solidarity between citizens and states. Only following a thorough revision of domestic and international structures could civilization be salvaged. The most significant enemies of this process fell into two main groups. In political terms, there were corrupt governments and the newly empowered 'dictators' in Germany, Italy and the USSR on one hand, and in economic terms, there were the capitalist corporations which had risen to international prominence by the mid-1930s. These two groups merged, however, as power was exercised across the world in accordance with the latter's division into competing imperial blocks. These blocks were key to the mechanisms by which the financial interests of capitalist elites took almost absolute precedence over the poor's need for food, shelter and warmth as well as the resources they required in order to flourish as social and creative beings. The elites produced and entrenched patterns of profound inequality both within and between countries. Elite dominance combined material and ideological power, for without true democratic control of the state, public policy based on orthodox capitalist thought would continue to serve the financial interests of the wealthy and powerful and to marginalize humanist conceptions of economics (examined below) which prioritized the health and flourishing of citizens and society. Corrupt politicians, dictators and corporations infected society. Only when the levers of power were controlled by 'freely elected representatives of the people' could individuals flourish, societies regain their health and democracy be made a reality.

Hobson saw democratization as particularly significant because extensive state intervention was required to counter the growing power of capitalist corporations. Yet, he held this growing power to be too complex and all-pervasive to be addressed effectively by any system of direct democracy. Against conservatives and individualists who retained their faith in limited government, Hobson argued that governing a modern complex society was an increasingly technical exercise. Consequently, governing a modern state could be done well only by large organizations that were dedicated exclusively to skilfully managing complex and rapidly changing data. Hence, direct democracy was no longer a realistic aspiration and, in light of the rise of extremist populist parties such as the fascists and Nazis, a very dangerous one. Nevertheless, specialized government had to be moderated through representative institutions, such as parliaments and elections. First, a centralized national government lacked the concrete knowledge and responsiveness required to implement policies in a nuanced and effective manner given local realities. Second, elites always tended to become dogmatic and unresponsive to changed circumstances and popular sentiment. For these and many other reasons, ordinary citizens, local administrations and non-state bodies had an obligation to monitor central government plans and actions, and to seek to change those plans where they judged the central government to be misguided. Hobson saw this as the most effective way to keep experts true to the public trust.

Achieving this critical citizenship required the democratic state to prioritize social justice and education. These policies should be based on awareness of the need to understand economics in human terms and of the organic nature of well-functioning societies. Certainly, while Hobson was a vocal opponent of the impersonal logic of capitalism, he did not claim that we should completely jettison monetary conceptions of 'wealth' and 'value'. Measuring wealth and value in monetary terms provided a relatively stable and universally-agreed basis for economic transactions. Nevertheless, as noted above, he insisted throughout his writings that the current capitalist obsession with understanding value in monetary terms tended to distort economic life in ways that favoured the vested interests of the wealthy at the expense of personal growth of the poor. An alternative was required. In one of his earliest books, a biography of the British art critic and social reformer John Ruskin, Hobson observed that:

> 'Goods' which are not 'wealth' in the [monetary,] 'mercantile' sense, the fruits of goodwill and self-sacrifice, friendship, family affection, neighbourly or civic feeling, intellectual efforts, not destined for the market, are, both in their 'production' and their 'consumption', in vital relation to industrial goods. The activities employed upon such 'goods' have the intimate reaction upon the distinctively 'industrial' activities, while the enjoyment of these higher moral and intellectual goods is a chief determinant of the nature of demand for mercantile wares.[3]

In consequence, monetary measures of value should be largely superseded by a more humanistic measure. For this humanistic alternative, Hobson turned to Ruskin's writings, and particularly Ruskin's famous claim that 'THERE IS NO WEALTH BUT LIFE. Life, including all its power of love, of joy, and of admiration.'[4] An object was valuable for Ruskin and Hobson to the extent that it helped the individual to live in the sense of being able to love and be joyful, and to admire and contribute to the beauty, virtue and truth found in the world. Given the marked differences between individuals' respective characters, circumstances, concrete needs and so on, there would be marked differences between the value that any particular object had for different people. All other things being equal, a guitar was useful to the extent that the owner could play it well, a book was valuable to the extent that its owner could read and understand it and so on. Nevertheless, some fundamental goods were always needed: food, warmth, shelter and so on. Similarly, other products such as heroin always had disvalue, because consuming them always made it more difficult for the user to feel love, joy and admiration and to enjoy other properly 'human' experiences. Consequently, society had an obligation to do what it could to ensure that individuals could always acquire the fundamental goods and avoid harmful products. Achieving the former required the maintenance of an economic system that allowed individuals to sustain themselves and their families through their own labour. Where self-provision proved effectively impossible the state had an obligation to maintain the poor via a welfare net. It was for this reason, and as noted above, that representative democratic states were required to protect individuals from harmful products via such mechanisms as education and legislation.

This shift of outlook had a transformative effect on the attitudes of democratic citizens and therefore on the governments that they elected. Specifically, reconceiving value in humanist terms tended to humanize the citizen's self-image and their attitude towards those around them. The citizen tended to reject the instrumental view of their social relationships and the institutions that structured those relationships. Hence, they tended to vote for political policies on humanistic grounds rather than narrowly materialistic ones. Consequently, democratic priorities tended to focus on social justice rather than profit-maximization.

Yet, this refocusing propagated a profound and, for many liberals, disturbing insight. The democratic citizen tended to recognize the necessary and intimate interconnectedness of their particular life and the life of the wider society. In other words, Hobson argued that by altering their conceptions of value citizens tended to arrive at the realization that they were part of a society which functioned in a way that was similar to the way in natural organisms functioned. As Hobson wrote in his 1909 essay 'The Re-statement of Democracy': 'Society is rightly regarded a moral rational organism in the sense that it has a common psychic life, character and purpose, which are not to be resolved into the life, character and purpose of its individual members.'⁵ He was emphatic that the society had value independently of the services that it provided to its individual citizens: 'This Spirit of the Hive or of the Herd is a true spirit of Society, a single unity of purpose in the community. . . . [T]he individual always is a means to the collective end of the maintenance of the good of the race.'⁶ (By 'race' here, Hobson did not mean some type of biological sub-species of human beings endorsed by far right political groups, but rather the population of a country or humanity as a whole.)

In claiming that the well-ordered community was an organic unity that possessed intrinsic value, Hobson was in clear danger of focusing on the collective good at the expense of the good of individuals. He responded in several ways. Firstly, he argued that merely holding an organic conception of society did not commit one to accepting uncritically the pronouncements of political, economic or military elites regarding what those interests required at any particular time. This point underpinned his rejection of dictatorships and his advocacy of representative democracy. Secondly, he was at great pains to point out that society was often regarded in popular and public discourse as having its own interests, and that great weight was placed on maintaining those interests even at the expense of the individual's interests. Here, he had in mind the need to preserve society during times of war (for example, through military conscription) and to use education and coercion to maintain the norms, conventions and institutions which were partly constitutive of the social organism. Thirdly, even though Hobson tended to ascribe greater weight to society than to the individual, he did not believe that society's interests automatically invalidated the individual's interests. In fact, he took great care to explore not merely the ways in which the interests of the social organism coincided with the well-being of its individual citizens, but also the ways in which serving the interests of the individual helped the social organism to flourish as well. He set out the key policy areas for a healthy society and individual in the following terms:

> Health, education, security, these three departments of the 'public good', adequately administered by society, would, by their reaction upon the standard of life in all classes of the community, so change the relative valuation of wealth, and so operate through changed demands upon industry, as to produce an incalculably great increase in subjective or real [i.e. humanized] wealth. . . . For health, education, and security will individualise the character, develop a varied personality in each, and give free play to all the faculties to seek the activities and enjoyments which belong to them. This individuation and variety of needs will create a corresponding character in the productive work required for their satisfaction.⁷

By attending to the 'health, education, [and] security' of the individual citizens, then, the whole society would be gradually transformed, the public culture would be oriented towards 'real' values and away from narrowly-monetized measures of wealth, new and varied types of product would be demanded and supplied, and more humane modes of production would flourish. One of Hobson's key objectives was to remove the inequalities of status and income that scarred modern societies and hindered the flourishing of citizens. In these and many other ways, the social organism would diversify and flourish with a new life that also accorded with citizens' real needs.

Control by democratically-elected representatives and humanist economics was crucial at the international level as well, as elite dominance and degeneration obtained there just as they did at the domestic level. This was especially true given the increasing dominance of international capitalist corporations. Hobson explored this problem at great length throughout his long career, and not least in his most famous work, his 1902 book *Imperialism: A Study*, the work which Lenin admired so greatly. For Hobson, contemporary capitalism strongly tended towards imperialism for four key reasons.[8] First, corporations needed new secure foreign markets because their domestic markets had reached a saturation point, or in other words domestic demand was insufficient to absorb domestic supply. Second, secure sources of raw materials and cheap productive capacity were required. Third, significant sections of wealthy countries sought to satisfy their jingoistic urges by conquering other nations. Fourth, imperial conflicts created a greater economic demand for domestically-produced military ordinance. In short, Hobson argued that imperialism grew out of 'capitalist-military nationalism'.[9]

Despite Hobson's profoundly critical analysis of contemporary corporate global capitalism, he did not believe that transnational trade should be brought to an end. Indeed, he was an ardent advocate of international free trade where it was conducted in a socially-beneficial, non-exploitative manner. His alternative to the current dangerous and exploitative international trade system was the creation of an economic League of Nations. This organization would be formed through a treaty signed by every state in the world, with each state being reformed internally to become a representative democracy. The League would be given the responsibility of maintaining a truly free trade system that nevertheless treated even the weakest states with respect and without exploitation. In this way, democracy might be made a reality across the world. Hence, one of Hobson's main concerns was to eradicate the domination of poor countries by the rich. In this way, a new economic League of Nations would bring profound benefits to societies and their citizens. As he wrote in 1931: 'The conscious ordering of world industry and commerce as the organic whole it is, can alone serve to give peace, prosperity, and progress to the economic life of the several parts of that organic whole. The simple fact that we are all members one of another underlies all the complexities of trade relations.'[10]

From the perspective of democratic theory and practice, the passage from Hobson's *Democracy and a Changing Civilisation* quoted at the beginning of this chapter is remarkable in many ways. It was at once prescient in the central role that it ascribes to corporate power in the corruption of political power and the process of capitalist development, and profoundly insightful in its critique of monetary measures of wealth and particularly its search for a humanized alternative. Certainly, many critics have expressed great concern about economic planning and Hobson's claim that society was best understood using an organic metaphor. Yet, ultimately the passage shows Hobson to have offered reasons for hope. Not least are the possibilities that he saw for the reform of capitalism and for the power of international institutions to control national and global economic development, as well as his optimism regarding the power of representative governments to give some reality to democratic ideals.

Notes

1. John Atkinson Hobson, *Democracy and a Changing Civilisation* (London: John Lane The Bodley Head, 1934), 133–4.
2. Richard Overy, *The Morbid Age: Britain and the Crisis of Civilisation, 1919–1939* (London: Penguin, 2010), xiii.
3. John A. Hobson, *John Ruskin: Social Reformer* (London: James Nisbet, 1898), 75.
4. John Ruskin, 'Unto this Last', in his *Unto this Last, The Political Economy or Art, Essays on Political Economy* (London: Dent, 1968), 168.
5. John Atkinson Hobson, 'The Re-statement of Democracy', in his *The Crisis of Democracy: New issues of democracy* (London: P. S. King, 1909), 73.
6. Hobson, 'Re-statement', 74.
7. John A. Hobson, *The Industrial System: An Inquiry into Earned and Unearned Income*, new and revised edition (London: P. S. King, 1910), 332.
8. John A. Hobson, 'Introduction to the 1938 edition', in his *Imperialism: A Study* (London: George Allen and Unwin, 1938 [1902]), ix–x.
9. Hobson, 'Introduction to the 1938 edition', xxi.
10. John A. Hobson, *Poverty in Plenty* (London: George Allen and Unwin, 1931), 81.

CHAPTER TWENTY-TWO

A New Reading on Authority and Guardianship (*wilayah*): Ayatollah Muhammad Mahdi Shamsuddin

Hamid Mavani

Islam categorically rejects dictatorship because it always leads to oppression, persecution, and uprising.[1]
From the Islamic point of view, only the divine (most exalted), who has no partner or associate in His Lordship, Authority, and Guardianship (wilayah), has the right to govern and enjoy absolute rule. In essence, no human being has any right to rule over others. The rule and control of God is the only type of guardianship and authority that complies with human reason and intellect.
Every mandate of authority and governance (hakimiyyah) *for a human being requires a definitive proof. In its absence, therefore, no one has authority over another person, any other existent in the universe, or over nature, including over one's own life and property. That these set limits cannot be transgressed is a fundamental principle under the subject of authority, as well as a matter that is well-established in jurisprudence and theology . . .*

> [I]nvoking democracy while the infallible Imam is among us would be religiously unlawful, but . . . this is not the case during his Occultation. My jurisprudential opinion is based on the foundation of the 'wilayah of the people resides with themselves' (wilayat al-ummah 'ala nafsi-ha).[2]
>
> During the Occultation, any government that is formed with the people's free choice and consent is religiously lawful. As such, one must obey it within the confines of the laws enacted with the people's consent . . . in fact, if the people intentionally and freely form a government during the Occultation, then it is not a usurped state. Not only would there be no objection to assisting and co-operating with it, but it would be mandatory to do so if the general social welfare were at stake . . .[3]
>
> For such a government (consisting of Muslims and non-Muslims), professing Islam should have no impact upon a citizen's rank, and one's religion [or lack thereof] should not lead to any differences in terms of rights or preference. The same applies to one's socio-economic status . . . From the perspective of dignity and personhood, in the sight of the law every person in an Islamic society is equal.[4]

Muslims subscribe to divine sovereignty and agree that only God, the True and Absolute Sovereign, has the authority and exclusive prerogative to legislate and determine the norms for the Muslim community. Muhammad, in his capacity as God's designated Messenger, became His intermediary via revelation and, as such, was endowed with comprehensive authority and guardianship (*wilayah*) over the community. Thus the latter was duty-bound to obey and exhibit unquestioning loyalty and devotion (*walayah*) to him: 'O believers, obey God, and obey the Messenger and those in authority (*ulu al-amr*)' (Q. 4:59).

There is no dissent among Muslims that God empowered the Prophet with some of His *wilayah*. For the Twelver Shi'is, a restricted form of this *wilayah* was then transmitted to the twelve infallible Imams in succession. The Imam's legitimacy derives from the explicit designation of the Prophet or the preceding Imam, as opposed to public acknowledgment. As such, so long as the Imam was present and accessible, the Shi'is had to submit to him as the ultimate authority on all matters. However, the Twelfth Imam's prolonged Occultation[5] raised the question: Upon whom should his authority devolve: The qualified jurist (*wilayat al-faqih*), the attentive and discerning general community itself (*wilayat al-ummah 'ala nafsi-ha*), or some other configuration?

In modern Shi'a political thought, two contrasting views of political authority can be found. For example, according to Ayatollah Mohammad Mojtahed Shabestari, the Qur'an prescribes no particular form of government as normative because it is more concerned about the final outcome – establishing a just and egalitarian society – than with how this goal is attained. Therefore, this matter is left up to the people and may assume different forms according to time and place: 'If we study the Qur'an carefully, we see that the fundamental criterion it lays down for government is not a particular form or type – which it does not even present as a religious concern – but justice.'[6]

In contrast, during his exile in Najaf, Iraq, in 1970 Ayatollah Khomeini promulgated his version of the guardianship of the jurist (*wilayat al-faqih*), which he incorporated as part of the Iranian Constitution after the 1979 Islamic Revolution. He argued that the jurist, by virtue of being the Imam's indirect deputy, has both the mandate and the responsibility to interpret Islamic rulings not only on matters of devotion and personal affairs, but also in the social realm, and to manage the state's affairs on the Imam's behalf. Toward the end of his life, he stretched the scope of this authority to its farthest limit by proclaiming, in January 1988, that this individual can bypass the Shari'a if (in his opinion) it conflicts with society's general welfare and best interests.

His concept of the jurist's full-fledged authority and mandate as being equivalent in scope to that of the infallible Imams was a novel and radically different reading of the classical Shi'i doctrine of Imamate, and one that had and still has a very limited following among senior and eminent jurists. Ayatollah Muhammad Mahdi Shamsuddin (1936–2001) of Lebanon,[7] who criticized it, offered another paradigm that both accommodates religious diversity and pluralism and promotes a civil and democratic culture with a degree of separation of church and state, as we observe in the extract of his work that opens this chapter.

Shamsuddin was born in Najaf, Iraq, into a family steeped in religiosity and scholarship that could trace its descent back to eminent Shi'i jurists residing in Jabal 'Amil (a Shi'i district in southern Lebanon). His father, Shaykh 'Abd al-Karim, was a famous cleric and teacher of religious studies who decided to move back to Lebanon when his son was 14 years old. When the teenager was asked what he wanted to do, he opted to continue his studies in Najaf despite the severe economic hardship that was the common lot of all religious students at the time. This experience left an indelible imprint upon his psyche and instilled within him a genuine empathy for the underprivileged and the dispossessed. He enrolled in the advanced and specialized stage of his studies under two pre-eminent jurists, Ayatollahs Muhsin al-Hakim and Abu al-Qasim al-Khu'i, and attained the rank of jurist with a license to issue legal opinions. He was also very familiar with the writings of Sunni scholars such as Jamal al-Din al-Afghani (d. 1897), Muhammad 'Abduh (d. 1905) and Taha Husayn (d. 1973), who greatly influenced his conception of Islam as a living religion that encompassed all aspects of individual and social life.

The July 1958 revolution in Iraq caused Shamsuddin to embark upon a career of social and political activism. He issued proclamations and wrote anti-British articles in the intellectual periodical *Al-Adwa' al-Islamiyya*. In 1969 he and Musa al-Sadr moved to Lebanon, where they established the Supreme Islamic Shi'i Council (SISC) of Lebanon. In 1975 Shamsuddin was elected its vice-chairman, a post that he retained until 1978, when he assumed its helm upon Musa al-Sadr's disappearance during a visit to Libya. An exponent and in many ways a pioneer of Muslim-Christian dialogue, he has a number of works to his credit on this subject and also advocated Sunni-Shi'a rapprochement.

Shamsuddin speculated early on that Islam, being a comprehensive religion, requires the apparatus of an Islamic state to implement its teachings. He surmised that Islam must have legislated both a political system and a perfect social system. In a later work he revised his position by stating that the revelatory sources contain no clear-cut evidence to sustain this viewpoint and that, as a matter of fact, the issue of government requires rational deliberation and does not belong to any jurisprudential category that demands unquestioned obedience.[8] The outcome of this deliberation was the concept that the mandate to govern resides with the community itself. Given that establishing a government is a necessity and that there is no categorical proof in favour of one group having a monopoly on governance, he favoured popular sovereignty. This is in stark opposition to Khomeini's proposed model, in which the public plays no major rule and all authority is vested in the jurist. Given the special context of Lebanon, namely, multiple faiths and sectarianism, Shamsuddin espoused a notion of 'civil government' (*al-dawlat al-madaniyyah*) with an explicit public role for religion in terms of providing ethical foundations for individual conduct. Matters dealing with personal status laws (e.g. marriage, divorce and inheritance) and acts of worship remained under the purview of the jurists for the latter requires expertise and also because he was apprehensive of the erosion of religion.

Shamsuddin contends that during the Imam's prolonged Occultation, as well as under normal circumstances and in the absence of any specific justification or explicit evidence, no person has any *wilayah* or special prerogative over another person. Instead, the nation's citizens (*ummah*) become the locus of political authority, which it exercises through elective and consultative bodies in which jurisprudential knowledge is not a requirement for serving as the nation's leader.[9] It therefore follows that jurists cannot claim to be privileged or possess a special mandate to manage the public's affairs for the 'rule and control of God is the only type of guardianship and authority that complies with human reason and intellect', as we see in the opening extract for this chapter.

Unanimously accepted textual evidence does endow the Prophet and the Imams with *wilayah* over the people; however, there is no proof to substantiate such a *wilayah* for the jurist. As such, the principle of 'no person has *wilayah* over another' must be considered the norm, which necessitates that the community's *wilayah* inheres within itself, a reality that favours public sovereignty. Shamsuddin buttresses his conclusion with Qur'anic verses on *shura*, among them: 'Consult (O Muhammad) with them about matters, then when you have decided on a course of action, put your trust in God; God loves those who put their trust in Him' (Q. 3:159), arguing that the *shura* commanded is in matters of social life, such as forming a government.[10]

'The holders of authority' (*wulat al-amr*) are the people themselves. They may opt to delegate a task to certain individuals, including jurists, hold them to account and, at some future date, withdraw it.[11] In other words, resolving social issues and establishing a government is the entire community's collective responsibility. Shamsuddin quickly adds that this scope is limited to matters for which no explicit religious rulings exist and that its results should not violate any established religious rulings.[12]

He praises certain characteristics of democracy's procedural and substantive aspects, such as the smooth, secure and peaceful transfer of power; benefiting from the experience and expertise of a vast array of individuals; being amenable to accepting constructive criticism; and being able to rectify errors and deficiencies through a self-corrective process.[13] However, he subscribes to these democratic principles only during the Imam's Occultation, for upon that individual's return the public is duty-bound to obey him without question.[14] In addition, he proclaims that every human being, regardless of religion, race, gender and culture, is entitled to equal and inalienable rights and, under normal circumstances, can neither be deprived of them nor have them reduced or limited by another person or a government. This is partly based on the Qur'anic verse that endows human dignity to all members of humanity without any discrimination: 'We have honoured the children of Adam' (17:70).

Shamsuddin goes to great lengths to underline the necessity of upholding women's rights on the basis of Qur'anic verses, hadith reports, rational proofs and the fundamental principle that no one has any *wilayah* over another person. Women are entitled not only to full political and social rights, but also to hold political offices. Hadith reports that bar their participation in the public domain are either deficient because of a weak chain of transmission, or are time- and context-bound to that particular era and society.

He does add, however, that their most important responsibilities are to manage the house, nurture the children and enhance the marital bond. Yet their role is most certainly not limited to these undertakings, for in actuality it stretches into the social and political fields, as the Qur'an attests: 'The believers, both men and women, support (*awliya'*) each other;

they order what is right and forbid what is wrong' (Q. 9:71). The clear disabilities placed upon women as regards testifying in court, inheritance, *diyah* (compensation for injury or death) and divorce are bound by certain time- and context-bound social structures that, as such, do not dilute their inherent nobility or ability to occupy political office.[15]

Shamsuddin is equally adamant in protecting the rights of non-Muslims and asserting their equality with Muslims in the political and social spheres. As Islam has enshrined freedom of belief and conviction, it appreciates the diversity of traditions, languages and cultures. By not privileging one over another, it promotes a culture of mutual recognition, appreciation (*taʿarafu*),[16] and rivalry to perform good deeds.[17] He opines that this principle is a fixed and timeless ruling derived from the Islamic corpus, meaning that it cannot be trampled upon or negated without a valid reason for doing so. The equality of all citizens also means that non-Muslims are entitled to compete for and occupy political offices.

Contrary to the claim of many Muslims, Shamsuddin argues that Islam does not provide a template for an ideal state or endorse and prescribe any particular form of government; rather, its general guidelines promote justice, equity and fairness and are designed to help promote good and prevent evil at both the individual and the social levels: 'We sent Our messengers with clear signs, the Scripture and the Balance, so that people could uphold justice' (Q. 57:25). In other words, the forms of governments that arose after the Prophet's death are historically contingent and relative and, as such, are neither universally applicable nor normative. This is also true of the notion that separating religion from the state is inconceivable under Islam. As such, Muslims are not required to replicate the state model supposedly espoused by the Prophet.

In the first edition (1955) of his major work on the system of governance and administration in Islam, Shamsuddin explicitly rejected any compatibility between Islam and democracy on the grounds that Islam, being a divine religion, should have a religious basis of assigning authority. However, after Khomeini implemented his concept of *wilayat al-faqih*, one obseves a major shift in Shamsuddin's viewpoint on juridical authority. In the second edition (1990) of this work he argued that his rejection of democracy only applies to the period when the infallible Imam is present; however, it did not provide a precise definition of 'democracy'. In the 1993 edition of the same work, Shamsuddin asserted that democracy, with its separation of powers, is the only feasible and effective option for dealing with issues and challenges facing Muslim communities.

This evolution of his thought was conjoined with a change of perspective on the role of women and non-Muslims in politics: Women are competent enough to be judges and to assume the highest political offices. In 2000, for the first time he made a case in favour of non-Muslims competing for and holding political offices. While being the most 'progressive' on the latter issue, there are many commonalities between his views and those of other jurists, such as Ayatollahs Husayn Ali Montazeri (d. 2009), Muhammad Baqir al-Sadr (d. 1980), Mohsen Kadivar, Mohaghegh Damad and Mojtahed Shabestari. His innovative and creative proposal appears promising for countries with large Shi'i and Sunni populations, such as Iraq, especially given the dismal failure of the Iranian experience after implementing Khomeini's version of the all-comprehensive authority of the jurist: *wilayat al-faqih*.

Notes

1 Muhammad Mahdi Shamsuddin, *Fi al-ijtima' al-siyasi al-Islami*, 2nd edn (Beirut: al-Mu'assasat al-dawliyyah li al-dirasat wa al-nashr, 1999), 98. My translation.

2 Shamsuddin, *Fi al-ijtima' al-siyasi al-Islami*, 234–5.

3 Muhammad Mahdi Shams al-Din, *Rudud samahat Ayatollah al-Imam al-shaykh Muhammad Mahdi Shamsuddin 'ala as'ilah al-ustadh Fu'ad Ibrahim* (n.p., 1997), 11–12.

4 Muhammad Mahdi Shamsuddin, *Nizam al-hukm wa al-idarah fi al-Islam*, 7th edn (Beirut: al-Mu'assasat al-dawliyyah li al-dirasat wa al-nashr, 2000), 391–2.

5 The Twelver Shi'is believe that the Prophet explicitly appointed his cousin and son-in-law Ali as his rightful successor on the basis of a divine decree. Ali inherited the Prophet's charisma and knowledge, and this was transmitted to the eleven succeeding Imams in the lineage of Ali and his wife Fatima, the Prophet's daughter. As each Imam's appointment is divinely inspired, popular legitimation is inconsequential. They are all considered infallible and the ultimate authority in expounding the law, doctrine and practices in both the temporal and religious domains. The Shi'is accepted the view that the Twelfth Imam was born in 869 and assumed his position, aged five or six, upon his father's death in 874. This initiated the period of Minor Occultation (874–941), during which he was accessible to his followers through one of his agents. In 941 his fourth and last agent declared that the Imam had entered the Major Occultation and would not be accessible until his return toward the end of time with Jesus Christ in order to inaugurate peace and justice on Earth.

6 Muhammad Mojtahed Shabestari, 'Religion, Reason, and the New Theology', in *Shi'ite Heritage: Essays on Classical and Modern Traditions*, ed. Lynda Clarke (New York: Global Publications, 2001), 253.

7 Farah Musa, *Muhammad Mahdi Shamsuddin bayna wajh al-Islam wa jalid al-madhahib* (Beirut: Dar al-hadi, 1993).

8 Shamsuddin, *Fi al-Ijtima'*, 16.

9 Mohsen Kadivar, *Nazariyye-ha-ye dowlat dar feqh-e Shi'eh* (Tehran: Ney Publishing House, 1993), 172.

10 Shamsuddin, *Fi al-Ijtima'*, 98 and 132, fn. 4.
11 Ibid., 92–7.
12 Muhammad Mahdi Shamsuddinin, *Ahliyyat al-mar'ah li tawalli al-sultah* (Beirut: al-Mu'assasat al-dawliyyah li al-dirasat wa al-nashr, 1996), 127.
13 Shamsuddin, *Nizam al-hukm*, 234. Shaykh Yusuf al-Qaradawi, a popular contemporary Sunni scholar, has concluded that 'Islam sanctions and even mandates democracy' because it is a means to accomplish one of the Shari'a's objectives: establishing just governance based on *shura*. See Noah Feldman, 'Shari'a and Islamic Democracy in the Age of Al-Jazeera', in *Shari'a: Islamic Law in the Contemporary Context*, ed. Abbas Amanat and Frank Griffel (Stanford: Stanford University Press, 2007), 110.
14 Shamsuddin, *Nizam al-hukm*, 234–5.
15 Shamsuddin, *Ahliyyat al-mar'ah*, 31–6.
16 Qur'an 49:13.
17 Ibid., 5:48.

Conclusion

Xavier Márquez

Democracy has always been a dangerous idea. The basic themes of democratic thought – equality, freedom and consent – have often been in conflict with existing hierarchies of power and prestige. Moreover, democratic values have also been thought to conflict with other reasonable ideals, like competence, effectiveness and leadership. Democracy cannot but be controversial. Nevertheless, democracy is also alluring. Even thinkers who did not approve of democracy could often see the attractiveness of a society based on democratic values.

The ambivalence of democracy is reflected in the set of texts discussed in this collection. The writers of these texts did not always have a high regard for democracy as a political system; but all of them made use of, and appreciated, many democratic themes, most prominently of course equality and freedom, even if sometimes ambiguously and reluctantly. And from Herodotus and Protagoras at the very beginnings of Western political thought to Gandhi, Sun Yat-sen and Shamsuddin in a 'post-Western' context, we also see how these democratic themes have had a global impact.

Four distinct 'democratic moments' are identifiable in these chapters. First, there is the original 'ancient' moment dominated by the interpretation of genuine experiences of democratic rule or popular participation in government in Greco-Roman antiquity. After these experiences recede in time with the end of the Roman Republic, we find a 'post-democratic' moment, when reflection on democracy was disconnected from any genuine political experience but central themes of democratic thought could still develop. With the re-emergence of experiences of self-government in the fifteenth century a 'republican' moment begins that transforms democratic thought extensively. Democracy eventually becomes *representative* democracy, but the problems with representation in diverse contexts give rise to a 'post-representative' and 'post-Western' democratic moment. Let us review the key themes of each of these moments by way of conclusion.

An engagement with the Greek (and eventually Roman) legacy of democratic self-rule is common to all the Ancient political thinkers included here. The interpretation of that legacy was at best ambiguous; it is striking that one of the only full-throated defences of democracy we have from that period was put into the mouth of Protagoras by Plato, and clearly meant to be refuted, even if we today find it compelling in its praise of the capacity for cooperation of ordinary people. But in any case democracy was a live political possibility, tied to a particular set of institutions, which could be analysed in concrete terms. In this analysis, most of the Ancient thinkers discussed in this collection shared a concern with distinguishing what was true and useful in democracy from what was disorderly and dangerous. They persistently attempted to *tame* the wildness of democracy.

In Herodotus, democracy was tamed in part by separating its core values of equality from their institutional embodiment in Athenian institutions. Democracy in the institutional sense was a contingent accident; but valuable forms of equality could be useful in very different contexts. In later thinkers, democracy was tamed by its incorporation into the theory of the mixed constitution. From Greek to Roman times this meant arguing that equality and popular participation had value only in the context of a set of institutions where elite social forces and other principles of rule were able to properly constrain democracy. Virtue, in particular, was often opposed to democracy: the point was to figure out which virtues could constrain the destructive features of democracy, rather than which virtues supported it.

After the end of the Roman republic, it is possible to argue that this concern with the disorderliness and destructiveness of democracy went into abeyance. In most of the world no large-scale institution of rule incorporated democratic principles in any important way; even the use of the word democracy atrophied. We can thus speak of a post-democratic moment during which democracy remained as an echo of an experience that no longer existed, ill-understood but still in some ways compelling. When Alfarabi talked about 'democracy', re-working Plato's discussion of the concept in the *Republic*, he had no clear example in mind of a form of government that could be called democratic. But Plato's description of democratic values could still resonate with his experience of Baghdad to weave a striking picture of a diverse and in some ways 'equal' society. Democracy here served less as a live possibility for political order than as a placeholder for a way of understanding society that emphasized equality, individual freedom and sometimes consent or accountability.

The loss of a genuine experience of democratic self-government at this time is also manifested in the lack of a clear connection between the *term* democracy and the discussion of values and ideas that have come to be associated with democracy. As we see in the case of Marsilius of Padua, ideas that are now very close to the core of what we mean by 'democracy', such as ideas about the consent of the people and their representation in assemblies, could be explored without being associated with the ancient terminology. This is not because that terminology was necessarily unknown; Marsilius knew his Aristotle. But the ancient language was associated with an experience that had no real parallel in the medieval era.

With the revival of *republican* life in Europe a new, broadly democratic, political experience could again become an object of theoretical reflection. Ancient problems about the role of the people in government, about the virtues they should or should not have, and about the ways in which law could or could not constrain their participation, again emerged as serious problems worthy of theoretical reflection; new *data* could be brought to bear on them. As we see in this book, Machiavelli, Harrington and Spinoza developed the 'democratic' aspects of their thought against the background of genuinely new experiences of republican self-rule – even when these experiences had just failed. In any case, their blending of 'republican' themes about civic virtue, consent and the rule of law with democratic themes of popular participation and self-rule was to prove enduring.

Democratic thought at this time was reborn as a kind of anti-aristocratic and anti-monarchical republicanism. What the 'democratic' thinkers in this collection had in common at this time was less a willingness to use the *word* democracy (though some, like Spinoza or Paine, did not shy away from it) or to refer to familiar democratic institutions of popular participation, but a groping towards a notion of accountable government respectful of individual liberty, and a new evaluation of the capacities of the people for the preservation of both liberty and accountability. This is evident even in Radishchev's thought, in the unfertile soil of absolutist Russia. Radishchev was no radical democrat – and unlike Spinoza or Harrington, had few useful models of republican liberty to refer to in Russia – but he too, was hoping for a way to hold governments accountable and protect certain individual rights against the depredations of the aristocracy.

Two other themes also emerge much more clearly than ever before in this new democratic moment: inclusion and representation. Ancient democrats had never been particularly inclusive in their definition of the people. Much ancient thought, even when not altogether hostile to democracy, carefully circumscribed who was *qualified* to participate in rule, and modern 'democrats' at first followed suit. Perhaps this was because of the close connection, in Greek and Roman times, between citizenship and military activity. But in any case the idea of the armed citizenry, so important for ancient democracies, could still prove important in the modern 'republican' moment. As the chapter on Bolívar notes, armies could be models for the people as a whole; and it is worth noting that manhood suffrage only became a reality in most of Europe after the total mobilization of the First World War.

But to a much greater degree than ever before, democratic texts show a definite tendency towards *expanding* the people. Spinoza seemed to argue for a much more extensive degree of inclusion than any ancient democrat. Bolívar thought the army merely *represented* the people, for as long as they were unable to select its own representatives wisely; he did not *define* the people in narrow terms. And in the nineteenth century, we find arguments for the formal inclusion of women that would have been unthinkable to ancient democrats. These arguments, as the chapter on Taylor Mill shows, appealed to a variety of grounds: the justice of inclusion, the corrosive effects of exclusion on civic virtue and the common good. But they generally reflected a much more inclusive tendency in the modern conception of democracy. The democratic 'social state' described by Tocqueville increasingly rendered formal distinctions in political rights untenable, especially as the concept of democracy became tied to the notion of representation.

The importance of representation is exemplified in this book in the thought of Sieyès, but was obviously crucial for most of the eighteenth and nineteenth century discussions of democracy, including the works of the American founders. It is hard to overemphasize how important this idea has come to be for the modern understanding of democracy as a property of large-scale states (to the point that the phrase 'representative democracy' can seem like a pleonasm). Democracy in modern states is a mediated, rather than an immediate, relationship to political power. And representation brings a whole new set of questions to the fore, without parallel in the ancient discussions of democracy.

Representation could be seen either as a problem or a solution to various pathologies of democratic societies. Rousseau famously attacked representation as a mask for oppression; but Sieyès, in opposition to the radicals of the French revolution (themselves often inspired by Rousseau), found in representation the solution to the problems the division of labour caused for securing the consent of the people to law. And Tocqueville, who was especially concerned with the self-undermining tendencies of democratic societies, saw in the indirectness of representative institutions a mechanism for refining public opinion and providing genuine leadership. Representative institutions suggested ways for democracy to overcome its own tendencies towards social levelling and the 'tyranny of the majority'.

But as representative institutions spread throughout the world eventually the focus shifted to their imperfections. These are a common theme in later thinkers in this volume. Both Marxists like Lenin or Luxemburg as well as liberals like Weber or Hobson noted the many ways in which representative institutions could be captured by class interests. Their responses, of course, were different; Marxist thought insisted on recovering more robust and direct forms of popular participation in politics, whether at the workplace or in the street, Weber insisted on the need for creating democratic institutions capable of producing genuine leaders, and Hobson put his faith in state intervention in the economy and international cooperation. Nevertheless, by focusing on the inadequacies of democratic representation while taking for granted the need for inclusion, these thinkers stand at the beginning of the current 'post-representative' democratic moment.

The discussion of democratic themes outside the West in the twentieth century also moved beyond representation, inflected by the particular experiences of writers with colonial and post-colonial society. Gandhi foregrounded dissent in his conception of democracy in part because of his understanding of the anti-colonial struggle; Sun Yat-sen depicted democracy as integral to China's construction of a strong state that could resist imperialist depredations, and stressed the need to combine people's power with expertise in government, drawing on the long Chinese tradition of meritocratic selection of administrators; Shamsuddin, like other Muslim thinkers, foregrounded the relationship between religious and civil authority (a relationship that is today still being worked out in places like Iran). Key themes of democratic thought remain, of course; Gandhi stresses the intrinsic equality of all, Sun Yat-sen the sovereignty of the people and Shamsuddin the lack of natural political authority in the absence of the Iman. But democracy in their hands is reinterpreted in ways that transcend a simple focus on representation.

In sum, democratic texts suggest that particular political *experiences* – remembered historical experiences, sometimes – were crucially important for the development, articulation and appropriation of democratic ideas. Without particular historical referents, the democratic idea becomes a mere echo; yet even this echo had power in the long centuries where democratic rule was not a live possibility. The diverse pieces collected in this book thus attest to the enduring appeal of equality, self-rule and individual freedom.

SUGGESTIONS FOR FURTHER READING

General Works on the History of Democracy

John Dunn, *Democracy: A History* (New York: Atlantic Monthly Press, 2005.
John Keane, *The Life and Death of Democracy* (New York: W.W. Norton & Co., 2009).
John Markoff, 'Where and When Was Democracy Invented?', *Comparative Studies in Society and History* 41, no. 4 (1999): 660–90.

Herodotus

E. Bakker, I. de Jong, and H. van Wees, *Brill's Companion to Herodotus* (Leiden: Brill, 2002).
C. Dewald and J. Marincola, *The Cambridge Companion to Herodotus* (Cambridge: Cambridge University Press, 2006).
J. Gould, *Herodotus* (London: Duckworth, 1989).
J. Romm, *Herodotus* (New Haven: Yale University Press, 1998).

Protagoras

N. Denyer, *Plato: Protagoras* (Cambridge: Cambridge Greek and Latin Classics, 2008).
G. B. Kerferd, *The Sophistic Movement* (Cambridge: Cambridge University Press, 1981).
G. S. Kirk, J. E. Raven, and M. Schofield, *The Pre-Socratic Philosophers* (Cambridge: Cambridge University Press, 1983).
C. C. W. Taylor, *Plato: Protagoras* (Oxford: Oxford University Press, 1996a).
C. C. W. Taylor, *Protagoras* (Oxford: Oxford World's Classics, 1996b).

Aristotle

J. Frank, *A Democracy of Distinction: Aristotle and the Work of Politics* (Chicago: University of Chicago Press, 2005).
G. M. Mara, 'The Culture of Democracy: Aristotle's *Athēnaiōn Politeia* as Political Theory', in *Aristotle and Modern Politics: The Persistence of Political Philosophy*, ed. Aristide Tessitore (Notre Dame: University of Notre Dame Press, 2002).

M. P. Nichols, *Citizens and Statesmen: A Study of Aristotle's Politics* (Lanham: Rowman and Littlefield, 1992).
S. G. Salkever, *Finding the Mean: Theory and Practice in Aristotelian Political Philosophy* (Princeton: Princeton University Press, 1990).

Cicero

J. W. Atkins, *Cicero on Politics and the Limits of Practical Reason: The Republic and the Laws* (Cambridge: Cambridge University Press, 2013).
B. Straumann, *Cicero and Constitutionalism: Roman Political Thought from the Fall of the Republic to the Age of Revolution* (Oxford: Oxford University Press, 2016).
J. Zarecki, *Cicero's Ideal Statesman in Theory and Practice* (London: Bloomsbury, 2014).
J. E. G. Zetzel, *Cicero: De Re Publica, Selections* (Cambridge: Cambridge University Press, 1995).
J. E. G. Zetzel, *Cicero: On the Commonwealth and On the Laws* (Cambridge: Cambridge University Press, 1999).

Alfarabi

Muhammad Ali Khalidi, 'Al-Fārābī on the Democratic City', *British Journal for the History of Philosophy* 11, no. 3 (2003): 379–94.
Muhsin Mahdi, *Alfarabi and the Foundation of Islamic Political Philosophy* (Chicago: University of Chicago Press, 2001).
Avraham Melamed, 'The Attitude Toward Democracy in Medieval Jewish Philosophy', *Jewish Political Studies Review* 5, no. 1/2 (Spring 1993): 33–56.
Fauzi M. Najjar, 'Democracy in Islamic Political Philosophy', *Studia Islamica* 51 (1980): 107–22.
Alexander Orwin, 'Democracy Under the Caliphs: Alfarabi's Unusual Understanding of Popular Rule', *Review of Politics* 77, (2005): 171–90.

Marsilius of Padua and Medieval Political Thought

Marsilius of Padua, *The Defender of the Peace*, ed. and trans. Annabel Brett (Cambridge: Cambridge University Press, 2005).
Cary J. Nederman, *Community and Consent: The Secular Political Theory of Marsiglio of Padua's Defensor Pacis* (Lanham: Rowman & Littlefield, 1995).

Cary J. Nederman, *Lineages of European Political Thought: Explorations along the Medieval/Modern Divide from John of Salisbury to Hegel* (Washington, DC: Catholic University of America Press, 2009).
Francis Oakley, *The Watershed of Modern Politics: Law, Virtue, Kingship, and Consent (1300–1650)* (New Haven: Yale University Press, 2015).

Machiavelli

Niccolo Machiavelli, *Discourses on Livy*, Harvey C. Mansfield and Nathan Tarcov (trans.) (Chicago: University of Chicago Press, 1996).
Niccolo Machiavelli, *The Prince*, Harvey C. Mansfield (trans.) (Chicago: University of Chicago Press, 1998).
John P. McCormick, *Machiavellian Democracy* (New York: Cambridge University Press, 2011).
Catherine H. Zuckert, *Machiavelli's Politics* (Chicago: University of Chicago Press, 2017).

Harrington

J. C. Davis, '"*de the Fabula narratur*": The Narrative Constitutionalism of James Harrington's *Oceana*', in *The Nature of the English Revolution Revisited*, ed. Stephen Taylor and Grant Tapsell (Woodbridge: The Boydell Press, 2013), 151–73.
J. G. A. Pocock (ed.), *Harrington: The Commonwealth of Oceana and a System of Politics* (Cambridge: Cambridge University of Press, 1992).
Jonathan Scott, 'James Harrington's Prescription for Healing and Settling', in *The Experience of Revolution in Stuart Britain and Ireland*, ed. Michael J Braddick and David L. Smith (Cambridge: Cambridge University Press, 2011) 190–209.
Blair Worden, 'James Harrington and *The Commonwealth of Oceana*, 1656', in David Wootton (ed.), *Republicanism, Liberty and Commercial Society, 1649–1776* (Stanford: Stanford University Press, 1994).

Spinoza

Douglas J. Den Uyl, *Power State and Freedom: An Interpretation of Spinoza's Political Philosophy* (Assen: Van Gorcum & Company, 1983).
Jonathan Israel, *The Dutch Republic: Its Rise, Greatness and Fall, 1477–1806* (Oxford: Oxford University Press, 1995).
Yitzhak Melamed and Michael Rosenthal (eds), *Spinoza's Theological-Political Treatise: A Critical Guide* (Cambridge: Cambridge University Press, 2010).
Steven Nadler, *Spinoza: A Life* (Cambridge: Cambridge University Press, 1999).

Rebecca Newberger Goldstein, *Betraying Spinoza: The Renegade Jew Who Gave Us Modernity* (New York: Schocken Books, 2006).
Raia Prokhovnik, *Spinoza and Republicanism* (London and New York: Palgrave Macmillan, 2004).
Stephen B. Smith, *Spinoza, Liberalism, and the Question of Jewish Identity* (New Haven: Yale University Press, 1997).

Paine

Gregory Claeys, *Thomas Paine: Social and Political Thought* (Boston: Unwin Hyman, 1989).
Eric Foner, *Tom Paine and Revolutionary America*. Updated edition (New York: Oxford University Press, 2005).
Jack Fruchtman, *The Political Philosophy of Thomas Paine* (Baltimore: Johns Hopkins University Press, 2009).

Radishchev

Stephen Baehr, *The Paradise Myth in Eighteenth-Century Russia: Utopian Patterns in Early Secular Russian Literature and Culture* (Stanford: Stanford University Press, 1991).
Franco Venturi e la Russia: con documenti inediti, ed. Antonello Venturi (Milan: Feltrinelli, 2006).
Richard Wortman, *Scenarios of Power: Myth and Ceremony in Russian Monarchy* (Princeton: Princeton University Press, 1995).
Andrei Zorin, *By Fables Alone: Literature and State Ideology in Late Eighteenth- and early Nineteenth-Century Russia*, Marcus Levitt (trans.) (Brighton: Academic Studies Press, 2014).

Sieyès

M. Goldoni, 'At the Origins of the Constitutional Review: Sieyes' Constitutional Jury and the Taming of Constituent Power', *Oxford Journal of Legal Studies* 2 (2012).
L. Jaume, 'Constituent Power in France: The Revolution and Its Consequences', in *The Paradox of Constitutionalism*, M. Loughlin and N. Walker (eds) (Oxford: Oxford University Press, 2008).
E. Sonenscher, *Before the Deluge: Public Debt, Inequality, and the Intellectual Origins of the French Revolution* (Princeton: Princeton University Press, 2009).
E. Sonenscher, *Sans-culottes: An Eighteenth-Century Emblem in the French Revolution* (Princeton: Princeton University Press, 2008).
E. Sonenscher, *Sieyès Political Writings: Including the Debate between Sieyès and Tom Paine* (London: Hackett, 2003).

Simón Bolívar

Diego Bautista Urbaneja, *Bolívar: el pueblo y el poder* (Caracas: Fundación para la Cultura Urbana, no. 24, 2004).
Simón Bolívar, *El Libertador: Writings of Simón Bolívar*, Frederick H. Fornoff (trans.) and David Bushnell (ed.) (Oxford: Oxford University Press, 2003).
John Lynch, *Simón Bolívar: A Life* (New Haven: Yale University Press, 2006).

Tocqueville

Jo Ellen Jacobs, *The Voice of Harriet Taylor Mill* (Bloomington: Indiana University Press, 2002).
Harvey C. Mansfield, *Tocqueville: A Very Short Introduction* (Oxford: Oxford University Press, 2010).
Cheryl Welch, *De Tocqueville* (Oxford: Oxford University Press, 2001).
Sheldon S. Wolin, *Tocqueville between Two Worlds: The Making of a Political and Theoretical Life* (Princeton: Princeton University Press, 2003).

Harriet Taylor Mill

Harriet Taylor Mill, *The Complete Works*, ed. Jo Ellen Jacobs (Bloomington: Indiana University Press, 1998).
John Stuart Mill, 'The Subjection of Women', in *The Collected Works of John Stuart Mill*, vol. XXI, ed. Ann P. Robson and John M. Robson (Toronto: University of Toronto Press, 1994).
Alice S. Rossi, 'Sentiment and Intellect: The Story of John Stuart Mill and Harriet Taylor Mill', in *Essays on Sex Equality*, ed. Alice S. Rossi (Chicago: University of Chicago Press, 1970).

Lenin

Tony Cliff, *Lenin*, 4 vols (London: Pluto Press, 1975–19).
Paul LeBlanc, *Lenin and the Revolutionary Party* (Atlantic Highlands: Humanities Press, 1990).
Marcel Liebman, *Leninism under Lenin* (London: Jonathan Cape, 1975).
Lars Lih, *Lenin Rediscovered* (Leiden: Brill, 2006).
Tamás Krausz, *Reconstructing Lenin* (New York: Monthly Review Press, 2015).
Alan Shandro, *Lenin and the Logic of Hegemony* (Leiden: Brill, 2014).

Rosa Luxemburg

Norman Geras, *The Legacy of Rosa Luxemburg* (London: NLB, 1976).
Peter Nettl, *Rosa Luxemburg* (London: Oxford University Press, 1969).
Mary-Alice Waters (ed.), *Rosa Luxemburg Speaks* (New York: Pathfinder Press, 1994).
Rosemary H. T. O'Kane, *Rosa Luxemburg in Action: For Revolution and Democracy* (New York and London: Routledge, 2015).

Max Weber

David Beetham, *Max Weber and the Theory of Modern Politics* (London: Allen & Unwin, 1985).
Peter Breiner, *Max Weber and Democratic Politics* (Ithaca: Cornell University Press, 1996).
Wolfgang Mommsen, *Max Weber and German Politics 1890–1920*, 2nd edition (Chicago: University of Chicago Press, 1984).
J. J. R. Thomas, 'Weber and Direct Democracy', *The British Journal of Sociology* 35, no. 2 (1984): 216–40.

Gandhi

M. K. Gandhi, *Constructive Programme* (Ahmedabad: Navajivan Publishing House, 1945).
M. K. Gandhi, *Economic and Industrial Life and Relations*, vol. I. V. B. Kher (compiled and ed.) (Ahmedabad: Navajivan Publishing House, 1957).
S. Kaviraj, 'The Politics of Performance: Gandhi's Trial read as Theatre', in *Staging Politics: Power and Performance in Asia and Africa*, ed. Julia C. Strauss, Donal B. Cruise O'Brien (New York: I.B.Tauris & Co. Ltd, 2007), 71–89.
Visvanathan Shiv, *Between Cosmology and System: The Heuristics of a Dissenting Imagination*, http://www.arvindguptatoys.com/arvindgupta/cvs-shiv.pdf.
Anuradha Veeravalli, *Gandhi in Political Theory: Truth, Law and Experiment* (Farham: Ashgate Publishing, 2014).

Sun Yat-sen

Marie-Claire Bergère, *Sun Yat-sen*, Janet Lloyd (trans.) (Stanford: Stanford University Press, 1998).
Chu-yuan Cheng (ed.), *Sun Yat-sen's Doctrine in the Modern World* (Boulder: Westview Press, 1989).
Sun Yat-sen, *Fundamentals of National Reconstruction* (Taipei: China Cultural Service, 1953).

Sun Yat-sen, *San Min Chu I* (The Three Principles of the People), trans. Frank W. Price. 2nd and abridged ed. (Taipei: Government Information Office, 1990).
Sun Yat-sen, *Prescriptions for Saving China: Selected Writings of Sun Yat-sen*, ed. Julie Lee Wei, E-su Zen, and Linda Chao (Stanford: Hoover Institution Press, 1994).

Hobson

Peter Cain, *Hobson and Imperialism: Radicalism, New Liberalism and Finance, 1887–1938* (Oxford: Oxford University Press, 2001).
Michael Freeden, *The New Liberalism: An Ideology of Social Reform*, 2nd edition (Oxford: Clarendon, 1986).
John Atkinson Hobson, *The Social Problem: Life and Work* (London: Nisbet 1901).
John Atkinson Hobson, *Imperialism: A Study* (London: George Allen and Unwin, 1938 [1902]).
John Atkinson Hobson, *The Crisis of Liberalism: New Issues of Democracy* (London: P.S. King, 1909).
Colin Tyler, *Common Good Politics: British Idealism and Social Justice in the Contemporary World* (Houndsmill: Palgrave, 2017).

Muhammad Mahdi Shamsuddin

Talib M. Aziz, 'Popular Sovereignty in Contemporary Shi'i Political Thought', in *Shi'ite Heritage*, ed. Lynda Clarke (New York: Global Publications, 2001), 181–98.
Zackery M. Heern, *The Emergence of Modern Shi'ism* (London: Oneworld Publications, 2015).
Moojan Momen, *An Introduction to Shi'i Islam* (New Haven: Yale University Press, 1987).
Vali Nasr, *The Shia Revival* (New York: W. W. Norton & Company, 2006).
Muhammad Mahdi Shamsuddin, 'The Authenticity of Shi'ism', in *Shi'ite Heritage*, ed. Lynda Clarke (New York: Global Publications, 2001), 45–54.

INDEX

absolutism 91, 92, 94
action (political) 141, 142, 143, 146
aidōs 19–20
Alfarabi 3, 41–8, 186
America 6, 15, 16, 88, 105, 107, 110, 123, 126, 127 *see also* United States
   Latin America 2, 5, 7, 106
   'Democracy in America' 113–20
aristocracy 5, 34–6, 50, 67, 84–5, 116–19, 151, 187
Aristotle 3, 21, 25–32, 35, 43, 47, 50, 51, 58, 73, 132
assembly (popular) 66, 67, 68
assent 148 *see also* consent
Athens 2–3, 5, 8, 10–15, 26, 39, 46, 109, 125, 131, 145, 146, 156
autocracy 33–4, 37, 44, 130, 164, 165, 167

Baghdad 2–3, 43–6, 48, 186
ballot 67, 132
   secret 67
Baxter, Richard 70, 72
Bolívar 2, 5, 6, 105–11, 187, 188
Bolsheviks 5, 90, 93, 133–5, 139, 141, 144
bourgeois 47, 131, 132, 133, 134, 139, 140, 142
bourgeoisie 129, 130, 141, 143
bureaucracy 130, 146, 149
bureaucratization 7, 146, 148, 150, 151

capitalism 6, 7, 130, 131, 132, 134, 136, 152, 169, 171, 172, 175, 176
charisma 7, 183
   charismatic demagogue 82, 147
   charismatic leadership 7, 145–51
China 2, 8, 117, 120, 161–7, 189
   Communist Party 163

Imperial censor 165
Imperial examination board 165
Nationalist Party 163
Chinese Communist Party 163, 166, 167
Chinese Nationalist Party (Kuomintang) 163, 167
Cicero 3, 8, 33–40, 50, 51, 52, 73
citizens and citizenship 6, 29, 32, 66, 68, 69, 70, 91, 92, 125, 156, 158, 172, 187
   definition in Aristotle 27
   virtues of 125
   critical citizenship 172
   free citizenry 34
city 3, 9, 13, 27–31, 41–6, 59, 60, 63, 77, 91, 100, 125
   cultural diversity 45
   parts of 28
   polis 99
   virtuous city 42, 46
civil disobedience 155, 156, 157
class (social and economic) 29, 30, 38, 93, 107, 125, 138, 142
   class conflict 3
   class division 30
   industrial class 117, 119
   interests 188
   middle class 28, 29, 115, 144
   ruling class 90
class structure or hierarchy 91, 94
class struggle 150
   subordinate class 91
class warfare 30
   working class 124, 133–4, 141, 143
colonial rule 156, 157, 163
   anti-colonial 189
   post-colonial 166, 189
Comintern 163
common good 4, 6, 35, 50, 54, 61, 62, 69, 77, 90, 109, 125, 188

commonwealth 66, 67, 68, 69, 70, 71, 72, 107
  'equal commonwealth' 67
  as *res publica* 35, 37, 38, 39
Communist Party, Germany *see* KPD
conformity 154, 158
Confucius 163
conscience 7, 17, 19, 20, 22, 66, 68, 142, 156, 157, 158
consent 3, 4, 5, 34, 49, 50, 51, 52, 53, 55, 77, 83, 89, 92, 114, 142, 148, 154, 178, 185, 186, 187, 188
constituent power 98, 101–3
Constituent Assembly, France 102
Constituent Assembly, Russia 129–30, 133–4, 139
constitution 1, 10, 12, 50, 55, 94, 98, 99, 101, 102–3, 105–6, 111, 113, 122, 131, 132, 145, 152, 157, 159, 166, 179, 186
  constitutional change 35
  'Constitutional Debate' 10, 12
  constitutional democracy 82
  five-power 165, 167
  mixed constitution 3, 34, 35, 37–9
  of Oceana 66–71
cooperative ability 18, 19, 20, 22
corruption 94, 107, 117, 121, 123, 124, 126, 140, 176
customs 11, 12, 41, 57, 85, 109, 110

Darius 10–13
decision-making 52, 53, 54, 66, 77, 100, 114, 142
demagogy 34, 36, 38, 145, 146, 151
  demagogues xii, 29, 35–6, 67, 68, 71, 145–8, 151
democracy
  assembly 2
  bourgeois 129, 132, 133, 139, 140, 141, 142, 143
  constitutional democracy 82
  direct 2, 7, 94, 103, 147, 152, 172
  liberal 1, 4, 130, 132, 139, 141, 143, 171
  as natural 28
  Plato's account of 35–6
  representative 6, 7, 22, 86, 103, 165, 173, 174, 185, 188

  Scipio's account of 35
  socialist democracy 141–3
  Soviet democracy 130, 133–4
democratic contempt 82–7
democratic social state 3, 6, 115, 118
democratization 66, 151, 166, 172
despotism 6, 91, 105, 107, 115, 117, 119, 124, 164
dictatorship 1, 130, 134, 135, 136, 139, 142, 174, 177
  military 149
  of the proletariat 131, 140
dissent 7, 39, 153, 154–60, 178, 189
  space for 154

education 5, 11, 30, 32 n11, 42, 44, 47, 59, 106, 108, 109, 111, 115, 122, 123, 140, 143, 170, 172–4
  civic 5
  democratic 30
  political 109
elections 7, 37, 43, 44, 61, 67, 77, 98, 102, 117, 129, 130, 133, 134, 138, 139, 140, 141, 143, 145, 166, 172
  ecclesiastical 53, 54
  indirect 114
elite 7, 22, 36, 67, 85, 92–4, 110, 116–18, 167, 171, 172, 174, 175, 186
  capitalist 171
  creole 106, 108
  manufacturing 118
  Persian 10
Epimetheus 18
equality 2, 3, 5, 25, 27, 29–30, 35–6, 39–40, 44, 46, 50, 51, 76–8, 82–6, 92–3, 95, 110, 117, 125, 129, 158, 164, 182, 185–6, 189, 193–4
  as *isonomia*, *isēgoria*, and *isokratia* 10–15
  before the law 9, 11, 36
  between men and women 122–3, 125, 138
  between poor and rich 3, 25, 29
  formal 133, 141
  and inequality 86, 108, 117, 141, 171

natural 76, 83–4
  of opportunity 169
  racial 108
  social 36, 39
Erfurt Programme (1891) 138
expertise 21, 53, 120, 149, 180, 181, 189

farmers 28, 29
First World War 6, 138, 146, 156, 170
freedom 12, 13, 21, 25, 30, 41, 44–7, 68–70, 77–8, 97, 101, 111, 117, 119, 123, 125–6, 129–30, 138–43, 156–7, 164, 182, 185–6, 189, 192; *see also* liberty
  excess of 35, 36, 107
  natural 75, 77, 107
  sexual 45
  of speech and the press 44, 138, 139, 141
  of thought 4, 75, 77–8, 140, 143
free trade 175
friendship 29, 119, 172

Gandhi 2, 7, 153–60, 185, 189
German Communist Party *see* KPD
German Revolution (1919) *see* revolution
German Social Democratic Party *see* SPD
guardianship (*wilayah*) 177–80

Harrington, James 4, 65–72, 73, 74, 187
Herodotus 2, 3, 9–16, 185, 186
heterodoxy (religious) 44
Hobbes 21, 77, 159
Hobson, John Atkinson 7, 169–76, 188
Homer 11
Humanism 171, 173–5
humours 59, 61

imperialism 7, 161, 175 *see also* colonialism
Independent Social Democratic Party of Germany *see* USPD
India 2, 128, 153–60
indifference, public 115
inequality
  economic inequality 86, 108, 141, 171

isēgoria 13–15
isokratia 10, 13–15
isonomia 10, 11, 13–16, 35

jimāʻiyya (collective) 43
juries 10, 29, 37, 61, 66, 116
Jurist 178–83
Justice 6, 13–14, 16–17, 19–22, 27, 28, 30, 31, 34, 40, 51, 74, 86–8, 91, 93–4, 105, 123, 138, 159, 160, 172, 173, 179, 182, 183, 188
  dike 19
  social justice 172

Khomeini 179–80, 182
Kings 36, 75, 83–7
KPD (German Communist Party) 139
Kuomintang *see* Chinese Nationalist Party

law 3, 4, 5, 9, 10, 11, 13, 17, 20, 28, 35, 51, 53, 60, 67, 109, 147, 156, 165, 187
  discovery of law 53
  authorization of law 53
  human law 49, 51
lawyers 52, 54, 68, 116, 150
leader 33, 58, 60–1, 94, 105–6, 114, 147, 188
leadership 7, 38, 94, 109, 113–17, 119, 142, 143, 145–51, 166, 185, 188
Lebanon 179–80
legitimation 146, 150, 156
Lenin, Vladimir Ilich 2, 6, 95, 129–37, 140, 141, 144, 170, 175, 188
liberal *see also* democracy, liberal
  discourse 126, 139,
  French liberals (Girondins) 99
  Institutions 106
  New Liberal government 170, 171
  tradition 75
liberalism 124
liberty 5, 33, 35–7, 59, 61, 62, 66, 68, 75, 78, 91–4, 97–8, 100–2, 107, 110, 125–7, 158, 161, 164, 187
Luxemburg, Rosa 7, 133, 136, 137–44, 188

Machiavelli 4, 57–63, 66, 70, 187
majority 9, 25, 27, 28, 29, 30, 31, 35, 53, 54, 55, 67, 70, 76, 77, 100, 113, 116, 117, 129, 133, 134, 157, 158, 159, 166, 188
  maioritas 53
  majoritarianism 54
  majority rule 11
Mao Zedong Thought 163, 167
market society 119
Marsilius of Padua 4, 49–55, 186, 187
Marx 2, 6, 7, 129, 130–6, 138, 139, 140, 141, 144, 167, 188
mass strike 133, 136, 142, 143, 144
masses 9, 35–7, 73–7, 131, 137, 139–43
Megabyzos 10–12, 15
Mencius 163
mestizos 108
military 33, 66, 68, 106, 108, 110, 166, 174, 175, 187
  dictatorship 134, 149
  rule 166
  virtue 27
Mill, John Stuart 123
Milton 70
minority 108, 134, 159
  protection for 142
multitude (rule of) 9, 28

obligation 138, 172, 173
oligarchy 10, 11, 12, 26–30, 31, 34, 38, 50, 67, 92, 95, 119, 132, 146
opposition
  ideological 111, 130
  to tyranny 13
organization (political) 11, 14, 76, 146, 147, 150, 151, 172, 175
  of masses 134
  of women 122
  of workers 141, 143
Otanes 10–13, 15

pacific internationalism 169
pacifism 138
Paine, Thomas 5, 81–8, 103, 187
parliament 52, 65, 69, 94, 110, 117, 131, 132, 133, 134, 138, 139, 140, 141, 146, 148–51, 155, 157, 164, 172
  bourgeois parliamentarism 141
participation 2, 13, 34, 66, 67, 70, 91, 115, 120, 123–5, 126, 140–3, 147, 181
  active 52, 139, 142, 154
  direct 91, 101
  mass 142
  popular 3, 4, 5, 44, 100, 101, 185, 186, 187, 188
parties, political 46, 66–8, 70, 71, 133, 134, 137–43, 145, 148, 150, 157, 163, 166, 167, 170, 172
passion 43, 44, 45, 46, 57, 61, 105, 113, 116, 117, 118
patriarchy 122, 124
Peisistratos 11
people (the) 1, 4, 5, 6, 9, 11, 12, 22, 25, 26, 29, 33–9, 43, 44, 46, 51, 52, 58, 59, 60, 62, 63, 65–7, 69, 70, 71, 75–9, 84, 86, 91, 92, 94, 97, 98, 100, 101, 102, 106, 109, 110, 111, 114–16, 129, 132, 133, 135, 137–42, 146, 148–51, 154, 155, 157–9, 161–3, 165–7, 169, 170, 172, 178, 179, 181, 187, 188
  demos 11
  native peoples 108
  people's principles (*San Min Chu I*) 162, 167
  populus 52
  power 7, 10, 37, 92, 95
  sovereignty of 107, 189
Persian empire 12
Plato 3, 26, 33, 36, 39, 43, 45, 47, 82, 158
political community 18–21, 27, 30, 51, 117
political judgement 124
political merit 8, 84, 117, 120
political philosophy 27, 31, 51, 114
political tutelage 166
politikē technē 18, 22
polity (as Aristotelian regime) 26, 27, 31, 50
power 2–11, 13–15, 21–2, 27–8, 30–5, 37, 42, 44, 46, 47, 50,

52, 54, 58–61, 65, 67, 69–71, 73, 76, 78, 81–3, 89–92, 94–5, 97, 98, 100–3, 105, 107, 109, 111, 114–17, 119, 122–6, 129, 130–7, 141, 142, 146–51, 158, 159, 161, 163–7, 170–3, 176, 181, 182, 185, 188, 189
  absolute power 74, 75
  economic 6
  political power 6, 58, 98, 100, 101, 114, 123, 131, 132, 141, 165, 188
Prometheus 18, 19
proportional representation *see* representation
Protagoras 2, 17–23, 185, 186
protest 143, 157
public good 78, 122, 123, 124, 125, 126, 128, 174
public opinion 140, 188

Radishchev, Alexander 2, 5, 89–96, 187
referendum 138, 165, 166
Regicide 65, 69
regimes (in Aristotle) 26–7
religion 61, 74, 75, 79, 84, 106, 126, 131, 156, 178, 180–3
  Catholic Church 74, 84, 126
  Islam 180–2
  liberty of conscience 68, 138
representation 4, 5, 6, 43, 53, 54, 55, 68, 92, 97–103, 116, 123, 124, 134, 139, 148, 158, 185, 187, 188, 189
  indirect 114
  proportional 138, 148, 149
  representative institutions 110, 172, 188
republic
  democratic republic 76, 77, 106, 107, 108, 130, 131
  Plato's *Republic* 26, 36, 158
  Roman republic 3, 39, 61, 94, 185, 18
republicanism 92, 94, 126, 187
  radical republicanism 4, 73
revolution 31, 59, 65, 83, 86, 98, 99, 100, 101, 129, 134, 135, 140, 141, 146, 161, 163, 164, 166, 167, 179, 180

American 2, 126
Aristotelian revolution thesis 50
French 88, 94, 95, 188
German Revolution (1919) 139, 146–7
Latin American 106
October (Russian) revolution 130, 133, 136, 138, 139, 142, 144
'The Russian Revolution' 138–42
Socialist revolution 130, 131
rights 1, 36, 68, 70, 76, 83, 87, 89, 90, 92, 110, 111, 115, 123, 124, 125, 127, 128, 138, 143, 147, 159, 163, 178, 181, 182, 187, 188
  civil 95, 122, 126
  economic 86, 126
  human 5, 93, 94
  individual 1
  natural 73, 76–8, 89–96, 123, 126
  of the people 91, 165
  of resistance 91
  'Rights of Man' 88
rule
  popular 41–7, 101, 107
rule of law 3, 28, 32, 43, 90, 187
rulership 41, 42, 44

SDKPiL (Social Democracy of the Kingdom of Poland and Lithuania) 142
self-rule 6, 68, 70, 73, 100, 103, 107, 108, 147, 186, 187, 189
senate
  American 109, 113, 114, 117, 118
  of Oceana 67, 68
  Roman 34, 38
Shamsuddin 2, 7, 43, 177–84, 185, 189
Sieyès 5, 97–103, 188
slavery 37, 107, 110, 111, 123
  slave trade 108, 111
  slaves 6, 62, 95, 99, 111
social contract 76, 77, 91, 94, 96, 106, 154, 159
social democracy *see* democracy, socialist; Erfurt Programme
Social Democratic Party, German, *see* SPD
social levelling 188

social reform *see* Erfurt programme
socialism 123, 130–1, 138, 152; *see also* democracy, socialist
socialist democracy *see* democracy, socialist
socialist revolutionary party (SR) 133
Socrates 17, 18, 26, 156, 157, 160
sovereign right 73, 76
sovereignty 3, 5, 7, 11, 49, 52, 65, 94, 95, 103, 107, 154, 155, 157, 158, 159, 163, 164, 178, 180, 181, 189
Spartacus League 138, 143
SPD (Socialdemokratische Partei Deutschlands, German Social Democratic Party) 138, 142
specialization of labour 99
Spinoza 4, 73–9, 187
state (political) 7, 11, 22, 34, 35, 38, 39, 50, 58, 61, 67, 68, 69, 70, 72, 74, 75, 76, 78, 79, 86, 93, 102, 106, 113, 115, 117, 120, 129, 131, 132, 133, 134, 138, 156, 157, 158, 165, 169, 171, 173, 175, 178, 179, 180, 182, 188
  absolutist 90
  Chinese 163, 164, 167, 189
  democratic social state 3, 4, 6, 118
  German 149
  modern 21, 145–50, 154–5, 164, 167, 172
  of nature 21, 77, 91
  regulatory 7
  Russian 90, 92
  Soviet 135
  strong 165, 189
statesman 26, 28, 31, 38, 106
strikes *see* mass strikes

Stubbe, Henry 70, 72
suffrage 5, 122, 124, 127, 147, 151, 152, 165, 166
  manhood suffrage 123, 187
  universal suffrage 6, 7, 113, 114, 117, 138, 139, 146
Suffrage Law (Russia) 144
Sun Yat-sen 2, 7, 161–7, 185, 189

Taylor Mill, Harriet 6, 121–8, 188
Tocqueville 3, 6, 113–20, 126, 147, 151, 188
toleration 77, 142
trade union 138, 142, 143
Trotsky, Leon 130, 134, 135, 137, 139, 140, 141

United States 6, 107, 109, 119, 122, 125
USPD (Independent Social Democratic Party) 138

Vane, Sir Henry 70
vote 12, 33, 143, 157, 173
  popular 102, 117
  right to 122, 123, 124, 126, 127
  voters 23

Weber, Max 7, 21, 145–52, 188
welfare 7, 90, 178, 179
  state 86
women 6, 11, 45, 68, 69, 121–8, 138, 181–2
The Subordination of Women 124
workers 117–18, 129–34, 138–43
working class *see* class (economic and social)